A CATHOLIC PHILOSOPHY OF EDUCATION

A CATHOLIC

PHILOSOPHY

OF EDUCATION

The Church and Two Philosophers

MARIO O. D'SOUZA

McGill-Queen's University Press
Montreal & Kingston · London · Chicago

© McGill-Queen's University Press 2016

ISBN 978-0-7735-4771-1 (cloth)
ISBN 978-0-7735-4772-8 (paper)
ISBN 978-0-7735-9978-9 (ePDF)
ISBN 978-0-7735-9979-6 (ePUB)

Legal deposit third quarter 2016
Bibliothèque nationale du Québec

Printed in Canada on acid-free paper that is 100% ancient forest free
(100% post-consumer recycled), processed chlorine free

This book has been published with the help of a grant from the Canadian
Federation for the Humanities and Social Sciences, through the
Awards to Scholarly Publications Program, using funds provided by the
Social Sciences and Humanities Research Council of Canada. Funding
was also received from the Basilian Fathers of the University of St
Michael's College.

McGill-Queen's University Press acknowledges the support of the
Canada Council for the Arts for our publishing program. We also
acknowledge the financial support of the Government of Canada through
the Canada Book Fund for our publishing activities.

LIBRARY AND ARCHIVES CANADA CATALOGUING IN PUBLICATION

D'Souza, Mario O. (Mario Osbert), 1956–, author
A Catholic philosophy of education : the church and two philosophers /
Mario O. D'Souza.

Includes bibliographical references and index.
Issued in print and electronic formats.
ISBN 978-0-7735-4771-1 (cloth). – ISBN 978-0-7735-4772-8 (paper). –
ISBN 978-0-7735-9978-9 (ePDF). – ISBN 978-0-7735-9979-6 (ePUB)

1. Catholic Church – Education – Philosophy. 2. Maritain, Jacques,
1882–1973. 3. Lonergan, Bernard J. F. (Bernard Joseph Francis), 1904–
1984. 4. Catholic schools. I. Title.

LC473.D76 2016   371.071'2   C2016-903463-1
                                 C2016-903464-X

Set in 11/14 Filosofia with Filosofia Grand
Book design & typesetting by Garet Markvoort, zijn digital

To Melanie and Michelle;
for your love, courage,
and panache!

CONTENTS

ACKNOWLEDGMENTS

This book would not have come to pass were it not for the steady, scholarly, charitable, professional, friendly, and patient encouragement of Dr Kyla Madden, senior editor, McGill-Queen's University Press. Dr Madden was encouraging from the start and the inception of an idea, and I am enormously grateful to her for all her care and attention in helping me realize this work. In every way, I cannot thank her sufficiently. I also thank Mr Ryan Van Huijstee, managing editor, and Ms Grace Seybold, copy editor, for their professional courtesy and kindness in bringing this work to completion. Like Dr Madden, all those with whom I have dealt at McGill-Queen's University Press have been, to a person, immensely and unfailingly courteous and helpful.

I thank the two anonymous reviewers chosen by McGill-Queen's University Press. This book was born from the solitary experience of locking myself in my office during my sabbatical and writing, 2014–2015. The reviewers saw merit in this effort. I thank them for their generous encouragement and helpful suggestions.

I thank Michael Vertin, emeritus professor, University of Toronto, who was always ready to help me during my sabbatical year while I wrote this book. He had lengthy meetings and telephone conversations with me, and replied to email inquiries on some of the more technical questions that are part of this work. I recall saying to him, many years ago, that a great peace and stillness descended upon my soul every time I read a work by Bernard Lonergan. Professor Vertin is a living embodiment of such peace and stillness.

Professor Julian Stern, dean of theology and education, York St John University, York, UK, is another friend and colleague who stood by me while I wrote this book, and he did this while being appointed as dean to a second faculty at his institution. Professor Stern read each of my draft chapters, and responded with helpful observations, comments, and suggestions, all dressed up very nicely in his dry and relaxed humorous manner. I am most grateful to him.

I thank my Basilian brother, His Grace, the Most Reverend J. Michael Miller, CSB, archbishop of Vancouver and the former secretary for the Congregation for Catholic Education, at the Holy See, for his help and readiness to speak with me as I explored the Catholic educational documents from the Congregation for Catholic Education.

Two other scholars were also very generous with their time. I thank Fr Peter Drilling, sometime rector of Christ the King Seminary, Buffalo, NY, and now rector of St Joseph's Cathedral, Buffalo, NY; and Fr Robert Doran, SJ, professor and Emmett Doerr Chair in Catholic Systematic Theology, Marquette University.

Professor Thomas H. Groome was my teacher when I studied at Boston College, and is my friend. I thank him for encouraging me to write this book. I also thank John Sullivan, emeritus professor, Liverpool Hope University, UK, for his thoughts and suggestions regarding this work.

I thank Professor Gerald Grace, editor of *International Studies in Catholic Education*, director of the Centre for Research and Development in Catholic Education, and visiting professor of St Mary's University, Twickenham, London, who has encouraged my work in Catholic education.

While writing this book, I visited and stayed with my old friend, Fergal Roche – whom I have known since 1981 – and his wife Heather and their family in Guildford, UK. As Fergal and I chatted one brisk Saturday morning, as he walked their new puppy Lola, I asked him what he thought of the title of the book – he was the first to hear it. He thought it catchy and succinct.

I thank another old friend, Fr Patrick Hume, SJ, whom I have known since 1976. Patrick invited me to stay with him and other old Jesuit friends when I began my university sabbatical. It was in that religious house that I sat, in the familiar summer solitude of a Dublin I know and love, and sketched out this work. Patrick's company, hospitality, generosity, and usual good humour provided the launching pad I needed to get started.

I wish to thank Ms Melissa Rae Horsman for her kind assistance and gracious spirit. And finally, I thank Fr Allan Smith, CSB; the idea for this book's cover was his, and I am most grateful for it.

In closing, I attended the World Congress on Catholic Education (*Educating Today and Tomorrow. A Renewing Passion*) in Rome, 18–21 November 2015, hosted and sponsored by the Congregation for Catholic Education. With nearly one thousand delegates from across the world, the Congress marked the fiftieth anniversary of the Second Vatican Council's document *Gravissimum Educations / On Christian Education* and the twenty-fifth anniversary of *Ex Corde Ecclesiae / Apostolic Constitution on Catholic Universities*, promulgated by Pope Saint John Paul II. The experience of attending this Congress was truly moving; it captured in living and breathing form the universality of the Church's educational mission as outlined in her educational documents.

A CATHOLIC PHILOSOPHY OF EDUCATION

INTRODUCTION

I have spent my ministry as a Catholic priest in researching, teaching, and reflecting upon Catholic education, and more particularly, Catholic philosophy of education, an interest that can be traced back to my own school experience. I grew up in an Islamic country – in Pakistan, in the city of Karachi – where I, like most Catholics, attended Catholic schools. Indeed, Catholic schools in the sub-continent of India are much-coveted educational institutions, and they have a long and distinguished tradition. Such institutions were administered by both diocesan clergy and religious orders, and Catholic schools and colleges not only dotted the main cities of the Indian sub-continent, but were also established in remote areas, and, by all accounts, welcomed and celebrated.[1] And in spite of the very changed and dangerous landscape of religious extremism and religious persecution of today, Muslims continue to be, as they were in the past, strong supporters of the Catholic school system.

What made my educational experience noteworthy was that the majority of my fellow students were non-Christian, and North America's leading Catholic educator, Thomas Groome, has duly recognized that model of education. In his recollections of visiting Catholic schools in Karachi, Groome recounts his experience of asking the Sisters who administered that city's celebrated St. Joseph's Covenant School "about their educational philosophy and sociocultural situation ... and if they felt that their mission was compromised by the exigency to avoid evangelization." He said that though the Sister principal was surprised by this inquiry, her response was swift and unequivocal: "Oh no, to educate well is always to do God's work – that is enough." Later, reflecting on this answer, Groome muses to himself, "My sister friends in Pakistan were correct. To educate *for life for all* is ever to give glory to God."[2]

Catholic education in that non-Christian land, in my opinion, had, whether intentionally or not, evolved into a model that was really revolutionary for its age and time, but particularly for its place. This model was an example of how Catholic education contributes to the common good, and was established well before the changed theological, social, political, and cultural worldview that emerged from the Second Vatican Council (1962–65) [henceforth "the Council"]. By the time I went to school, which was while the Council was still in session, the aim and purpose of Catholic schools in Pakistan was, like any school, to educate students in the curriculum. But given that such an education was being imparted in a non-Christian country, I have often later wondered whether the founders of these schools were also looking ahead at the impact of these institutions upon society, upon the common good, and upon the general welfare of a newly created nation, founded in 1947 and marked by staggering poverty and widespread illiteracy. Catholics not only ran schools and colleges, they also administered hospitals, orphanages, and other social services, and cared for those left on the margins of society. There was a clear social mandate and thrust to the Church's apostolates, and to looking beyond those who were Christians. Whatever the implicit and explicit purposes of these Catholic schools were, and whether or not the founders of these schools were circumscribed by a bookish conception of education, or whether they actually expected their educational influence to extend beyond the school and into society, I have no doubt that my fellow students and I were the recipients of a form of education that recognized the social nature of diversity and plurality, and well before those designations were made popular, as they have become in our age. While the social nature of the Catholic school would come to be emphasized later in the Documents of the Second Vatican Council, these schools were streets ahead of their time. Charles Taylor expresses philosophically what our young hearts seemed to understand, in an unarticulated and undifferentiated, though enthusiastic, way within our being: "thus my discovering my own identity doesn't mean that I work it out in isolation, but that I negotiate it through dialogue … my own identity crucially depends on my dialogical relations with others."[3]

And what is the model that I am referring to? The school day was broken up into the usual subjects: English, history, physics, geography, mathematics, Urdu (the national language of Pakistan), chemistry, biology, civics, etc. All the students in the school, most of whom were non-Christian and mainly Muslims, studied together. And our response to what appeared to be a natural religious pluralism was to think nothing of the experience of students of quite different worldviews and cultural backgrounds studying together – most Catholics in the era I am referring to would have spoken English at home, dressed in Western clothing, listened to Western music, and read Western literature, and their social, cultural, intellectual, aesthetic, and emotional worldview and sensitivities would have been decidedly Western, influenced by both the British Raj and the Portuguese. Amidst this religious and cultural plurality, enduring and happy friendships developed between Muslim and Christian students. While teachers were, by and large, Catholic, it was not unusual to have a non-Catholic teacher. However, what I think was the most distinctive feature of this model, and I say this in light of all the scholarship and attention to pluralism, diversity, and multiculturalism, was that we studied everything together, the one exception being religion: Catholics went to their class in catechism, or whatever model of religious instruction was emerging during those pedagogically bumpy years after the Council, and the Muslims went to study the Koran. To us, such going apart for one class – for religious instruction – but remaining together for the rest and most of the school day seemed as natural and expected as the assurance of the sun rising and setting each day. Indeed, what was extraordinary is that the state allowed Catholic schools to flourish, and, further, that it allowed Muslim students to attend such schools. Following high school, I spent two years at a Catholic college studying the liberal arts in preparation for university. This institutional educational experience was again in the company of a majority of non-Catholic students, though religious instruction was no longer offered. I did go on to the University of Karachi, but only for a year before moving to Ireland, and eventually to Canada. However, that part of my autobiography is not relevant here.

I wish to return, though, to this model of education, and for one principal reason. On reflection many years later, and given my interest in the Catholic philosophy of education, I cannot help but admire how

my schooling was modelled, and what my education stood for and proclaimed, even though the proclamation was implicit, and carried out
through what today might be referred to as the *covert* or *hidden* curriculum. And it is this: that in the context of institutional education, knowledge and learning are communal and decidedly social activities and
engagements, and they are fundamental, decisive, and natural sources
of humanization, natural in the sense that human beings are *naturally*
social. And while knowing and learning are, in the context of the school,
not the *only* sources of humanization, they are, nonetheless, extraordin-
arily powerful, decidedly humanizing and formative, and utterly irreplaceable sources. We recognize that education is a life-long process
and a journey, and that while schooling brings to conclusion a stage of
learning particular to an educational institution, education is hardly
concluded at the end of one's time in school, college, or university. However, the model that I went through proclaimed a simple but powerful
truth: that though we were living amidst religious, cultural, and other
significant diversities, and even though the majority of those being educated in the nation were not attending Catholic schools or colleges, for
those of us who were, this was the natural and expected thing to do. Our
neighbours were Muslims, our parents worked alongside Muslims and
often had Muslim friends, as did we, and so it seemed perfectly natural
and thoroughly matter-of-fact and quite ordinary to be educated side by
side. Our differences did not separate us; we recognized and were aware
of our differences, but we went beyond them. The philosopher Jacques
Maritain says beautifully and convincingly what we, again, seemed to
know in an intuitive, though unspoken, way: as citizens we are called
to transcend our religious differences and work for unity that is "not
supradogmatic; it is suprasubjective. It does not make us go beyond our
faith, but beyond ourselves. In other words it helps us to purify our faith
of the shell of egotism and subjectivity that we instinctively tend to en-
close it."[4] I believe that in our own unsophisticated ways we were learning, each day, what this *going beyond ourselves* meant and entailed.

The Catholic tradition has long celebrated the dignity of the intellect
and the freedom that comes from pursuing truth through knowledge
along with goodness and beauty, wherever they are found. What my school
experience implicitly proclaimed, though it was unarticulated, was that
learning – the acquisition of knowledge and the pursuit of truth – is

something that human beings seek naturally, that it is undertaken in common, and that it is carried out in the context of friendship, thus confirming its social dimension. That in spite of our differences – and in this case the religious and cultural differences were significant – as students, all of us needed to study geometry and history, English literature and Urdu poetry and physics, and go off together to the laboratory to do, as I thought, dreadful things to unsuspecting, anaesthetised frogs. But more importantly, that while learning and knowing and being educated were communal and social activities, and our friendship and fellowship confirmed this conviction, our pluralist experience widened what it meant to be educated, and in this it went far beyond the explicit curriculum. In many ways the truths that we learned were important dimensions of the education of the *whole person*.

This second part of this model also implicitly contributed to unity: that while we recognized the primacy of religion, and though we were divided by religious doctrine and worldviews, our education, with the exception of religious instruction, was in common, enabling it to transcend religion. Religion was hardly being ignored, but neither was it being unduly emphasized, in the sense of eclipsing or dominating the other subjects of the curriculum. This transcending of religion in an educational context was achieved by recognizing the legitimate place and the primacy of religion in the curriculum and within the environment of the school day. However, such transcendence also suggested that we, the students, were united by much more than the obvious divisions of religion, culture, and worldviews. We were friends, we studied together, and we encountered all that went on in the school day together. What this suggested was that being educated, learning, knowing, deciding, choosing, and acting were human activities, and while religion and culture certainly influenced these activities, religion did not need to overpower, overwhelm, or overshadow the rest of the school day. This was what was *extraordinary* about this model, and all contained within the *ordinariness* of the school day. And whatever the primary reasons that led to the establishment of these Catholic schools and colleges may have been, on reflection many, many years later, it seems to me to have been an admirable model for education in a religiously pluralist society. More recently, there has been a similar call to realize that though religion and religious distinctiveness certainly contribute, indeed very fundamentally, to human identity, they are not, and need not be, the only source of identity; and to realize also that in the context of living in religiously pluralist and multicultural societies, citizens are more than just religious beings: they have multiple and intersecting identities. In his timely work *Identity and Violence: The Illusion of Destiny*, Amartya Sen draws attention to this realization: "a person's religion need not be his or her all-encompassing and exclusive identity … People see themselves – and have reason to see themselves – in many different ways." Today, "despite our *diverse diversities*, the world is suddenly seen not as a collection of people, but as a federation of religions and civilizations."[5]

In the ensuing years, and in the context of my study, reading, reflecting, and teaching in the area of Catholic education, I am increasingly convinced that Catholic schools, precisely because they are able to be grounded upon a distinct anthropology, a decided understanding of society and of its transformation, the pursuit and contribution of the common good, upon moral and religious values, and particularly upon an emphasis on the humanizing and transforming power of learning, knowledge, and understanding and their implications for human behaviour, choice, decision, and action; in short, a comprehensive and expansive worldview – that such schools have a distinct role to play in a religiously pluralist and multicultural society. It is precisely because of a worldview that encompasses all of reality – indeed, a broad curricular and school-day experience attests to such encompassing; the *diversity of the curriculum* and *the rest of the school day* attest to the *diversity of reality* – that Catholic schools have an important unifying role to play in modern pluralist societies. Such unity depends upon the dynamic and integrating power of truth through knowledge and learning.[6] It is a potential unity, and it is actualized and realized through the choices, decisions, judgments, and actions that flow from the students' learning, knowing, understanding, and choosing. In ultimate terms, this is what *educational maturity* means and entails.

In the context of pluralism and diversity, and recognizing that this context is hardly smooth or universally agreed upon, Catholic schools should consider the model that I am referring to – acknowledging that it did, like any system, have its own difficulties and shortcomings – in bringing a religiously and culturally diverse student body together and educating them in the context of fellowship and friendship. However, such a model must recognize the right of those who are non-Catholic and non-Christian to be educated in their own faith traditions in the Catholic school. In my experience, Muslim students had to be taught the Koran because it was an Islamic country; the state would simply not have tolerated Muslim students not being educated in their religious tradition. However, in the model I am suggesting – that is, a model for Western nations and for other democratic countries that practice religious tolerance – Catholic schools would offer religious instruction to the diversity of their student body not because they *had* to, but because they *wanted* to, because they saw it as a matter of pedagogical justice, but also because of its wider educational coherence. Such a choice would confirm that religious instruction in the school contributes to the human identity and human unity of the individual student. In addition, the decision to offer religious instruction according to the diversity of the school population would confirm that Catholic education possesses a distinct educational philosophy. And to the objector who might suggest that non-Catholic students should go elsewhere if they want a particular religious instruction, one would reply that Catholic education is doing precisely what it is meant to do: reading the signs of the times. In responding to religious diversity, Catholic schools contribute to bringing together a diverse citizenry and educating them to seek and contribute to the common good, which is neither a collection of individual goods, nor a collection of the goods of different religions all lumped together in one unmanageable and, more seriously, unintelligible heap. Thus, the Catholic school contributes to intelligible human living.

First, the Catholic school recognizes the primacy of religious identity; but, second, human identity is varied and complex, and in the context of the school, the common identity of knowing and learning, and being transformed, is what unifies a student body, with enormous consequences for adulthood. Such a model would enable Catholic educators to show how such an education can transform society and culture in the midst of plurality and diversity, a transformation brought about by persons *in spite of* their religious differences. In its opening paragraph, the Council's document *Declaration on the Relation of the Church to Non-Christian Religions / Nostra Aetate* affirms the unity of the human race and their journey to God: the Church "considers above all in this declaration what men [*sic*] have in common and what draws them to fellowship.

One is the community of all peoples, one their origin, for God made the whole human race to live over the face of the earth. One also is their final goal, God."[7]

Now such a proposal to constitute the Catholics school has, I realize, some practical, pragmatic, and logistical difficulties. Catholic schools in many Western societies often educate students from multiple religious traditions; the student body is often made up of Catholics, Christians of various other denominations, Muslims of various denominations, Hindus, Sikhs, Buddhists, Zoroastrians, etc. Added to this mix, there may be students who come from families who have no faith tradition or who are atheists. How would this work practically in offering each student religious instruction in their own tradition? Or, indeed, how would the school be respectful of those who choose not to receive religious instruction? The latter question is particularly charged, but prescinding from it, the other, more practical question about how one would manage such religious diversity, while difficult, is hardly insurmountable. A bit of creative thinking can be envisaged, on how Catholic schools, especially those governed by school boards, could be grouped together, depending on the makeup of the school population. And challenging as some of these difficulties are, I do not think this is the real challenge facing the place and role of Catholic schools in a religiously diverse society. Further, I do not believe that the real challenge is to trying to ensure the Catholicity of the school through mandatory Catholic religious instruction for all students, whatever their faith. Rather, the real test is to show how the rest of the curriculum and the school day — while recognizing the primacy of instruction in the Catholic faith — are universally educational because of who human beings are, based upon a philosophic-anthropological vision of the student as a person, and thus worthy to be offered to all students. Such a vision can be philosophically unifying in the midst of doctrinal and theological diversity. The absurdity of having to refute the suggestion of a Catholic physics, Catholic mathematics, or Catholic biology is just too obvious, but there remain, nonetheless, the broader and more important questions as to the distinctiveness of Catholic schools, and whether such distinctiveness is confined to their religious identity alone, or whether it includes all that is learned during the school day.

Let me say, and without any qualification, that I recognize that Catholic schools, colleges, and universities are all arms of the Roman Catholic Church, and in Canon Law – the law that governs the spiritual and temporal life of the Universal Church – such institutions have an intrinsic relationship with the Universal Church, with the pope, and with the local bishop.[8] These are relationships that are inherent to the nature of the Catholic school and are fundamental to its identity, particularly to ensure that Catholic students are not just receiving adequate religious instruction, but that they are being educated to develop and appropriate a Catholic worldview and values as they prepare to take their place as active citizens. However, I suggest that it is this Catholic worldview that is educational for all students, irrespective of caste, creed, or culture. Such a worldview is wider and deeper, and is not limited to the religious beliefs and doctrinal teachings of the Catholic faith, though it arises from those beliefs and teachings; but it then moves to a broader philosophical stage, for example, the dignity of the human person, the freedom of conscience, distributive justice, the pursuit of truth, the right to education, and the freedom that comes from truths learned and understood. While the Catholic Church teaches that everything that happens in the school should be influenced and shaped by this Catholic worldview and values, I maintain that this worldview (particularly when one moves outside of religious instruction), educationally considered, offers all students the capacity for critical engagement and reflection, both from the context of their own faith traditions and as fellow students being educated communally, as to what it means to grow in authenticity, integrity, and responsibility, both personally and communally, thus contributing to the common good. What is noteworthy about such a sense of unity is that it goes beyond the particularities of race, culture, or creed. These are surely some of the constituent elements of what it means to grow as a human person, to grow as a *whole person*. School education is wider than the curriculum, of course, but staying with the curriculum for a moment, what is being suggested is not some absurd process of baptizing the curriculum to ensure its Catholicity, but rather to show why it is that a student deprived of the diversity, the breadth, and the unity of the curriculum would not be educated as a *whole person*; indeed, such a deprivation would mean that Catholic education had not been imparted, for it is intrinsically dependent upon the diversity of the curriculum. Secular and non-religious schools could make such a claim as well, and I am not contesting that. All I am suggesting is that the Catholic worldview is broad and comprehensive and claims to be able to educate the whole person, and such a holistic education is of particular interest in the context of religious diversity and cultural plurality. Institutional education is more than the curriculum, but the curriculum is the skeleton. The flesh that drapes this skeleton and the life that pours through it depend upon how truth and knowledge are gained from each subject, all according to their own methods of teaching and knowing the truth, and are appropriated in the life, living, and choosing of each student, contributing to their own inner unity. Thus the curriculum and all the learning of the school day is the means by which the Catholic school educates the whole person, of which religious instruction is one dimension, albeit occupying a place of primacy.

Often, Catholic schools appear to be caught between the devil and the deep blue sea: on the one hand, identifying their mission in theological and religious terms alone, thus, I maintain, narrowing it unduly; and, on the other hand, struggling to articulate what makes the rest of the school day (the rest of the curriculum other than religious instruction) unique and distinctly Catholic. Both positions open themselves up to criticism from non-Catholics. There is no denying that the identity of the Catholic school is, in the first instance, fundamentally religious, and secured upon the beliefs and assumptions of faith, doctrine, and theological and moral principles. However, the critic, especially in situations where Catholic schools receive state or other forms of public funding, and sometimes to the exclusion of other religious traditions, is quick to take exception in a number of ways. First, it could be maintained that either the state funds all religious schools, or none at all, and that this is simply a matter of equity and justice; second, one can hardly claim state support by an appeal for funding in exclusively religious or theological terms; all faith traditions are religiously and theologically distinct, as could be their schools; and third, if non-Catholics and non-Christians are attending Catholic schools supported by state funding, how are their distinct religious traditions and faith practices being attended to and respected; how are they receiving a religious education in *their* faith? Indeed, how are they being educated as whole persons?[9]

The Catholic school is not the stage to convert non-Catholic students; minors and children are hardly in a position to make such a fundamentally and essentially adult decision. Conversion from one faith to another – unless an entire family were to convert – must be limited to adulthood, and beyond the walls of a school. Thus in the context of diversity and plurality, the Catholic school need not shy away from the thorny and understandably divisive issue of the faith education of non-Catholic students. The model I referred to at the start is an example where the diversity of faith traditions are not only accommodated, but also, and more positively, sewn into the very fabric of Catholic schools, whose mission is always situated in a particular social and historical environment, a specific culture, and must therefore respond to ever-changing contexts, thus reading the signs of the times, an expression that frames the Catholic response to living and being in the world.

Today it seems that the preparation of Catholic teachers usually moves through the steps of earning a degree in a secular university; acquiring state or provincial qualification to teach, usually through a secular faculty of education, sometimes with the possibility of receiving instruction in religious education; and then making one's way to assume the mantle of Catholic educator, either as an administrator or as a teacher. From the perspective of the Church, teaching is fundamentally a *vocation*, without, of course, ignoring the necessary and important *professional* dimensions of the teacher's vocation. However, how student teachers are being educated and prepared to teach as Catholic teachers is a pressing and urgent matter. How are such candidates, in the context of an essentially secular teacher-education program, being prepared to become Catholic teachers? Is a course in Catholic religious education sufficient? Alternatively, does the emphasis on such a course alone run the danger of narrowing the mission and mandate of the Catholic school, rendering it vulnerable to the criticisms of non-Christians, as raised above? Added to this, is the delicate and sensitive issue of the faith life of Catholic teachers. What does it mean for Catholic teachers to be committed to and to practice their faith? In the context of the Catholic school, is there more to Catholic education than a class in religious instruction, prayers and occasional celebration of the Eucharist, and a general goodwill among teachers and administrators to enhance a Catholic climate, with accompanying claims, though these can easily slip into platitudes, of *educating the whole person*? This, given my own vocation and ministry as a Catholic priest, is not meant to be a disrespectful question. I have said that the faith dimension of a Catholic school occupies a place of primacy. However, the Church teaches that there are three agents of education, parents being the first educators of their children, followed by the Church and the school. Each educates in their distinct way, and while all three are fundamentally related to each other, they are distinct, and must each show forth their particular educational method. The Catholic school must manifest its unique role in the midst of diversity and plurality.

To speak about a *Catholic philosophy of education*, as distinct from a *philosophy of Catholic education*, is to formulate a wider and more universal approach. First, a Catholic philosophy of education is distinct from a general philosophical approach to education, not in its method but rather in its historical context of certain philosophical enterprises. Second, in speaking of a Catholic philosophy of education, the term *Catholic* is used to modify *education*, but also *philosophy*. How the Catholic intellectual tradition understands *education* and *philosophy* is hardly unified or uniform, but neither is it so disjointed and fragmented as to provide no unity in the way *Catholic* modifies *education* and *philosophy*. Third, a Catholic philosophy of education would admit to a unity and a hierarchy of knowledge. And while within such a hierarchy theology and Scripture occupy a higher place and order (and, in ultimate terms, while Scripture leads this hierarchy), nevertheless philosophy plays an integrative and unifying role, as it recognizes the various orders of knowledge but also seeks to relate and unify them. Fourth, a Catholic philosophy of education is distinct from a Catholic theology of education whose starting point would be Scripture, the teaching tradition of the Magisterium, and the Catholic moral and theological tradition, as itself distinguishable from the traditional philosophical starting points such as knowledge, learning, and understanding, while, of course, not forgetting their place in a theology of education as well. Here the term *Catholic philosophy of education* is being used in a universal sense of the Roman Catholic Church's understanding of education. I maintain that while the Church places Scripture and the Teaching Tradition of the Church – including the intellectual tradition – as the foundation of the Catholic School, it does possess a philosophy of education that is grounded in traditional philosophical themes such as knowledge, learning, and understanding; and I maintain too that these themes are in service of unifying the student as a person. Finally, today, a Catholic philosophy of education, as evidenced by the most recent documents from the Congregation for Catholic Education, seeks to serve a religiously and culturally diverse world by unifying the student through an integral education. And here again, while this service continues to be primarily inspired and strengthened by the Gospels and the teaching tradition of the Church, it is a philosophical service for the freedom and autonomy of the student as a person.

On the other hand, the more particular application of a *philosophy of Catholic education* is thoroughly important as well, precisely because a broader and universal *Catholic philosophy of education* must be applied to local historical and cultural situations. In this context, a philosophy of Catholic education is understood as the application of the Church's universal teachings on education to particular local, cultural, and historical contexts.[10] So given this approach, one could speak, for example, of a Canadian philosophy of Catholic education or a South African philosophy of Catholic education. Another distinction between a *Catholic philosophy of education* and a *philosophy of Catholic education* is that the former would be a wider and more general investigation, while the latter would be a distinct and specific investigation determined by the particularities of historical, social, and cultural context. Since the Council, there have been many studies of Catholic education in the particularities of geography, history, politics, and culture. The *International Handbook of Catholic Education* and *The Contemporary Catholic School: Context, Identity and Diversity*, referred to elsewhere in this volume, are two internationally recognized works in this tradition.

Two more points in this regard. First, while the title of this book, *A Catholic Philosophy of Education: The Church and Two Philosophers*, suggests a universal and philosophical approach, my aim is not to suggest it is *the* definitive approach. By making detailed references to the Church's educational documents and the thought of Jacques Maritain and Bernard Lonergan, what I present is one way of understanding a Catholic philosophy of education. Other ways could be envisaged, for example, using these documents in reference to the thought of Paulo Freire, Luigi Giussani, or Josef Pieper. The works of all three thinkers could be employed to extricate the universal and general approaches to a Catholic philosophy of education that transcends particularities of history, culture, and geography. Second, and more will be said about this in the next chapter, while the focus of this work is a Catholic *philosophy* of education, the theological shift that came from the Council, and the subsequent attention to Christian personalism and existentialism, and Lonergan's own transcendental method, now means that one can no longer propose a Catholic philosophy of education that is isolated from or ultimately independent of the wider theological method of the Catholic intellectual tradition. This is particularly noticeable in the scholarship and reflection on the theoretical and systematic approach to Catholic education that has occurred since the Council. There is a decided theological shift. However, that shift is inclusive and accommodating in envisaging a philosophical understanding of Catholic education. For example, the scholarship in Catholic religious education attests to this more inclusive and accommodating bent. What I attempt to show is that in spite of this shift, the Church does have a philosophy of education, and that philosophy is developed and incrementally added to by the documents from the Congregation for Catholic Education.

This work, then, examines what the Catholic Church understands by a Catholic philosophy of education, as developed primarily in her educational documents, issued from the Congregation for Catholic Education. This is then placed in parallel relationship with the thought and writings of two philosophers, Jacques Maritain and Bernard Lonergan, who help in providing variations and varieties of philosophical muscle. These documents are addressed to the whole Church, but particularly to Catholic educators across the world. Thus this work is a more universal reflection of what the Church teaches about education. However, by employing the thought of Maritain and Lonergan, this work explores how Catholic education, with its emphasis on learning and understanding, can be a source of integral unity for all students, regardless of their faith traditions. The Catholic educational documents envisage knowledge, learning, and understanding as transformative, personally as well as for communal living, including the search for and the contribution to the common good. What this book does not do, therefore, is offer an analysis of how such an education might be implemented in a particular national and local context. That crucially important task is for those who are familiar with and knowledgeable about their own situation and context, and the issues and concerns that must be addressed given these documents. It is my contention that the Catholic Church does generate

Catholic philosophy of education, and the challenge remains, in the face of the universal mission of the Catholic Church, to apply this universal mission to particular situations, to local and national contexts, with particular histories and cultures. Such an application is both an empirical process – that is, remaining open to such new discoveries and innovations as arise in a particular context – as well as dependent and relying upon tradition and the teaching authority of the Church. It is a dynamic relationship between the faith of the Church – ever ancient and ever new – and the Catholic school existing in particular moments of time, and thus responding to the particularities of history and culture. Such application is challenging and must of itself remain open-ended, as an essential means of reading the signs of the times. This work offers one way to consider a Catholic philosophy of education; it is not an exclusive model, of course, nor does it preclude other ways of envisaging such a philosophy of education.

This work will be divided as follows. I maintain that there are two influences that have shaped Catholic philosophy of education in our time, Thomistic philosophy and the Second Vatican Council. The first chapter, "Catholic Philosophy of Education: Before and after the Second Vatican Council," examines these two influences. In modern times, Thomistic philosophy received public and universal acclamation with the encyclical of Pope Leo XIII, *Aeterni Patris / On the Restoration of Christian Philosophy*, promulgated in 1879. Thomism, particularly Neo-Thomism, which shaped a Catholic philosophy of education, grew in prominence after the encyclical and remained centre-stage until the close of the Council in 1965. What was distinct about this approach was not a philosophy of education that emerged and was formulated from the official documents and teachings of the Church, but rather the application of Thomistic principles by individual Catholic intellectuals: theologians, philosophers, and educators. The second influence was the Council, one that shaped a Catholic worldview, opening the Church to the modern world, as is evidenced by its documents that span a variety of issues in the Church's relation with the world. A foundational change was a shift away from, though not an official rejection of, a Thomistic and Neo-Thomistic worldview, toward one determined by the singularities of history and culture. While the worldview of Thomism was more philosophically based, the Council's worldview was comprehensively theological. However, the Catholic educational documents that were issued after the Council, while acknowledging this theological worldview, also sought to develop a Catholic philosophy of education. Employing the thought of Maritain and Lonergan, in relation to the Catholic educational documents, shows that these Thomistic approaches still contribute to a Catholic understanding of education.

Given more than two thousand years of Christian experience and history, commenting on a Catholic philosophy of education that spans such a history is a herculean undertaking; the aim of this chapter is thus much more modest. It reflects upon what was understood by a Catholic philosophy of education between *Aeterni Patris* and the close of the Council, and how that understanding shifted after the Council. The works considered in this chapter are works in English, though even these are hardly an exhaustive list. Today, a Catholic philosophy emerges from the documents of the Congregation for Catholic Education. And while a Catholic philosophy of education is never completely defined in any one of these documents, it is clear they form the essential structure of such an educational philosophy, which also, and necessarily, is open-ended and heuristic.

Chapter 2 is titled "Jacques Maritain and Bernard Lonergan: Two Catholic Philosophers of Education." These two philosophers have influenced me greatly, and have helped me shape a Catholic understanding of a philosophy of education. Both wrote works on this subject. Jacques Maritain was a Neo-Thomist and Bernard Lonergan was also influenced by the Thomist tradition. Maritain, by applying his philosophical *habitus* to a wide array of issues, from political philosophy to aesthetics, and from metaphysics to philosophy of history, wrote extensively, including works on educational philosophy. Lonergan, like Maritain, also produced a vast intellectual corpus, but his work is, by and large, in the area of philosophy and theology, with writings on culture, economics, political economy, and educational philosophy as well.[11] These two thinkers, while sharing the Catholic faith and a dedication to the thought of Saint Thomas Aquinas, did differ, particularly in the area of metaphysics and epistemology. However, what they have to say about knowledge, learning, and understanding, particularly for institutional education, offers two Catholic perspectives through which one might read the Catholic educational documents. They provide useful *before* and *after* lenses for

Catholic education – that is, before and after the Council. While Maritain's and Lonergan's works on educational philosophy were written before the Second Vatican Council, Lonergan's thought, bolstered by his later works (written after the Council) advocates for a worldview that would emerge from the Council. Nonetheless, Maritain's educational philosophy remains extremely relevant.

The next four chapters are thematic, and follow a similar structure examining the Catholic educational documents, with parallel perspectives from Maritain and Lonergan. Chapter 3 is titled "The Aim and End of the Catholic School: The Role of Knowledge and Learning." The Catholic school, as stated previously, is both an arm of the Church as well as one of the three agents of Catholic education, parents and the Church being the other two. The Catholic school is one of the sites of the formation of the *whole person*, and such a formation is intrinsically bound by the divine destiny of the student as a person created in the image and likeness of God, and consequently promotes a distinct worldview that is theological, philosophical, social, cultural, moral, and communal. The Catholic school responds to this divine destiny through its intellectual mandate. While it must protect this divine destiny, it must also show how it is closely linked with everything that happens in the school, and it must do so through this intellectual mandate upon which the religious and moral dimensions of the school are secured. The religious dimension of the Catholic school is undoubtedly central, but the whole curriculum – and, again, *curriculum* is being used in the widest sense possible to encompass the total school day and the school environment – is also essential as to how students grow in their personhood. Knowledge and learning are fundamental in realizing the aim and end of the school. They are also essential for the personal freedom and autonomy of the student, and for the communal and societal contribution of the Catholic school.

Chapter 4 is titled "The Unity of the Student." The student is the primary agent in the learning process; learning is an active, dynamic, and unifying process. It is not, on the one hand, a Platonic exercise of introducing the student to some idealized form of the good, beautiful, and true; nor does it consider the student to be an empty vessel who must be filled to the brim as a complete and finished product once schooling concludes. Students are active learners, and an integral education, the education of the student as a whole person, is not a monologue but a dialogue. Students must also be taught the art of questioning, which ensures the understanding and appropriation of what has been learned. In the Catholic school the student must be educated to understand what is entailed in personal freedom and autonomy – religiously, intellectually, morally, culturally, socially, and politically – and their implications for communal living. Students mature and grow by participating in their own learning, and such participation spans the depth and variety of the curriculum. Human beings encounter the world in many different ways, and while the senses have a place of initial primacy, it is through reasoning, understanding, and deciding that one knows, and hence the claim to be educated, and thus moving beyond the senses. In an electronic age where the visual and the ubiquitous power of the image loom ominously and disproportionately large, students in a Catholic school must be assisted to understand that though they primarily encounter the world through their five senses, that encounter must move to the more integrative levels of reasoning, understanding, deciding, and choosing what one has learned, and the implications thereof for the living of life. It is only through such integration that learning and knowing can occur. All of this is crucial to the personal unity of the student.

Chapter 5 is titled "The Vocation of the Teacher." The interaction and relationship between the teacher and the student is not just primary, it is irreplaceable. It is the living, emerging, and heuristic encounter of one human mind with another. And while the professional relationship of a teacher and students must never be compromised, education, Catholic education, is primarily a human encounter, one that no amount of technological sophistication can substitute for or replace. While teachers' professional and intellectual competencies are the foundation of their public claim to teach, teachers' commitments and convictions are, in ultimate terms, more important than their professional skill or academic competence. The teacher's example, particularly their intellectual, religious, moral, and social example, is the primary source of the student's true and lasting learning and understanding; and it is the teacher's lived and appropriated Catholic worldview that is ultimately and foundationally educational for the student, and an important source of the student's personal unity and freedom. In addition, the spirit of inquiry that the teacher engenders by encouraging students to ask their own questions enables the teacher to remain faithful to the claim that

Catholic education seeks to know the truth, wherever it is to be found. The art of teaching is a living activity that must activate the student's dynamic ability to think and to reason, appropriate to their stages of mental and moral growth. The teacher also ensures the personal unity and freedom of each student, without which the education of the whole person would be untenable.

Chapter 6 is titled "Society, Culture, and the Common Good." The social teachings of the Catholic Church, and not just since the Council, have consistently emphasized why the Catholic faith and by implication the Catholic school needs to be situated within a wider social context and respond to the cultural issues of the day.[12] Each believer, of course, must enter into a personal relationship with God, but the social and communal dimension of faith is undeniable – *love of God and love of neighbour*. The challenges of relativism and pluralism, on the one hand, and gross social and economic inequities, on the other, make this care for society, the transformation of culture, and striving together for the common good all the more urgent. The ecological concern for the world's environment is a compelling example of the contemporary understanding of the common good. The later educational documents speak of an *educational emergency* not only in communicating values to the student, but in relating these values to life in common, particularly in striving for the common good. The values being communicated are *anthropological* and *ethical*, and in this, once again, the Catholic school can play an integrative role in the midst of plurality and diversity. Communal living and striving for the common good have an undoubted and necessary terrestrial quality; they are an end in themselves, not an absolute end, but an end nonetheless. Students of a Catholic school must grapple with the personal and social dimensions of freedom and liberation. The Church's understanding of culture has also shifted, having moved from a principally Western and European conception to an understanding of culture as a theatre for human growth; thus culture in one sense transcends the confines of one's geography. The understanding of culture as the environment where, among other things, one strives for human growth, human responsibility, the search for truth, the pursuit of the common good, and freedom has resulted in expanding the notion of culture. In previous ages, culture or a cultured person were often narrowly understood as possessing and acquiring knowledge, tastes, and sensitivities associated with the finer things of life by those who were economically and socially in positions to do so: an elitist understanding of culture. Now, culture is understood broadly as the necessary and ever-present environment that should enable human persons to grow into their personhood. Culture is now the context that either frees or imprisons a person.

The final chapter is not a conclusion in the traditional sense of gathering positions or arguments together. Chapters 3 through 6 involve textual readings of the Church's position and those of Maritain and Lonergan on the topic of *Catholic philosophy of education*. Each of those chapters is a pillar of a Catholic philosophy of education, and closes with a conclusion, as do chapters one and two. The seventh chapter is titled "Teach Me Goodness, Discipline, and Knowledge," the motto of my religious congregation, the Congregation of Saint Basil, also known as the Basilian Fathers, and is I think a fitting title under which to present a personal reflection in light of the previous chapters. Goodness, discipline, and knowledge are essential sources of the freedom and liberation that education offers the student.

The principal mandate of an educational institution is primarily intellectual in nature; this is confirmed by the Catholic educational documents, and by Maritain and Lonergan. The intellectual mandate has essential religious, social, moral, cultural, political, and anthropological implications. A student comes to a school to be educated, and that process is really an enlightenment of the mind, in which the student is an active and not a passive agent. A Catholic school educates in concert with the other two agencies (parents and the Church); but it does so via the intellectual enlightenment of the mind, however (and this is worthy of repetition), never isolating knowing, learning, and understanding from human becoming, choosing, deciding, and acting. In Catholic education, knowledge and learning would surely be deemed to have failed if they became avenues to intellectual snobbery and an elitism of ideas for their own sake. After all, knowledge, learning, and understanding are one of the principal means of freedom and liberation, an invitation offered to all God's children.

Knowing and learning are never concluded or completed at the end of institutional education, but neither are they so open-ended and so tentative as to be unable to assist students, after sufficient investigation, to choose, decide, and act, thus manifesting themselves through their living – how they will choose to grow in their personhood. Of course, like knowing, learning, and understanding, the growth in and towards personhood is perennial; it is never ever achieved nor completely realized at any one stage of life. Yet knowing and learning are inextricably linked to human becoming. In this, the Catholic school has a particular contribution to make amidst religious and cultural plurality and diversity.

Finally, and again this bears repeating, in employing the thought of Jacques Maritain and Bernard Lonergan, this book is offering *a* reflection on Catholic philosophy of education. The Church has a very detailed and reasoned educational vision, particularly amidst religious diversity and cultural plurality; it is a vision for the unity of the student and for the communal unity of all students. The philosophies of Maritain and Lonergan supplement and confirm this. Both wrote on religious diversity and cultural plurality. Maritain did so throughout his philosophical corpus, but principally in his works on political and social philosophy and educational philosophy. Lonergan wrote in the context of the change from a classicist conception of the world, secured upon enduring and universal truths, to a world now encountered through the particularities of history and culture: an empirical approach. No longer is there thought to be one culture, one Western conception of culture; there are now many cultures and human becoming is always in the context of one's history and culture, but never confined by it; hence the freedom through self-transcendence. Both these philosophers have important contributions in situating Catholic education for our time, and their response is remarkably close to my own Catholic school experience, one marked by diversity and plurality.

The educational documents, Maritain, and Lonergan all emphasize, each in their own way, how a Catholic philosophy of education serves and can unite a religiously diverse society. And while, in ultimate terms, such a philosophy of education is related to theology, its philosophical distinctiveness and independence is not compromised or diminished by its ultimate relationship with theology, thus enabling it to serve religiously pluralist school societies. This, of course, is not a work on a Catholic theology of education. Therefore, I hope, it is a work that attracts a wide readership as it points to the universality of Catholic education, universal in bringing together a religiously and culturally diverse student body, based upon an anthropology and worldview that promotes the unity of the student as a person and thus unifies community and society, implicitly securing the common good. One group that I hope will profit from this work is Catholic educators in general, but particularly Catholic teachers, given my own commitment to their ongoing education and formation. During my academic career, I have had the privilege of teaching many Catholic school administrators and teachers, and I have concluded the semester by saying to my students how much I have learned from them. Adult education has shown why and how the experience of adults is often heavy and laden with educational meaning, and adult learning environments are truly educational when teaching and learning are collaborative and interactive. I also hope that this work will contribute to the corpus of Catholic educational studies. Finally, I will be most pleased if it goes beyond a Catholic readership, as the transformation, freedom, and liberation that come from education are of interest to all educators.

One note is required regarding references. As the documents from the Congregation for Catholic Education and works by Jacques Maritain and Bernard Lonergan will be used frequently, the titles of these works will be abbreviated in the endnotes, with the full title given in the bibliography at the end of this book. While a cardinal prefect and an archbishop secretary usually sign the Church's documents on their promulgation – those issued from Congregations, Pontifical Councils, etc. – the endnotes and the bibliography will simply cite the individual Congregation or Pontifical Council as the author.

1

Catholic Philosophy of Education: Before and after the Second Vatican Council

I Introduction

The purpose of this chapter is to situate Catholic philosophy of education before and after the Council. However, its scope is modest, and is limited to literature in English; I make no claim, therefore, to universal coverage of this topic.

I shall first outline the contents of this chapter. The second section then considers the influence of Thomism and Neo-Thomism in shaping and influencing a Catholic philosophy of education. This influence was largely in the context of the encyclical *Aeterni Patris*. Part 3 is an overview of Catholic philosophy of education between *Aeterni Patris* and the close of the Council in 1965. Catholic educators in the English-speaking world at that time would have known the literature examined in this section. Part 4 considers the change of worldview that emerged from the Council. The depth and diversity of that transformation was breathtaking, and this brief section looks at some of those changes, and how they shaped Catholic educational theory. Part 5 offers some comments on the Council's document *Gravissimum Educationis / Declaration on Christian Education*. While it has been said that this was not a particularly strong document, its strength is derived from its place among the other fifteen documents of the Council, and consequently the changes that it ushered in, reshaping Catholic education, were nourished by these other documents. Part 6 reviews the thoughts of five Catholic educators and the changes they saw emerging from the Council, particularly the change in emphasis from a Catholic philosophy of education to a Catholic theology of education. The relevance of philosophy for a Catholic educational theory is recognized, but under a wider theological umbrella. The chapter closes with some conclusions.

II Thomism and Neo-Thomism

Since the close of the Council in 1965, the Roman Catholic Church has not promulgated a fully fledged and formally articulated Catholic philosophy of education in any one document. The Church's philosophical understanding of Catholic education is wider than the sharp and specialized distinctions between philosophy and theology. However, various statements, documents, and encyclicals have been issued on Christian and Catholic education, by popes and the Congregation for Catholic Education in Rome[1] (cce), all of which show the breadth of what is entailed in the Church's understanding of Catholic education.[2] Given that such a philosophy has never been formalized in a single document, the Catholic educational documents issued since the close of the Council develop a Catholic educational philosophy in an incremental, cumulative, and heuristic way.

The term *Catholic philosophy of education* has a specific historical context, and is situated within the overall resurgence of *Thomism*, which flourished between the promulgation of the encyclical *Aeterni Patris* and the close of the Council.[3] The golden age of a Catholic philosophy of education, within the context of the revival of Thomism in general and its evolution and manifestation as Neo-Thomism in particular, can be traced to *Aeterni Patris*. In one sense, the encyclical attempted to give Catholic intellectual life a public dimension, and theologians and philosophers have mapped the responses to it.[4] However, the pope's primary concern was with the quality of seminary education, which prepared candidates for the priesthood.[5] Catholic intellectual life since the time of St Thomas, had, of course, undergone many changes. These changes were first in relation to the Church itself, and then, most notably, in response to external pressures – for example, the calling of the Council of Trent in 1545 and its closing in 1563, in the face of the Protestant Reformation. In responding to Luther and Zwingli, the Catholic Church was also faced with the ecclesiastical turbulence created by Henry VIII. With the burgeoning of a plurality of positions, counter-positions, and teachings regarding the Christian faith, "one question [among Catholics] was on everybody's lips: What are we bound to believe as an article of faith, and what is merely theological opinion?"[6] The First Vatican Council, 1869–70 (three hundred years after the Council of Trent), was faced with challenges of a different kind, mainly philosophical, but which had a profound impact on the doctrinal, theological, and moral teachings of the Catholic Church. In addition, Gallicanism was a real threat to papal authority, particularly the Vatican's teaching authority.[7] Among the doctrinal and theological issues discussed at the First Vatican Council was the most famous and controversial declaration on papal infallibility.[8]

Pope Leo XIII was anxious to restore the integrity of a single philosophical system based on St Thomas Aquinas – though he did not name or identify specific Thomistic positions – as a means to prepare students in seminaries, but also as a response to the various philosophical challenges that had arisen since the time of the Council of Trent, associated with philosophers such as Hobbes, Descartes, Locke, Kant, and Hegel, as well as the scientism of Darwin, the materialism of Engels and Marx, and the birth of various and often conflicting social theories. The pope was responding to "the failure of contemporary systems ... marked by a strong tendency of individualism."[9] Philosophies of materialism, rationalism, liberalism, idealism, monism, pantheism, scientific naturalism, socialism, and positivism marked the philosophical landscape. While the history of philosophy is, of course, a history of intellectual turbulence and often-sharp disagreements, what the Church perceived was intellectual disarray and confusion. What it sought was intellectual unity. "Since all those systems could not offer an adequate and satisfactory solution, while men, by force of their endowment, were 'seeking ultimate, fixed foundations and standards for thought and action,' what was more natural for the truth-seeking mind than to return to the past?"[10] However, Pope Leo's response was not meant to ghettoize the Catholic intellectual tradition; rather he sought to open it to the world, using the unified and systematic thought of St Thomas as its foundation: "We exhort you ... in all earnestness to restore the golden wisdom of St. Thomas, and to spread it far and wide for the defense and beauty of the Catholic faith, for the good of society and for the advantage of all sciences."[11] Leo XIII was not advocating an intellectual return to the Middle Ages; he was sounding, rather, "the recall to Thomas' basic doctrines in order to meet modern needs."[12] He was a learned and cultured man, and recognizing the importance of knowing and learning for one's particular age, he was endeavouring to improve the intellectual coherence of his own time and responding to the challenges that faced his age. In his encyclical he "envisioned two main paths he was confident would lead to the recovery and authentic development of St. Thomas' own philosophy." One was the "ongoing dialogue between Thomists and contemporary philosophers; the other, rigorous research into Thomism's historical sources."[13]

The historical period between the close of the First Vatican Council and *Aeterni Patris* saw the rise, indeed the supremacy, of Thomism[14] – that is, a worldview, a particular philosophical and theological worldview, secured upon the writings of St Thomas Aquinas.[15] An entry of "Thomism" into the library catalogue of a Catholic university or Catholic seminary should reveal a rich and varied literature. St Thomas, who had distinguished himself from another great Christian thinker, St Augustine,[16] was a theologian who "philosophized abundantly and with great originality, but he did not think that a Christian should stop at philosophy. To Thomas, philosophy was a help and a consolation to the Christian on the road to salvation, and a vehicle for defending the faith and removing errors."[17] The strict division today between philosophy and theology emerges with the dawn of modern philosophy (a period that begins with René Descartes and the Cartesian *cogito* in the sixteenth century), a division that would certainly have seemed alien and artificial to Christian intellectuals of the Middle Ages. The preeminent historian of philosophy and renowned Thomistic scholar Etienne Gilson says, "the parts of his philosophy in which St. Thomas shows the most originality, are in general included within his theology ... The theology of St. Thomas is a philosopher's theology; his philosophy is a theologian's."[18] St Thomas's writings, mainly the *Summa Theologica*, were a great and encyclopaedic exposition of the Catholic faith. Also known as the Angelic Doctor, St Thomas "brought Aristotelian natural philosophy and metaphysics into the heart of theology and developed a unique synthesis known as *Thomism*."[19] Hence, Catholic scholars have used the framework of Thomistic thought for more than just theology and philosophy. His works have been applied to jurisprudence, political theory, ethics, theory of natural law, educational philosophy, and aesthetics, among other disciplines. Gilson welcomed *Aeterni Patris*, as his copious research attests. What "caught Gilson's attention" was the pope's emphasis on Christian philosophy, "not so much as a doctrine, as a special *way* of philosophizing," but rather the "special mode that is appropriate to that of philosophy." This mode, this disposition of philosophizing, caught his attention. It was a method that was known to the Church Fathers, as well as to St Augustine, St Bonaventure, and St Thomas Aquinas.[20]

In the late nineteenth century, Thomism evolved, forming a distinct branch known as *Neo-Thomism*. "The second strand [the first being traditional Thomism] might be called neo-Thomism. These more speculative thinkers attempted to open up Thomism, willing to engage in dialogue with twentieth-century science, art, and scholarship, and even to assimilate aspects of modern thought."[21] It has also been maintained that some in this group would be better designated "Neo-Scholastics."[22] Neo-Thomism, the application of the thought and writings of St Thomas Aquinas to a particular historical context, spans the late nineteenth and the middle part of the twentieth century.[23] Disciples of this school were convinced that while St Thomas was understandably silent on particular philosophical and theological issues and topics that arose subsequent to him, especially all that ensued after the advent of modern philosophy, nevertheless his works were broad, dynamic, and versatile enough to contain the principles and method that would enable his thought to be applied to any given age and time, irrespective of history and culture.[24] (Indeed, given the unified worldview of the Middle Ages, transcending one's history and culture would have seemed meaningless.) This Neo-Thomistic application was not limited to the areas of philosophy and theology, but was also adapted to a philosophy of art, political theory, educational philosophy, social and family life, music, culture, etc. "In almost quixotic manner, literally thousands of Catholic authors worldwide, in monographs, periodicals, and in all the standard teaching venues, offered Thomistic cures for modern ills."[25]

Education is always contextual and historical, and the history of education is never isolated far from, or unrelated to, the history of ideas. Education is always shaped, and subsequently either enhanced or diminished, by philosophical and ideological currents, some of which have been referred to above, and many of which are categorized under the designations of "modern" and "contemporary" philosophy. More recently, postmodernism and poststructuralism, deconstructionism, critical race/ethnicity studies, postcolonial/decolonial theories, theories related to diversity and multiculturalism, and various positions related to individualism have added to this intellectual and philosophical smorgasbord of pluralism. While Thomists sought to apply the thought of St Thomas to divergent issues, but within a stable intellectual and conceptual universe and unified by a Christian worldview, Neo-Thomists, on the other hand, did not have the benefit nor the luxury of such intellectual stability or philosophical unity.[26]

The writings and thought of St Thomas span a vast intellectual universe. Apart from his three major works – the *Summa Theologica*, the *Summa Contra Gentiles*, and the *Commentary on the Sentences* – he wrote thirteen commentaries on the works of Aristotle; four commentaries on the books of the Old Testament; commentaries on each of the four Gospels; sixteen commentaries on other works of the New Testament; various responses to disputed questions, short works, and popular writings on the Creed, the Lord's Prayer, and the Ten Commandments; and other works as well. The staggering breadth and diversity of his thought could be summarized as a quest for harmony and for unity as a response to the diversity of the created order, and the place and role of human beings within that diversity. At the heart of this quest for unity is order, ultimately found in God, in whom all creation is both ordered and united.[27]

Brief mention needs to be made of the crisis of modernism in the Catholic Church, a vast subject in itself. In his encyclical, Pope Pius X condemned modernism as "the synthesis of all heresies," a description that is not immediately enlightening.[28] While the terms *modernism* and *modernist* are "inescapably imprecise," in Catholic circles a modernist was one "whose thinking and methodology led him to challenge the over-all philosophico-theological *schema*, or any significant element therein, of the then prevailing neo-scholastic conception and method of doing philosophy and theology."[29] Liberalism, particularly its intellectual variety, was viewed with suspicion, as were any attempt to dethrone Neo-Scholastic metaphysics in favour of hermeneutics, new and advancing biblical studies, the methods of the social sciences, and the rise of various forms of subjectivism. In the religious context, modernism claimed the "modern mind is entitled to judge what is true or right in accordance with its own experience, regardless of whether or not its conclusions run counter to tradition and custom." It was a synthesis of "the basic truths of religion and the methods and assumptions of modern thought."[30] It is maintained that the "foundations of Modernism," as envisaged in the encyclical, "were the broad philosophical and theological tendencies towards agnosticism, immanentism, evolutionism and democratism." The real crisis of modernism was "the question of authority" in interpreting Scripture: the hierarchy of the church versus scientific and historical scholarship.[31] For Rome, modernism "meant, among other things, the derision of the sacred, the theft of age-old endowments, the imposition by an elite of a positivist and agnostic mindset upon formerly Christian peoples."[32] Modernism was viewed as the "dethronement of reason," with "pragmatism [as] a prior condition." It was thought that with modernism, "the external standards – revelation, dogma, doctrine as well as the Church's magisterium – would be entirely devalued and uprooted. Ultimately the Church would lose its criterion of truth," leading to its destruction.[33] Given its breadth, modernism has been described as the "compendium of all heresies." The crisis of modernism was addressed at the Second Vatican Council, marking the "Church's departure from a classicist to an historical world view."[34]

III   Catholic Philosophy of Education: Some Literature Prior to Vatican II

The purpose here is less a review of the literature and more an overview of how a Catholic philosophy of education was understood between *Aeterni Patris* and the close of the Council. Furthermore, this overview is hardly an exhaustive or comprehensive list of works on the Catholic philosophy of education. The list proceeds chronologically, and the works would have been familiar to Catholic educators in the English-speaking world.

Mayer's *The Philosophy of Teaching of St. Thomas Aquinas* (1928) offers the text and a commentary on St Thomas's *De Magistro* (*On the Teacher*). While the author refers to Dewey and to modern influences such as behaviourism and pragmatism, the book concentrates on St Thomas's conception of education in the context of "an orderly universe." St Thomas sees the universe "in the order and connection of causes." The *De Magistro*, says Mayer, anticipates the perennial and persistent problems of education: the experience of the student, the teacher's role in integrating this experience, and free choice and the integration of character. St Thomas would have considered all these problems "as aspects of his theory of the educability of man, the potentiality for self-stabilization of human plasticity into an integrated character, under the influence of an ideal." Given this thirteenth-century text, the reader is offered a glimpse of what school life was like at the time. The book's purpose is modest, and there is no inclusion of an apologia defending the perennial versatility of Aquinas's thought. Rather, the methodical and systematic manner of St Thomas's text is self-evident proof that a vision of education depends on the ultimate and created nature of the student in relation to the divine Teacher.[35]

Marique claims that his work *The Philosophy of Christian Education* (1939) is "emphatically antifaddist," and "catholic, in its most comprehensive meaning." Apart from setting out the nature of philosophy of education and philosophies in relation to education, the work is divided traditionally into physical, intellectual, aesthetic, moral, and religious education. While Western education benefited from Plato and Aristotle and from the early Church Fathers and the schoolmen – the teachers of philosophy and theology in medieval universities – the last three hundred years, presumably from the date of this publication, witnessed the displacement of this unified system by "new philosophies that ignore or reject principles which Christianity considers as fundamental." The main social theories (naturalism, socialism, and nationalism) and their relation to education are presented and critiqued. Apart from being comprehensive, a Christian conception of education is decidedly democratic, thus emphasizing the relationship between education and society. The reconstruction of society – its inevitable building and rebuilding with every generation – must not be an "organic reconstruction," which is a "purely mechanical process," but a "psychical process." Of historical interest is the inclusion of the *state* as one of the agencies of education, referring to Pope Pius XI's encyclical *Divini Illius Magistri / On Christian Education*. In spite of having "Christian" in the title, the book is clearly a work on a Catholic philosophy of education.[36]

In the essay "The Thomistic Concept of Education" (1942), Slavin maintains that if larger questions such as the purpose of life and attaining happiness, which are what drive human beings, ignore "an objective interpretation of man and his place in society," then education will be confined to "minds and bodies," rather than "hearts and souls" as well. Education is framed in the context of four philosophical causes – material, formal, final, and efficient. The limitations of Aquinas's thought are outlined, especially given the advances of educational psychology, teaching methods, and other scientific and technological progress. Despite these limits, however, the versatility of his thought lies in his understanding of human beings created by God and invited to a divine destiny. This understanding was particularly relevant for education, and Aquinas understood "the nature of the educable." The order of a created universe is intrinsically related to the order that human beings must seek to follow in pursuing the questions of life and happiness. Human beings will be imprisoned by turning in on themselves, or failing to allow the natural light of reason and intelligence to flower in relationship to the order that God has called each person to by virtue of their divine destiny. Thus Thomist education is "wider than a classroom," and can "never be restricted to any particular period of a person's life but encompasses the whole of life."[37]

Leen's *What Is Education?* (1943) is somewhat like Marique's work, though it intersperses chapters relating to the philosophy of education with chapters pertinent to the school day, such as positive sciences, religious instruction, the catechism, and art. The Church is identified as the "chief educational institution," and it teaches its followers "that it is only in organic union, each with the other, that they attain full Christian perfection." If educators fail to grasp the end of education (that is, its goal and ultimate purpose), then education becomes trapped in pursuits that fail to liberate the student. By acknowledging original sin, the Catholic educator understands the "two sets of tendencies" intrinsic to every person: original sin and "divine grace given at Baptism." A true education must concentrate on potencies that develop the latter, and employ mental and physical growth as a means to realize the fruits of such grace, thus curbing the former. However, the chapter on "Education and Womanhood" would not be well received today. While the author is eager to protect the "characteristic graces of womanhood" from being compromised and falling prey to a false equality that renders women simply

imitators of men, the chapter, unintentionally, shows the historical limitations of that period, and how today our understanding of society and
culture would see such "protection" as far beyond just condescension.[38]

It is no exaggeration to state that Redden and Ryan's work, *A Catholic
Philosophy of Education* (1949), is a classic of this genre. The "position of
philosophy in education" frames this book. Catholic philosophy of education "makes religion the foundation of life and education"; further,
"it is universal and objective in its application regardless of time, place,
or social conditions"; and "it is traditionally sound in its principles as
proved by the experience of the past, and its comprehensive possibilities for the constructive guidance of the future." Chapters devoted to
naturalism, socialism, nationalism, and communism frame historical
concerns. St Thomas's view of the student is seen as "developmental
and evolutionary," but not in a Darwinian sense; rather, "learning is a
passing from potentiality to actuality brought about by self-activity." The
purpose and goal of the curriculum is impressive: "the curriculum implies a body of subject matter, activities, experiences, directed and un-
directed, involving instruction and sequences which the individual must
pass in order to attain the goals of education." The author recognizes the
distinction between the ultimate aims of (Catholic) education and those
aims that are "proximate" and "immediate." Immediate ends, while independent, are related to the ultimate end, and enable the student to
"carry out his work with interest and zeal, in conformity to unchanging
moral principles." Thus to "interpret the Catholic philosophy of education, it is necessary to comprehend the Catholic philosophy of life."[39]

Pegis's short work *Christian Philosophy and Intellectual Freedom* (1955)
is a reflection on the role, particularly the integrating role, of philosophy
in the context of *Aeterni Patris*. He is critical of the "anti-intellectualism
of progressive education," which has transformed the school "from a
center devoted primarily to intellectual instruction to a social service
agency." Perhaps Catholics have presented their educational philosophy badly, and consequently it is perceived as "authoritarian in form
and structure, dogmatic in spirit and expression, and hence without
intellectual freedom." Worthy of note is that "Catholic philosophy" is
equated with "Catholic education." Such a philosophy seeks to "understand the ways of the intellect within faith." The chapter "Christian Philosophy and Catholic Education" comments on St Thomas's conception

of the "Christian view of the unity of knowledge, truth and reality." The Thomistic relation between philosophy and theology is emphasized. The separation of philosophy from theology, in the name of "rationality," has created a "modern scholastic philosophy" that has forgotten its "metaphysical moorings" and has thus become susceptible to the "changing winds of philosophical doctrine from rationalism to ... empiricism." Finally, Catholic education has produced "bifurcated Catholics ... partly religious and partly secular in their formation," and "truncated Catholics ... wholly religious in their formation but cut off from a supposed alien world of knowledge beyond the frontiers of faith." Pegis calls for educating "integral Christian" persons, "wholly religious" in their dedication to their humanity, including dedication to the intellect, and "wholly open to the world of knowledge, of thought, and of truth."[40]

Cunningham's *The Pivotal Problems of Education* (1953) opens by considering education from the perspective of the individual or society, combining them into one view of education. The distinction between science and philosophy leads to clarification of the role of philosophy, which is "interpretation and unification"; its method is "reflection" and its subject matter is the "general." These distinctions enable one to examine the four basic philosophies of education – idealism, materialism, humanism, and supernaturalism – an examination that begins by considering ends and means. The hierarchy of educational objectives comprises the psychological, the sociological, and the philosophical. For a philosopher of the school of supernaturalism, such a hierarchy is predominantly religious in nature, thus enabling the "emergence of personality through education," a "complete personality," perhaps what today would be referred to as *the education of the whole person.* The culmination in the Catholic philosophy of education depends upon a fourfold development: "physical, social, religious, and mental." And while a "Catholic theory of education ... has its theological foundations in the Catholic theory of man," it is human unity, which functions as a whole, that is "at the very center of the Catholic theory of education."[41]

In *New Life in Catholic Schools* (1958), Ward offers a wider reflection on the Catholic school by expressing a broad understanding of Catholic learning, a challenge especially given "the interrelationship between common natural knowledge and divinely-directly revealed knowledge." Such learning becomes clear in the context of the Catholic school whose end is intellectual: "a Christian intellectual end ... the end of our schools is Christian intellectual life." The Catholic school is much more likely to reach this intellectual end than are those institutions that have other ends, such as "military, political, religious, or financial." Two points therein have implications for my work. First, one philosophizes not from just any conditions, but from one's own conditions, thus giving rise to the possibility for Christian philosophy, the Christian who philoso-phizes. This is hardly an un-contentious claim, but philosophers have claimed such an existential state.[42] "A real being exists and operates in particular conditions, and so of course does the Christian philosopher." The second point, related to the first, and referred to in the Introduction above, is the question of Catholic subjects in the curriculum; Ward's ex-amples are *Catholic poetry* or *Catholic art*. While subjects remain art and poetry, biology and physics, the disposition of the one teaching them in a Catholic school is the disposition of a Christian, and this disposition or "climate" is "sure to leave its mark on what is said by poet or philosopher or anything else working creatively in an art or in a human science."[43]

Smith's *The School Examined: Its Aim and Content* (1960) begins with a chapter on teaching, and two sections are noteworthy: "the authority of St. Thomas" and "the intellectual aim of the school." This intellectual aim, or "perfection," is related to charity and to "moral perfection," the aim of any institution of the Church, the school included. However, the aim of moral perfection is realized in a particular way in a particular in-stitution, and the Catholic school must bring this to realization through its intellectual aim. It is also noted that "teaching is intellectual in aim." Metaphysics plays an integrating role in such education, and is a "prin-ciple of teaching." Such study also "supplies a principle of order to the curriculum because it brings us to a knowledge of the source of all order who is God." It would be unusual for a Catholic school, as distinguished from a college or a university, to teach metaphysics as a distinct subject, but given the emphasis on its integrating role, and the statement that "the various sciences are put in order by metaphysics," it would appear that the author would consider the study of metaphysics to be an es-sential part in the preparation of Catholic teachers. Another theme is the education of the *whole person*: "the happy man is the whole man – mentally, morally, physically, economically, and socially adequate"; the growth towards wholeness is governed by prudence, an "integrating virtue." Wholeness, while never achieved or realized at any one stage of life, is developed in the context of the Catholic school by attending to the Thomistic understanding of the "powers of the soul."[44] Thus this work situates the education of the whole person within the framework of a Thomistic psychology.[45]

Philosophy and the Integration of Contemporary Catholic Education (1962), edited by McLean, is a collection of twenty-three essays. And while they are written in the context of Catholic higher education, they are most instructive for the vision and mission of the Catholic school in the era prior to the Council. Integration is defined as "the unification of a multitude of parts ordered by subordination to some principle." The teacher imparts knowledge and is in relation to the rational nature of the student. Thus, the last end of the human being cannot be considered apart from knowledge or from intelligibility. The integration of the curriculum is based on both unity and truth: truth as distinguished and discovered in each subject, and unity as realized by the subjects participating in a hierarchical order. Such an order "is presented with a series of relationships to be discovered by thought." Philosophy provides the leadership of integration, as it is the only discipline that "studies truth as such." Truth "includes being and being is not chaotic, each truth has its proper place, which is known to the degree that truth is known." This has important implications for the unity of the curriculum in a Catholic school. The validity of knowledge is not in question, as it is "an inescapable fact of consciousness." And though human knowledge begins with the senses, "truth more strictly taken is of intellectual knowledge alone." Human knowledge, while beginning in the senses, moves beyond the senses to the intellect; truth is "therefore implicit in the difference between the two intellectual functions of apprehension and judgment." The chapter on "Curricular Integration" refers to *Aeterni Patris* and the dependence of the human arts and disciplines upon a true philosophy. The subjects of the curriculum are to "reflect reality faithfully and accurately." A failure to do so results in placing "the intelligence in confinement." And it is precisely because each subject must represent and reflect reality accurately, that "the curriculum cannot be something subjective in the learner." The subjects of the curriculum are diverse, but they are united: the curriculum "is a pedagogical mirror which reflects reality, it has always been looked on as a unified thing because the reality which it reflects is a cosmos not a chaos."[46]

Goodrich's essay "Neo-Thomism and Education" (1962) begins with a historical note that while the philosopher Jacques Maritain influenced American Catholic education, he did not have the same influence upon its British counterpart. The essay confronts the charge that some dismiss Thomism as an "outmoded synthesis of Aristotelianism with Christian Orthodoxy, and thus is irrelevant for education, as for all departments of living." This charge is faced by reference to the work *Aquinas*, by the renowned historian of philosophy Frederick Copleston,[47] who says that while Neo-Thomism gets its inspiration from Aquinas, it conducts "its meditations on his writings in the light of subsequent philosophy, and of subsequent cultural developments in general." Aquinas's theory of knowledge contributes to education. While empiricism restricts knowledge to sensory experience, for Aquinas "the human mind is not confined only to discursive reasoning but ... it also has an intuitive power of apprehending the intelligible and grasping truth." This has important implications for the curriculum, which, while acknowledging the importance of the scientific method, cannot emphasize it exclusively. The Thomistic-inspired curriculum stresses discursive and analytical knowing as well as contemplative knowing, to develop "the capacity for intellectual wonder," whatever the subject. The author advocates that philosophy be included in the final year of the school. Given a Catholic understanding of who the human person is, in responding to this nature, "Thomism rightly asserts the fundamental educational aim in terms of shaping the human person, subordinating to this all social and vocational claims." Finally, the acknowledgment of metaphysical and religious knowledge "restores to the curriculum a rightful element of hierarchy ... in which all the sciences, natural, human, and divine, have their appointed place as reflections of a unified reality creatively through the mind of God."[48]

IV The Second Vatican Council: A Change in Worldview

Between *Aeterni Patris* and the close of the Council, Neo-Thomism shaped Catholic life, not only in the way the Church saw herself, but also socially, politically, morally, and academically. The Neo-Thomistic call for a Christian philosophy was not without its critics. Some maintained that the distinctions between philosophy and theology were clearly demarcated; adding *Christian* to *philosophy* only confused the divisions and drew scorn and criticism from the academy. "While Catholic philosophers were willing to concede that philosophy was subordinated to theology, and even that it served a propaedeutic function with respect to the teaching and learning of theology; however most of them balked at accepting a position that undercut the autonomy of their discipline. But they had to contend with a pedagogical disagreement that grew out of the Christian philosophy question."[49] The ground beneath the seeming impenetrable intellectual edifice, the all-encompassing structure of Thomism, shifted after the Council.[50] Among the seismic shifts was the advance in the study of Scripture. No longer was Scripture just a source of dogmatic theology; "the Council shifted from a propositional view of revelation to one that centered on the living Word Incarnate as Jesus of Nazareth."[51] The Church was also opening itself to dialogue with other cultures, other intellectual traditions, and other philosophical and theological positions. Indeed, the very ecumenical nature of the Council, its spirit, its intent, its very shaping of Catholic identity for the modern world, all influenced the Church's self-understanding.

The Council fundamentally transformed how the Church saw herself in matters of change itself, how she perceived herself as a truly world Church, and the style in which she preached the Gospel to all nations. This new style was "not [a] superficial ornamentation but the vehicle for conveying a significant shift in values and priorities," and it gave a profound unity to the documents of the Council.[52] The sheer breadth of the Council's sixteen documents, including *Christian Education*, addressed such matters as relations with other Christians and other cultures, moving beyond a Western classical worldview to understanding the world in the context of history and culture, and a renewed pastoral emphasis on the Church's relationship with the laity. It is said that the Second Vatican Council was "very much a council about the Church," and that "its documents make a comprehensive statement about ecclesial life," both in its "internal operations" and in its "complex of external relations." There was a practical dimension as well, and that was that in order to advance the cause of the Gospel, the Church had to take the world *seriously*. In this self-conception, the Church now saw herself as a community of persons, a *communion*; Christians were now constituted as "an entirely new form of human community, a society whose very principle of unity and identity was the felt presence of God's own self."[53]

There were significant theological changes that emerged from the Council. Among them was the Church's transformation from a *suspicious* and *guarded* institution to one anxious to reach out to non-Catholics and non-Christians, and from having "viewed the world as alien to itself" to now seeing the world as "a partner in dialogue." Perhaps most profoundly, the Church's shift in self-understanding led her to look on herself as "an instrument of the kingdom and hence always in need of renewal and reform." Changing also was a mainly monolithic approach to theology in a "new key," one that needed to respond to the various intellectual, cultural, and social influences. Such a shift was in concert with the changes in the approach to Scripture studies, with a new emphasis on the language of the author, the cultural and historical period of the text, and the religious, political, and social concerns of the people for whom it was written. Prior to the Council, the presuppositions of the theological method were drawn from medieval philosophy. There was new attention now being paid to the sensitivities to culture, history, languages, and the various hermeneutical ways of reading the texts of Scripture, all leading and contributing to a new breadth and expansiveness in theology, primarily shaped by a movement from a classicist worldview to a "historically conscious worldview."[54]

Another shift was in the Church's understanding of *Tradition*. With the Council, the notion of Tradition expanded from the "handing on of doctrinal propositions from age to age" to Tradition understood in the context of "*communio*." Among these changes was a shift from a hierarchical to a *communio* model of the Church as the "visible expression in prayer, action, teaching, relating, speaking and working. *Communio*, therefore, suggests a weight to the notion of 'Tradition' that is greater than the mere accumulation of information."[55] Theologians further enriched the Church's understanding of Tradition. Faith is itself a living transmission, reception, and communion. The person receiving the faith is actively engaged in that reception. "Thus tradition will not be merely a transmission followed by a passive, mechanical reception; it entails the making present in a human consciousness of a saving truth." There is a sense of "entrusting something to someone" when speaking of Tradition, a personal entrusting, one that goes beyond what is handed down in the written word as it concerns the living and loving reception and engagement of the one who has received the Tradition. Tradition is not set permanently, but rather renewed and given life in each age through "a living and unchanging principle of identity," realized through "the relations between Christ and the Holy Spirit."[56] Further, Tradition always exists in relation to one who believes and who is committed to what is contained in the tradition: "Tradition, like the body and its organs, is best known in a subsidiary way by dwelling in it, rather than in a focal way, by looking at it. Hence the doctrinal implications of the tradition will presumably be clearer to one who is existentially committed to the tradition than to the outsider."[57] Thus the Council's document on divine revelation states that Tradition and Scripture "form one sacred deposit of the word of God."[58] This widening in the understanding of Tradition had implications for education in the Catholic school.[59]

The Council also contributed to the understanding of the human person. The response to God's invitation at baptism was now lived within the transition from a classicist worldview to one of historical-mindedness, and amidst rapid cultural, technological, scientific, and economic change. One of the Council's most significant documents, *Gaudium et Spes / Pastoral Constitution on the Church in the Modern World*, has at least one hundred entries on *person* and *personality*, including a chapter "On the Dignity of the Person." One striking sentence: "Man's social nature makes it evident that the progress of the human person and the advance of society itself hinge on one another ... the subject and the goal of all social institutions is and must be the human person which for its part and by its very nature stands completely in need of social life."[60] Added to this understanding was the new relationship between a person and their giftedness, responding to their own "personal gifts" and accompanying "duties"; but also the relationship between a person and their "vocation." A vocation was no longer linked exclusively to the religious life and priesthood; it was now understood as the response of each Christian to God's call, including engagement with and transformation of the temporal order.[61] People were no longer simply passive recipients of Church teaching and doctrine, but were invited to enter into active and transformative participation. The growing appreciation of the relationship between theology and history, and theology in the context of history, further contributed to understanding the human person in the context of history and culture. A person is characterized by *subjectivity* – as opposed to a self-centred *subjectivism* – and characterized by "historicity," the human person is shaped by and inseparable from history; is characterized by "relationality," both with others and with the world, a relationality through which a person grows in self-awareness; and finally is characterized as "the creator of meaning and language."[62] All these profoundly shape the perennial growth in and towards personhood.

One way of summing up the breadth of the Council's documents is as *aggiornamento*, a spirit of openness and change; a spirit anxious to interact with the world where the Gospel continues to be proclaimed. This *aggiornamento* marked the breadth of the sixteen documents of the Council. Given this breadth and diversity, it now appeared that it was no longer possible for any one philosophical system, understood in classical terms and distinguished by hierarchical categories, to synthesize, categorize, or organize the Church's new emerging self-understanding. This contributed to "Thomism's loss of primacy as a systematic philosophy."[63] This shift meant that the mantle of leadership was moving from philosophy to theology, a leadership of theology and theological method, rather than the more circuitous route of philosophy, classically understood and exclusively Western in its approach and focus. What was clear, however, was that the approach had to be theological, and wider than one housed in a single philosophical framework, and it had to be open to the contingencies of history and the historicity of culture. Thus it is maintained that "if the chief aim of nineteenth-century Catholic theology was the relationship between faith and reason ... the chief theme of twentieth and twenty-first century theology is the relationship between history and theology."[64] This is not to suggest that this new approach to theology emerged, Athena-like, fully formed from the head of the Council. Rather, it developed and grew as a result of the Council, and continues to do so in our day, as is attested to by the significant body of literature and scholarship devoted to the Council.

It would be erroneous, however, to conclude from these brief comments that Thomism as a system came to an end with the close of the Council. That field of study continues to be ever-vibrant today, as is evidenced by both the scholarship in that field and the distinguished journals covering Thomism and Thomistic studies, such as *The Thomist*, *The Modern Schoolman*, and *The New Scholasticism: The Journal of the American Catholic Philosophical Association*. Some see a "Post–Vatican II Thomism" and refer to philosophers in this group as "progressive Neo-Thomists," including therein such eminent names as Yves Congar, Marie-Dominique Chenu, Edward Schillebeeckx, Karl Rahner, and Bernard Lonergan.[65] While the claim that "Vatican II really nailed the lid on the coffin of neo-Thomism"[66] may be referring, if somewhat too dramatically, to the change in intellectual approach since the Council, there are those who may well take exception to the finality of such an obituary, preferring, rather, a more subtle approach of change in perspective, emphasis, and nuance.[67] It is said, "the intellectual heritage of the contemporary Catholic school is a rich blend of Neo-Scholastic principles that are lightened with a humane spirit and deepened with a symbolic richness that was reclaimed at Vatican II."[68]

V *Gravissimum Educationis / Declaration on Christian Education*

The Council's declaration, *Gravissimum Educationis*, may be put in context with very brief comments on two previous Roman documents on Christian education in the twentieth century.[69] First, *Acerbo Nimis / On Teaching Christian Doctrine*, an encyclical of Pope Pius X in 1905, focuses on the religious instruction of the young, and the role of the priest in such instruction. It makes five references to the Council of Trent, and none to the First Vatican Council, which was closer to it historically. The encyclical identifies two chief obligations that were emphasized by that earlier Council regarding religious instruction: to preach "the things of God to the people on feast days; and second, that of teaching the rudiments of faith and of the divine law to the youth and others who need such instruction." Also worth noting is language that today we would find to be impersonal and disembodied: for example, "We by no means wish to conclude that a perverse will and unbridled conduct may not be joined with a knowledge of religion."[70] The second, *Divini Illius Magistri / On Christian Education*, encyclical of Pope Pius XI in 1929, is longer and much broader than the previous encyclical. Among the more regular concerns regarding religious instruction is the role of parents and the Church in the formation of the young. There are references to

"educational rights and systems in different countries"; "new pedagogical theories"; that "education is essentially a social and not a mere
individual activity"; the contribution of "letters [scholarly knowledge],
science and art" to Christian education; and the declaration that while
Christian education does not remove students from society to "save their
souls," there is an urgency in the young being "forewarned and fore-
armed against the seduction and the errors of the world." The following
would appear, at best, curious to contemporary ears: "False and harmful
to Christian education is the so-called method of 'co-education.' This
too, by many of its supporters is founded upon naturalism and the denial
of original sin ... upon a deplorable confusion of ideas that mistakes a
levelling promiscuity and equality, for the legitimate association of the
sexes." That historical extremism aside, the encyclical sees education as
preparing the student's Christian identity, both in being and in doing,
and thus regards it in relation to earthly existence, though recognizing
that "a 'true education' is always linked to one's last end."[71]

In spite of the understandable limitations of their historical contexts,
both encyclicals provide a frame for the Council's document on Christian Education. The future Pope Benedict XVI referred to *Gravissimum
Educationis* as "a rather weak document."[72] Compared to the Council's
four principal constitutions – *Dei Verbum*, on Divine Revelation; *Lumen
Gentium*, on the Church; *Sacrosanctum Concilium*, on the liturgy; and
Gaudium et Spes, on the Church in the modern world – and some of the
other documents, *Gravissimum Educationis* does seem weak, but it is also
different from the others: "it states specifically that it deals only with
a few fundamental principles and that a more developed point of view
is being left to a special postconciliar Commission and to the Conferences of Bishops. This may explain why the Declaration breaks little
new ground and limits itself to a strong statement of basic positions."
Furthermore, "the whole concern of the Council is with education in one
form or another."[73] Since the Council, the ongoing work of that post-
conciliar Commission has been undertaken by the CCE, and Catholic
education has received sustained attention.[74]

The Council's declaration on education is not long, and is divided into
twelve sections, including sections on Catholic colleges and universities
and faculties of sacred sciences, such as theology and canon law. While
the declaration does not refer explicitly to the *education of the whole*

person, it does see education holistically and as something to be nurtured across many dimensions. Thus, "a true education aims at the formation of the human person in the pursuit of his ultimate end of the good of the societies of which, as man, he is a member, and in whose obligations, as an adult, he will share." The human person, a new being through baptism, is "created in justice and holiness of truth," and must strive for "the development and spread of culture" amidst "the peaceful association of citizens and ... [amidst] the pluralism that exists today in ever so many societies." In attending to moral and religious education, there is the recognition that education be "imparted in all schools according to the individual moral and religious principles of the families," and mention is made of the role of parents in fostering a "well-rounded personal and social education." In this the school has a wide mandate: "not only to develop with special care the intellectual faculties but also to form the ability to judge rightly, to hand on the cultural legacy of previous generations, to foster a sense of values, to prepare for professional life."[75] In twelve relatively short sections (compared to the Council's other documents) the declaration covers some broad areas within which the Catholic school finds its place. And though it spends relatively little time on the Catholic school per se, the document "does not see schools in general as being in any way isolated from other means of communication and education, but rather as being continuous with them."[76] Finally, it makes only a single reference to St Thomas Aquinas.

It is said that this declaration had a "tortured history," essentially because of the different understandings of the term *education* across the world. Also what "agitated the deliberations ... was the role the document should accord Aquinas."[77] Others say that *Gravissimum Educationis* "was a rare document in that agreement seemed in abundance and histrionics were minimal" and that "contemporary educators recognized in the document many of their own priorities."[78] However, in spite of the criticisms and reservations about this document, it does possess a unity in "approach and style" with the other documents of the Council.[79]

VI Catholic Education after the Council: Some Literature

There has been a wealth of literature on Catholic education since the close of the Council. Offered here are five snapshots of how Catholic educators have understood the shift in the understanding of Catholic education as a result of the Council. Again, this glimpse is chronological.

Donohue in *Catholicism and Education* (1973) says that in the midst of the changes, particularly the change of worldview since the Council, "there cannot be many Catholic educators who think it possible ... to produce a satisfactory account of the meaning of Catholicism for education." The breadth of issues situates the Council's call to Catholics to see themselves as part of the human family, and to thus strive for the integrity of the social, cultural, moral, and intellectual order. They are called to work for "secular or terrestrial values – the whole range of arts, sciences, technology, and civic enterprise involved in building civilization as both the support and the expression of humane life." What is noteworthy is how wide and challenging Catholic education has become since the Council: wide as attested to by the documents of the Council, and challenging given the call to personal responsibility and authenticity; and also demanding, given the breadth of application required. The breadth of issues is in the context of phenomenally rapid growth and change across a variety of dimensions, from technology to a more inclusive, and not an exclusively Western, conception of culture. The Church's self-understanding, how she sees herself and her mission in the world, now places a new responsibility on each person; thus the two calls to "interiority and to responsible work for the common human welfare are the council's basic implications for Catholic education." Donohue's work is less a philosophy and more a theology of education, but with philosophical aspects. He is interested in that part of educational theory that is derived from Catholic "religious convictions." While he refers to the relationship between philosophy and education, he understands a Christian theory of education as a harmonious combination of "the contributions of philosophy and religious faith." He points out that while the Gospels do not elaborate on most details of educational theory, many of the "perennial educational problems have religious connotations." This book attests to a seismic shift from a Catholic theory of education grounded exclusively upon philosophy, where religious instruction is based upon catechesism and apologetics, to a Catholic theory of education now inspired by a sense of call and vocation, as expanded upon in the documents of the Council. The world is at the stage where, with the grace of God and the gifts of the Church, Catholics must work out their salvation both personally and communally. Consequently, Catholic education is much broader than the Catholic school; it is life-long, and is much more than merely the acquisition of information, for it is inspired by Christian discipleship and serving the world and the common good through one's personal vocation. The following encapsulates this wider frame for a Catholic theory of education:

[T]hat portion of educational theory which is derived from the Gospel is delivered not by philosophy but by religious faith, and this faith is not a profession of abstractions and purely speculative conclusions. It is, for each Christian, a crucial and profoundly personal affirmation about certain historic events and present realities ... the Christian not only affirms that God *is* but also that He communicates with men and that this communication, at a determined point in history, took the supreme and unimaginable form of divine incarnation so that Jesus who lives is authentically God and authentically man.[80]

Boys' *Educating in Faith: Maps and Visions* (1989) is very helpful in mapping some of the key shifts in Catholic education since the Council. The wider relationship of "faith to society" meant that Catholic education could not "merely be equated with Catholic schooling." Boys says that while *Gravissimum Educationis* is "not among the documents generally regarded as the most significant," it does express the Church's interest in formulating "an explicit philosophy of education." She goes on to say that while the document was really based in the frame of nineteenth- and twentieth-century papal teachings and scholarship in the Catholic philosophy of education, that "ironically, what the council participants did not foresee was that the ecclesial revolution set in motion by the council changed the theological and philosophical assumptions upon which *Catholic education* rested. Vatican II represented a rethinking of 'timeless truths' and the emergence of new categories." Two shifts of the Council have particular relevance for Catholic education. One was a "conciliatory tone," a move from the condemnation of heresy and error to a "spirit of charity and reconciliation." A Catholic philosophy of education defined as true and condemning other systems as false was now in need of rethinking. Second, the two-tiered world of "nature" and "supernature" led inevitably to the "Christ against culture" position, the "natural/supernatural schism." The Council's understanding of revelation, the Scriptures, the Church, the Christian vocation in the world, etc., brought about fundamental changes in catechesis and in the relationship between catechesis and evangelization, all shaped by the "emphasis on conversion" and "a deep change of one's life, a commitment to live anew in Christ." The Council's key concepts, such as "truth, knowledge, salvation, humanity, conversion and revelation," had an enormous influence on religious education and on Catholic education as a whole. The contribution and the limitations of reason are acknowledged; knowing now has an existential dimension, thus bridging the chasm between belief and action.[81]

Moran, in "Religious Education after Vatican II" (1997), says that, at the time of the Council, it was unthinkable how "traumatic and far reaching the changes would be." And two decades after the publication of Moran's work, the process of renewal is ongoing and "the shape of the Church is still emerging." Moran highlights some of the work that had already begun in the United States that would help shape the reform of Catholic education, particularly in what would become the field of religious education. He also thinks that the Council's document on education was weak, and did not provide a theory of Christian education as its title suggests, and that the document is essentially a "plea for Catholic schools." And while he says the Council's documents only make a single reference to *religious education*, he goes on to say that "Vatican II as a whole was an exercise of Christian or religious education. It began an educational reshaping of the Catholic Church, and it fundamentally altered the relation of Roman Catholicism to the rest of the world." He sees religious education as comprising two parts: "formation, initiation, or induction," and "providing ... an understanding of religion"; these are "two faces" of religious education, not "two separate compartments." Also helpful is the evolution of the term *religious education*, which Moran says is "an idea born in the twentieth century." Since the Council, the language of Catholic education has "revolved around the word catechetics." However, "the educational formation of a Catholic rests first not on catechetics but on worship and service."[82] This essay assists scholars in understanding the place of prominence that religious education has come to occupy since the Council. While Catholic education is much more than attending a Catholic school, religious education should play an educationally integrative role in the Catholic school.

Kelty, in "Towards a Theology of Catholic Education" (1999), maintains, "it is no longer self-evident that Catholic schools should simply serve the purpose of initiating the next generation into active church membership as practicing Catholics." *Gravissimum Educationis* "tends to repeat verbatim" principles from Pope Pius XI's encyclical, while the Council's document on the Church, *Gaudium et Spes*, "contains ideas that have enormous implications for educational theory" – thus the shift in understanding Catholic education. Kelty says that "the vastly changed philosophy of Catholic education [can be categorized] through the use of four common thematic headings ... the nature of the person; the function of knowledge; the view of history; and the social goals of Catholic education," themes that have found consistent expression throughout the history of Christian education. Two reasons are provided for the disappearance of a clear Catholic philosophy of education. First, the Council's declaration on education was "uninteresting ... and repetitious of the past," whereas the "major agenda of the Council was to face modernity"; this left Catholic education with "its traditional heritage." Second, given the new emphasis on "the internalization of individualized Christian conviction," the emphasis shifted to religious education. Kelty follows this with a thought-provoking observation that this "was at the expense of an articulated educational philosophy, which might have built on the best theological insights of Vatican II." He concludes with a pressing question: "does this philosophical shift constitute a theology of education?" He answers in the affirmative "because this modified philosophy of education takes faith in God and religious practice seriously." This essay is provided as a map of the signposts that marked the shift and the evolution from a Catholic philosophy of education to a Catholic theology of education. Also noteworthy is how theology is understood to perform an integrative and unifying function in a way that philosophy, maintains Kelty, no longer could.[83]

Finally, the purpose of Elias's essay "Whatever Happened to Catholic Philosophy of Education?" (1999) is "to explain the eclipse after Vatican II of a distinctive Catholic philosophy of education based on the

principles of Thomas Aquinas." It moves to describe the main elements
of such a philosophy, and refers to *Aeterni Patris* as well as to works by
Redden and Ryan, Donohue, and Cunningham, and some of the sources
on Neo-Thomistic philosophy of education referred to above. Elias identifies six distinct headings for a Neo-Thomistic philosophy of education:
philosophy of persons; *social philosophy*; *aims of education*; *curriculum*;
learning, knowledge, and method in education; and *the role of teachers*. He
attributes the decline in that philosophy of education to changes within
the Church and within the field of philosophy of education itself. The
changes within the Church arose from the Council having moved from
an absolutist and certain philosophy to a "more modest church that ad-
mitted it did not have the answers to all problems and that expressed
a willingness to work with others to discover solutions to the pressing problems of our times." The rise of philosophies of existentialism,
personalism, phenomenology, and existential phenomenology stood
in contrast to the "authoritative aura and dogmatic attitude of the Thomists." Since the Council, few Catholic educators identify themselves as
philosophers of education, while more tend to prefer the designation
"religious educators," whose work, while possessing a philosophical
component, does "not attempt to provide a philosophy for all of Catholic
education." The author adds two more reasons to account for this decline
in a Catholic philosophy of education: the interest of Catholic theologians
in conversing with a variety of philosophical schools – "Neo-Thomism
no longer has its pre-eminence either in philosophy or in theology" –
and the fact that courses in Catholic philosophy are no longer offered in
most universities today, thus cutting off a vital source for Catholic philosophy of education. The essay concludes with "a modest proposal for a
Catholic educational theory," suggesting its interdisciplinary nature, and
develops it using the thought of Bernard Lonergan and Paulo Freire and
employing the six categories listed above, which Elias says were used in
a Neo-Thomistic philosophy of education.[84] This essay captures some of
the most significant points in the evolution of the Catholic philosophy of
education (in English), both before and after the Council. By employing
the thought of Lonergan and Freire, Elias broadens how a Catholic philosophy of education may be conceived in the light of the Council and
the change in emphasis from an exclusively Neo-Thomistic philosophy
of education.

VII Conclusion

This chapter has covered a wide variety of issues that have influenced and shaped Catholic philosophy of education. The two major influences on this educational philosophy have been Thomism (and Neo-Thomism) and the Council. Both influences were decisive, and both were formative.

What is important, of course, is the conclusions that one may draw from an overview such as this chapter has attempted to offer. There is little doubt, given the shape and evolution of Catholic educational theory today (whether formulated locally in school boards or in diocesan and national Catholic educational agencies, or in the documents that are issued from the CCE), that the Council, and the thought and research that have emerged as a result of the Council, continues to shape Catholic educational theory. There is also little doubt that religious education has come to occupy a place of prominence and leadership, and also plays an integrating role today in a wider way than a Catholic philosophy of education would have played in the era prior to the Council.

What is of significance, as this overview has attempted to illustrate, is that since the Council, it is no longer possible for a single philosophical system to lead and inspire Catholic education as it did in the past. The reasons are many and varied, but chief among them is the very self-understanding of the Church, and as a result, the interpretation of whom Catholics are called to become amidst this self-understanding, through personal conversion and an authentic personal responsibility, with irreplaceable social and communal implications, and, of course, striving for all this through God's grace. The Church is now understood not simply as the hierarchy – the pope and bishops – but as the whole people of God, amidst which the pope and bishops are called to a ministry of service. Such a ministry has profound implications for Catholic education, and can only be fruitfully contained within a wider theological tent.

It does seem, however, that in some circles the condemnation of Thomism and Neo-Thomism was too swift, almost relishing their seeming downfall. Admittedly a change, a significant change, had occurred since the Council, and again, admittedly a single philosophical system or school of thought could no longer govern Catholic intellectual life. Nevertheless, philosophy continues to occupy a place of importance in the intellectual life of the Church. Candidates for the Catholic

priesthood, for example, must spend a significant part of their formation in philosophical study, thus confirming the relationship between
"theological work and the philosophical search for truth."[85] Philosophy
continues to play a part in Catholic intellectual life, both in relationship
to theology and in understanding the wider questions, trends, and influences in every age.

The educational documents of the cce do not refer to a Catholic philosophy of education, but there is no doubt that they do contain an implicit Catholic philosophy of education; in fact, they use the very term
educational philosophy.[86] The documents frame Catholic education in
wider terms than a traditional Catholic philosophy of education would
have done, but they do, nevertheless, see education in philosophical
terms, placed within a wider theological framework. Such a framework
has enormous and far-reaching implications for a universal institution
like the Catholic Church. In such a framework, while it is useful and
important to think about and construct *Catholic theologies of education*,
this need not to be at the expense and eclipse of *Catholic philosophies of
education* – that is, reading, reflecting on, and contributing to an understanding of the documents of the cce through the lens of a Catholic philosopher or philosophers of education.

Undoubtedly, any attempt to formulate *one* universal Catholic philosophy of education, with or without the help of the documents from the
cce, would be at best a herculean task, and very likely impossible. Consequently, the intention of this work is modest and contained. Jacques
Maritain and Bernard Lonergan wrote extensively, including on philosophy of education. In the next chapter, I shall examine their works
in more detail, particularly their philosophies of education in the context of religious diversity and cultural plurality, and in parallel with the
Church's educational documents.

2

Jacques Maritain and Bernard Lonergan:
Two Catholic Philosophers
of Education

I Introduction

The preceding chapter gave an overview of the terrain of Catholic philosophy of education prior to and after the Council in the English-speaking world. Today, the evolution of the *Catholic philosophy of education* could also be designated as *studies in Catholic education* or *Catholic educational theory*, though educators continue to speak of a *Catholic philosophy of education*. In the midst of this evolution, and given the changes that emerged after the Council, the discipline of *religious education* has assumed a leadership role in Catholic schools, at least in the English-speaking world. It is wider than a catechetical approach to religious instruction, though the place of catechesis is recognized in the overall religious preparation of the Catholic student. Catechesis is usually a parish-based program, though it has implications for the Catholic school as well. As mentioned in the conclusion of the previous chapter, the educational documents from the CCE continue to associate *philosophy* with *education*, and thus refer to an *educational philosophy* for the Catholic school. A Catholic philosophy of education is wider than, though of course it includes, the Catholic school. The chapters that follow explore the Catholic philosophy of education for Catholic schools, and how the thought of Jacques Maritain and Bernard Lonergan can help expand such a philosophy. Again, this is merely one reading of Catholic philosophy of education. In the context of diversity and plurality, and the breadth of the Council, there can be many other such philosophies, depending upon context, approach, geography, history, and one's philosophical school. What is explored here are the Church's universal teachings on a Catholic philosophy of education, rising above regional and national particularities. I maintain that Maritain and Lonergan complement and enhance this universal approach, particularly amidst diversity and plurality.

As stated, this chapter introduces the philosophy of education of Jacques Maritain and Bernard Lonergan. Maritain was a philosopher, with some later works after the Council. Lonergan wrote extensively in the areas of philosophy, theology, economics, and culture, and on the relationship between philosophy and education. Maritain was a Thomist in the Neo-Thomist tradition prior to the Council, whereas Lonergan, who was also influenced by the thought of St Thomas, proposed a self-transcending transcendental method by turning to the human *subject*, a term which he preferred to human *person*. This chapter is divided as follows: the second section examines Maritain's philosophy of education, and the third Lonergan's philosophy of education. The fourth explores why these two philosophers of education can be helpful in understanding a Catholic philosophy of education. Section five closes with some conclusions.

II Jacques Maritain: Catholic Philosopher of Education

Maritain did not care for designations such as Neo-Thomism. This has important implications for the philosophical application of his thought, particularly to education. In 1951, he was awarded the Cardinal Spellman-Aquinas Award, the first award and medal of the American Catholic Philosophical Association, and in his citation, the Thomist scholar Gerald B. Phelan said of Maritain, "you have explicitly repudiated the attempt to classify you as a 'New-Thomist' – an epithet which (like all *ists* and *isms*) suggests a party line in philosophy – yet you have shown us St. Thomas Aquinas as the seer, the wise man whose wisdom is always contemporary because it is true."[1] In accepting the medal, Maritain confirmed his unease with such designations. Referring to St Thomas, he said, "He was intent only on the truth, – more, to be sure, than on what was to be called Thomism, and which would have sounded like a strange word to his ears; he was Thomas, he did not need to be a Thomist, or a Neo-Thomist, or a Paleo-Thomist. And if we are Thomists, it is surely because we love truth first, and hold Thomism to be the most appropriate means to cling to truth."[2] Maritain's position has implications for understanding his philosophy, particularly applied philosophies such as the philosophy of education. His academic career spans France and North America; he taught in Paris at the Institut Catholique, and at St Michael's College and the Institute of Mediaeval Studies in Toronto, as well as at Princeton and Columbia in the United States of America.

Maritain's two works in English on education are *Education at the Crossroads* and a collection of eight essays and two appendices titled *The Education of Man: The Educational Philosophy of Jacques Maritain* (with an inspiring introduction by its editors, Donald and Idella Gallagher, "Toward a Christian Philosophy of Education"). These books will be referred to in detail in the subsequent chapters. However, in order to understand how Maritain envisions the relationship between philosophy and education, this chapter will rely on three essays: "Philosophy and Education," "Thomist Views on Education," and "Some Typical Aspects of Christian Education," all from *The Education of Man*.

Maritain wrote extensively on political and social philosophy, aesthetics, philosophies of nature and history, science, metaphysics, epistemology, moral philosophy, culture, and the philosophy of education. His writings aim at unity, the unity of the human person. His philosophical attention is focused on such applied areas as society, education, political theory, and aesthetics, fields that he believed required particular attention, given his historical reality. He lived through two world wars, seeing the rise of political, ideological, and intellectual movements from Marxism to fascism, and from scientific materialism to existential atheism. Given Maritain's concern for the personal unity of each person, his diverse philosophical scholarship is united, interrelated, and all in search of the meaning of human living for his time.[3] Amidst the influences upon his philosophical approach, one stands out: his conversion, and his wife Raïssa's, to Catholicism. Jacques grew up as a Protestant, while Raïssa was raised in a Jewish household. They had met at the Sorbonne – Raïssa notes that she believed herself to be atheist, while Jacques was an agnostic – and their studies in philosophy and science were in the context of a looming relativism and scepticism. In 1901, this young couple experienced a profound emotional, spiritual, and intellectual crisis. Their age was one of "metaphysical anguish, going down to the very roots of the desire for life ... capable of becoming a total despair and of ending in suicide." Raïssa notes that suicide was not uncommon at this time, given the intellectual and moral state of Europe. They made a solemn promise, as they sat in the Jardin des Plantes on a Parisian afternoon, that if they were "so unhappy as to possess only a pseudo-intelligence capable of everything but the truth," thus robbing them of their dignity, then "everything became absurd – and impossible to accept – without our ever knowing what it was in us that thus refused acceptance," that they would continue to remain open with a certain "confidence in the unknown ... in the hope that the meaning of life would reveal itself ... and deliver us from the nightmare of a sinister and useless world." This promise closes with a chilling commitment: "But if the experiment should not be successful, the solution would be suicide ... We wanted to die by a free act if it were impossible to live according to the truth." However, they experienced a spiritual and intellectual conversion, encapsulated in Raïssa's *Memoirs*: "It was then that God's pity caused us to find Henri Bergson."[4] The thought of philosophers such as Bergson and the example of holy men such as Leony Bloy resulted in Jacques and Raïssa embracing the dignity and the unity of life, and the Roman Catholic faith as well. An account of their conversion is movingly recounted in Ralph McInerny's *The Very Rich Hours of Jacques Maritain: A Spiritual Life*. It was Bloy who answered the question that Jacques and Raïssa had been asking about life, about the meaning of life: "Why am I alive? The answer: in order to become a saint. Learning what that meant defined Maritain's life from then on."[5] The power of the conversion stayed with them from then on, shaping their thought, writings, and lives.

For Maritain, a philosophical understanding of education is rooted in his understanding of *Christian philosophy*. This is not the place to explore Christian philosophy per se, though we should recognize that Christian philosophy is not without its critics.[6] Some have also examined Maritain's understanding of Christian philosophy.[7] For Maritain, Christian philosophy shapes the applied discipline of philosophy of education. Without delving into philosophic technicalities, he refers to the "Christian state of philosophy" as the method and way of one's philosophizing.

Hence he distinguishes between "philosophy considered in its *nature* and philosophy considered in its *state* in the human mind."[8] By *nature* he means philosophy, as it is, a historical discipline, whereas *state* of mind refers to the existent person philosophizing, with a particular history and a distinct intellectual stance. Such a philosophical state is referred to as a *habitus*, a manner and state of one's intellectual, moral, and religious disposition; hence one's existential and historical condition situates one to philosophize as a Christian.

Maritain contrasts Catholic education with the various theories of education, noting that while Catholics must learn from the progress of educational theory, they must be cautious of incomplete educational systems that emphasize one aspect and ignore others. Education and philosophy are interrelated, as education is concerned, ultimately, with the meaning and purpose of life, and hence is implicitly philosophical. Another reason is that education is a practical activity; it depends upon philosophy to guide it towards its goals and ends. Thus, education cannot help but be influenced by the shape and evolution of philosophical thought, and in this it is not independent from philosophy. Once a discipline has the human being as its object, it cannot help but refer to values. He notes the movement to situate education in the field of psychology, and while affirming its contribution to educational theory, maintains that psychology is one aspect of education.[9]

There is another principle woven through his educational philosophy: "It is clear that the teacher must adapt himself to the child, but education properly so called does not begin until the child adapts himself to the teacher and to the culture, the truths and the systems of value which it is the mission of the teacher to transmit to the child."[10] While the teacher exercises an instrumental role in the student's learning, Maritain insists on the dynamic nature of the student's own learning. While education is a form of transmission, it is a living transmission from one human being to another, where the transmission, reception, and integration are all part of the unified dynamism of the educational process. While the teacher is responsible for the communication and transmission of knowledge, he or she acts as an "instrumental and not as an efficient cause" – that is, a cause that helps bring about change, but is not the actual source of the change. The teacher does not shape the student, a spiritual being, in a whimsical manner, but assists the student's mind to grow in freedom and liberation through what is learned. Thus it is the student, and not the teacher, who is the main agent in the learning process. So, while methods and techniques are important, what is more important is the truths that teachers profess and live by, at all levels of education; witness to truth becomes the formative influence for the intellect and personality of the student. It would be a mistake to conclude that Maritain isolates intellect and personality as two independent realities that can be observed or educated apart from the integral unity of the student. It is because institutional education is primarily concerned with forming the intellect, and because ultimately personality is the foundation of human unity, that he singles them out.[11]

Maritain grounds his educational theory upon Thomistic philosophy, which provides knowledge and structure, and engages all dimensions of reality. Such a philosophy provides a firm foundation for a systematic educational theory, and he elaborates using the example of the relation between the individual and society, a relation that has social and rational aspects because the true nature of society is fulfilled when persons actualize their truly human and moral nature. This is evident in Maritain's social and political philosophy, particularly regarding the purpose of society and how it serves the person and persons, and the relationship of freedom to those transcendental dimensions such as morality and the search for God. All these themes appear across his educational philosophy, one framed within the social mission of education and the transformation of society, a society, his society, torn apart by the terrors and horrors of the Second World War. These transcendental dimensions lead to the distinction and the relationship between the natural and the supernatural orders, which serve the social mission of society, within which education is situated.[12]

Ever aware of the dangers of the purely theoretical in a practical discipline such as education, Maritain's philosophy is an interplay between philosophical principles and practical application. Though his preference is for a Thomist philosophy, he recognizes that while progressive education looks to pragmatism for support, and such an education does have truths to offer, the educator, however, must take care not to curtail the internal and spiritual nature of the student as a person. And any organized system, such as education, that deliberates on human life must take into account values that are hierarchically organized and based on the nature of the student as a person, which, in turn, influence the purpose and the structure of the curriculum.[13]

Maritain then moves to a *philosophy of knowledge*, saying that all educators subscribe to such a philosophy, whether they are aware of it or not. He advocates a Thomist philosophy of knowledge that distinguishes between the senses and the action of stimuli upon bodily organs, for human knowledge begins with, and is dependent upon, the senses and the intellect. The immateriality of the intellect attests to its spiritual nature, transforming what is gained through the senses into what is known, whereby the known becomes intelligible. Empiricists disagree, saying that there is no difference in nature between the senses and the intellect; the only difference is in the levels. For the empiricist, human knowledge is just a more evolved and sophisticated form of sense knowledge, and ultimately human knowledge has no other sources of integrating and synthesizing what is experienced through the senses, and is dependent upon sense knowledge from the start of the knowing process to its completion. Maritain notes the circular irony of the empiricist position using reason to refute reason. The error of terminating human knowing with sense knowledge is all the more poignant given that "the senses are, in actual fact, more or less permeated with reason." An educational program based upon an empiricist philosophy may well attend to the rational and spiritual capacities of the mind, but it will be unable to identify the source and nature of those powers, and so will ignore what the mind requires and needs for its flourishing.[14]

Another distinction between a Thomist and an instrumentalist theory of knowledge is that the latter, based upon an empiricist theory, makes the mistake of reducing the mind and thinking to response and to one's environment. This reduces thinking and thought to simply the interaction between stimulus and response. Maritain says that in fact the opposite is the case. Thinking engages *being*, that is, knowledge of what is. Human knowing includes intelligibility, that is, knowledge that depends on the senses but is ultimately more than just sense knowledge; it includes meaning and understanding beyond the sensory, hence the claim that something is *intelligible*. Maritain, like Lonergan, uses the term *insight*, saying that that thinking both commences and concludes with and in insights, whose truth is confirmed though "rational demonstration or empirical verification, not by pragmatic sanction." It is because of such activity that thought is able to illuminate experience and work for the common good in new ways. Ultimately it is truth that is attained through such activity; human knowing is, seamlessly, from the start to the finish, a quest for truth. A Thomist philosophy affirms that knowledge is of value in itself, and is also an end itself. There is a disinterested quality in knowing – that is, knowing for knowing's sake, and not necessarily with a utilitarian end in mind. Maritain realizes that what pupils learn in schools must serve the living of life, personally and communally, including practical aspects of living. In this, he affirms the primary bent of the mind to know: knowledge for knowledge's sake. What one knows, of course, has implications, including moral implications, for action; but such implications follow, and are grounded upon, the disinterested desire to know.[15]

The reader will recall from the previous chapter the emergence of Catholic educational theory after the Council, and the shift from philosophy to theology in the development of such theory. Within his strong philosophical position, Maritain recognizes the relationship between Catholic education and theology. Human beings encounter a hierarchy, and so educational theory is more than just a quest for metaphysical and philosophical values and principles.

> If the conception of man, of human life, human culture, and human destiny is the basis of all education, we must insist that there is no really complete science of education, just as there is no really complete political science, except such as is correlated with and subordinate to the science of theology. The reason is simple. Man is not merely a natural animal ... but is called to a supernatural end. He is in a state either of fallen nature or of nature restored. The existence or non-existence of original sin and the effects thereof ... is a question of no small significance to education. As a practical science dealing with the complete formation of man, it is a theological discipline.[16]

This detailed quotation frames Maritain's understanding of a Christian philosophy of education, one that is hierarchically organized, not just in the curriculum, or the aims of education, or the overall structure of the Catholic school, but more fundamentally a hierarchy based upon the nature of the person, who is created in the image and likeness of God. Within such a hierarchy, educational theories are neither absolutely independent, nor are they so subservient and so overpowered by the ultimate spiritual nature of the students as a person that they ignore essential pedagogical realities. The practical order of the school has a specific end. Maritain distinguishes – mainly within his social and political philosophy, but with implications for education – between *ends* and *absolute ultimate ends*, particularly in the practical and moral realms. This distinction is further refined: "human life [is] ordered simultaneously to two different *absolute ultimate* ends, a purely natural *ultimate* end, which is perfect prosperity here on earth, and a supernatural *ultimate* end, which is perfect beatitude in heaven."[17] In the context of education, he distinguishes these ends in order that they should be united in the student as a person. Within this overall unity, and given the ultimate divine destiny of the student, and the overall governance of the *absolute* ultimate human end – union with God – the Church is an indispensable educator. Critics may see Maritain as bowing before the Church and so confusing the distinctions of ends, practical ends that permeated his philosophy, particularly in the social and political orders. Not so. On the contrary; his educational theory is a delicate and sophisticated elaboration of how these ends must be protected and their independence recognized, and how they are united. Within the mysterious identity of each person lies an ultimate desire and satisfaction that can only be fulfilled by God. So the task of the teacher is to "co-operate with God, Who is the Source of Truth and the First Cause ... Who can obtain results that no human teacher can obtain."[18]

Finally, a Christian philosophy of education must begin with and be based upon a Christian anthropology. Christians believe in the immortality and individuality of the soul. This confirms that body and soul are not two separate entities but one unified being, thus distinguishing it, for example, from Platonism. Christianity repeatedly emphasizes the unity of the human being, the person. Second, and this is a theme that we shall return to in later chapters, education is not to be reduced to intellectual or rational skills alone that fail to acknowledge the unity of body and spirit as one being, and that ignore the senses and sensory knowledge – a "Cartesian or angelistic" type of education.[19] Sense perception grounds education, and the school must relate such perception to the intellectual life. The aim of an integral Catholic education must include integrating and sharpening that perception. This is a fundamental pillar, and widens the conventional understanding of education, which, while grounded upon a liberal education and the humanities, includes an education of the student as a whole person. Thus Maritain sees manual labour as bound up with the human dignity of the student.[20]

In conclusion, both *Education at the Crossroads* and *The Education of Man* encompass a liberal education, the role of the humanities, the social and communal dimensions of education, the distinction between the person and the individual, and what today is referred to as the education of the whole person. Maritain develops a Christian philosophy of education, but one in which the distinct orders of human interaction, and those relationships in the world, are maintained and respected and these orders, in one way or the other, all influence and shape the person, the student. Maritain returns to the theme of human unity, and how the various dimensions of an integral philosophy of education ensure and enhance such unity. From his theory of knowledge to the nature and purpose of the curriculum, and from the social dimension of education to the dynamic primacy of the student in the knowing and learning process, Maritain formulates a philosophy of education that is attentive to perennial educational issues, but all within the frame of the unity of the student as a person. He sees human unity as fundamental to the educational process, and enhancing and nourishing such unity as the primary task of institutional education.

III Bernard Lonergan: Catholic Philosopher of Education

Bernard Lonergan's intellectual and spiritual journey was different from Maritain's, and he was younger than him by about twenty years. Lonergan, a Canadian, was born a Roman Catholic, and joined the Society of Jesus where he received a traditional Catholic education. He studied philosophy at Heythrop College in Oxfordshire, and theology at the Gregorian University in Rome, where he earned a doctorate on the theology of grace and human freedom in St Thomas Aquinas. He taught in Rome and in Toronto. His work has been described as "attempting to modernize Roman Catholic thought by freeing it from the shackles of classicist notions of culture, static theological manuals, and ahistorical propositions."[21] Though his intellectual career began before the Council, his writings anticipated the changes that the Council would usher in.

Modernity is a category heavy with meaning and implication; it is a multiple-layered concept, with a complex history. It is, therefore, unfair to typecast Lonergan's thought as simply a trend of modernity, particularly if that means an uncritical embracing of rationalism. On the other hand, Lonergan is certainly very modern, as his "work is grounded in the concrete struggle to adequately engage human reason. In Lonergan's thought there is an explicit critique of the weakness of modern or Enlightenment interpretations of subjectivity."[22] While he wrote extensively as a theologian and as a philosopher, his main contribution was in *method*, which, while begun in his work *Insight*, was developed in his later work *Method in Theology*, with implications for all branches of human knowing. Among those who helped shape his thought were Plato, Aristotle, St Augustine, St Thomas Aquinas, and John Henry Cardinal Newman. His two major works are *Insight: A Study of Human Understanding* and *Method in Theology*. The former has been described as "his own highly original solution to the problem of the nature of the relation of the subject and object of knowledge, of thought and reality."[23] *Insight* is essentially about intellectual conversion, while *Method in Theology* is an invitation to a more personal form of conversion, at three levels: intellectual, moral, and religious. The book's invitation is "to examine ourselves existentially, either to be converted or to reappraise our conversion, to examine our values and ourselves in relation to them, to resolve the conflicts that may lead us to differing interpretations of the same gospel message and to different accounts of what is going on in the world."[24] A feature of Lonergan's philosophy is that knowing cannot be reduced to looking. Though the senses are essential to knowing, knowing is more than sense knowledge and more than just looking, what he refers to as *picture thinking*.

Lonergan's thought should also be considered in the context of *Aeterni Patris*. He took seriously the invitation for a restoration of Christian philosophy; in fact, he uses the designations "Christian philosophy" and "Catholic philosophy."[25] Lonergan realized that "Cartesian/Kantian philosophy could not be outwitted by being regarded as a total mistake; rather, Thomas had to be reread in the light of modern philosophical considerations."[26] Lonergan's method seeks to engage the wisdom of

St Thomas with modern scholarship, all in a dynamic and open manner where the human *subject* (rather than human *person*) comes to understand what consciousness means, and to distinguish the various levels of consciousness, as well as the implications of consciousness for knowing and understanding. He situates this in the context of three transcendental precepts: experience, understanding, and judging. Later he introduces a fourth level, deciding, and it is primarily at this level that the human subject comes to understand that every major existential decision and choice has implications for one's life. These transcendental principles become the bridge between one's being and becoming, either in the direction of the good and right, or in the direction of error and evil: "The subject has more and more to do with his own becoming ... There is a critical point in the increasing autonomy of the subject. It is reached when the subject finds out for himself that it is up to himself to decide what he is to make of himself."[27]

Lonergan's method is an affirmation of the unity of the subject in and through the process of knowing, choosing, and deciding. Human knowing, choosing, and deciding have a normative pattern – for him normativity is not essentially external, such as first principles or perennial truths unrelated to human knowing; rather, normativity is linked to the knowing and choosing subject. There is thus a cognitional and a volitional unity in his method, a method that can be applied to any field. His four transcendental precepts are: "be attentive, be intelligent, be reasonable, and be responsible." His transcendental method consists in making one's consciousness more alert and intentional, of "objectifying" consciousness. And what does this objectifying mean? It consists in applying these transcendental precepts or operations – being attentive, intelligent, reasonable, and responsible – "as intentional to the operations as conscious." This means not only experiencing, but proceeding to experience one's experiencing, understanding, judging, and deciding, and carrying out this cumulative process of consciousness and intention at each of these four levels.[28] There are two further points regarding these operations: first, they are not experienced individually and apart from one another, nor do they arrive separately in asking questions or coming to insights and conclusions. Rather, subjects are unified by their consciousness, "and the pattern of these operations is part of the experience of these operations." Thus, inquiry and discovery are not charged with bringing about a synthesis of a series of unrelated experiences, but rather are intended "to analyze a functional and functioning unity." And second, when the subject achieves a knowledge of what is, not what one *wishes* or *hopes for*, but what *is*, this "gives way to conscious freedom and conscientious responsibility."[29] There is an integral relationship between one's intending and one's consciousness.

Lonergan recounts his intellectual history in a number of his essays.[30] Frederick Crowe devoted much of his scholarship to Lonergan's thought, and remains a recognized authority on such scholarship. His work *Lonergan* is a compact and illuminating intellectual and spiritual biography.[31]

Lonergan's work on education is titled *Topics in Education*, though educational implications are found across his writings. Here we will concentrate on the first chapter of this work, "The Problem of a Philosophy of Education." He begins by recognizing the influence of Dewey, particularly in relation to reflection and action. Lonergan formulates the relationship and interdependence between philosophy and education as follows:

> Philosophy is reflection on the human situation at an ultimate level. It is fundamentally thinking about the human situation. And education is the great means for transforming the human situation. It changes people's minds and wills, and it does so at the age when such change can be most easily produced ... Consequently, philosophy and education are interdependent. Philosophy is the reflective component, and education is the active component, at the ultimate level of reflection and action in human life. Philosophy is the guide and inspiration of education, and education is the verification, the pragmatic justification, of a philosophy.[32]

He distinguishes between the traditionalist and modernist approaches to education; both affirm the value of a liberal education. Proponents of the latter believe that the methods of the empirical sciences are the only measure of the values and the aims of education, and are thus in disagreement with the traditionalists. While they are both anxious to simplify the curriculum, they go about it in opposite ways using different criteria. Modernists are concerned with details, with methodologies and other forms of technique, as well as with examining information, while the traditionalists focus on first principles. While both admit to the importance of the past, the modernist proposes, and the traditionalist disagrees, that the way forward is to measure the wisdom of the ages through the methods of scientific hypothesis and forms of verification alone.[33]

Both groups also propose radically different views of philosophy. However, while the modernists have tailored their philosophy specifically for education, the traditionalists have not formulated a philosophy of education that makes a positive contribution for its evolving historical context. The modernist position on philosophy has five features: first, nothing is accepted on authority, and thus everything is open to question; second, "there is no fixed reality to be known; reality is in process"; third, "the methods of empirical science are the only valid methods; and the significant word … is *only*"; fourth, philosophy needs to be recast, and before any claim to knowledge is made, it must submit to a scientific method; finally, "experience always in the process of being reevaluated – is not only the best teacher; it is the *only* teacher."[34] For its part, the traditionalist position is founded on permanence and a suspicion of change: truths that exist for every age and every time. However, appealing to unchanging truths, irrespective of the age, does not offer a vision of education in light of human progress and intellectual development. But Lonergan's criticism goes further. The traditionalist position maintains educational truths that are as applicable to Romans as to Egyptians, for the Middle Ages or for the Renaissance, for citizens of the Industrial Age or for those of the twenty-first century. Such a vision fails to account for the challenges and progress of history. It reduces education to abstract principles, and is left with an abstract understanding of human nature. In the Catholic context, philosophy of education needs to be more positive than proposing a traditionalist vision. Lonergan elaborates on the various relationships between philosophy and other disciplines, including theology. This evolution arrives at the stage of "historicism," whose chief characteristic is meaning. Meaning unites human beings, and reason and freedom take on a dynamic and heuristic hue in the context of meaning. However, in a secularist conception of education, reason and freedom become disengaged from life, and are declared as the supreme arbiters of human life.[35]

Schools can be reduced to conveyors producing vast numbers of human cogs who will take their place in the great machine of the work force. However, the education of large numbers of students is a particularly recent challenge. A second issue is the advancement in learning, not only new subjects being included but new ways of understanding, particularly the modern understanding of science. A third change is the addition of languages, literature, and history, and the progress of the human sciences, and all require new ways of thinking and understanding, culminating in infinite forms of specialization. No longer can one person claim to be knowledgeable in a wide diversity of intellectual fields. The age of the Renaissance person is at an end. Such a view of specialization leads to a "notion of education as the information belt supplying students with a great number of pieces and leaving to them the task of putting together what the professors cannot put together themselves." Attempts to bring about a unity amidst this specialization themselves result in another specialized field.[36]

Lonergan concludes this chapter by reflecting on the nature of a Catholic philosophy of education, and a single sentence sums up the caution that needs to be exerted: "In much of today's education ultimate criteria come from philosophy in the sense of human reason and human freedom as ultimate." What is not needed is a secular philosophy that becomes the next phase after religion, nor a Cartesian philosophy that affirms the primacy of theology but then proceeds according to its own lights. The uniqueness of Catholic institutions of learning is based upon their Catholic identity, including their intellectual identity. Thus a Catholic philosophy of education today will not be Cartesian-based – that is, using and applying methods and means that are independent of the Catholic religion. A Catholic philosophy of education must include the new forms of knowing and knowledge and their implications upon human understanding. Today a Catholic philosophy for education cannot be based on a secular philosophy, a Cartesian philosophy entirely separated from either faith or religion, or a philosophy based on a medieval relationship between philosophy and theology.[37]

Given these distinctions, Lonergan then moves to the nature and identity of a *philosophy of ...*, such as the *philosophy of education*. In the medieval model of philosophy, there was no possibility of an applied philosophical discipline, such as a *philosophy of nature* or a *philosophy of education*. In the medieval model, philosophy was a discipline unto itself with its own divisions, such as metaphysics, epistemology, logic,

natural theology, ethics, aesthetics, etc. Lonergan asks how one gets to
an applied philosophy such as the *philosophy of education*. One way to
begin is in terms of universals and particulars, with the universal being
philosophy and the particular being the application. However, if one
begins a philosophy of education in terms of "intelligence and understanding as insight," and as the ground of forming concepts, then one
takes quite a different approach from abstract concepts such as universals and particulars. For Lonergan, understanding and knowing and
making judgments are personal: not private, but personal. Knowing and
understanding are not realized through abstract concepts, but through
personal insight, understanding, and judgment. Thus, he says, "there
are ... at least two ways of having a theoretical discipline connected
with particulars: one through insight into phantasm, the other through
subsumption of particulars under universals."[38] By this he means that
we have an insight through a mental image, and this mental image, the
phantasm, has the same relationship to the intellect as sensible objects
have to the senses.[39]

Lonergan notes that medieval thought was not historical in the modern
sense; it was concerned with first principles and unchanging truths, and
did not account for historical progression. Education, on the other hand,
must deal with the present, and apart from the history of education, it
deals with *today*, educating people *today*. What is required is to bring the
issues of today into philosophical reflection. But how is this realized?
Lonergan links this question to the notion of the development of both the
individual and society; after all, development always unfolds in a historical context. Development stands opposed to unchanging truths, which
stand outside time. In this search for a timely philosophy, he raises the
matter of a Christian and Catholic philosophy, and given that Catholic
physics or Catholic chemistry are distracting chimeras, can there be a
Catholic philosophy of education?[40]

Continuing to explore the possibility of a philosophy of education,
Lonergan says that the Catholic position or understanding of philosophy has not been existential; it has not been concerned with the human
subject "coming to grips with the meaning *for him* of true propositions."
Lonergan's philosophical quest is how human understanding works,
with existential human subjects engaged in acts of understanding for
themselves. However, as soon as one enters the realm of *meaning* for
personal living, there is a shift from philosophy to theology, because

human subjects exist in the world, and while affected by original sin, are offered redemption through divine grace. In spite of this shift, Lonergan notes that a Catholic philosophy of education cannot be formulated without adequately considering one's age and historical context. In order to affirm the existence of a Catholic philosophy of education, one must first confirm a Catholic philosophy.[41]

The medieval understanding of a perennial philosophy proceeds as if it is established for all ages, and on encountering a specific challenge in any age, one simply refers to a textbook to find the appropriate answers. Such a philosophy is steeped in concepts, particularly such concepts as first principles. However, if one understands philosophy as a stage, and affirms that philosophy grows and develops in each age by responding to the previous ages, then such an understanding can lead to a Catholic philosophy of education. The characteristics of such a philosophy include historical developments, but it can also be existential – in the broadest sense, and not linked to a particular philosophical school – and historical. With such distinguishing features, one can envisage a Catholic philosophy of education. Such a philosophy can take into account, but not be determined or defined by, fixed terms such as universal principles and timeless truths. Such an applied discipline is essential also to theology, in that it must also enter the concrete, and to do this it needs the assistance of philosophy. Furthermore, philosophy assists theology in making the necessary differentiations of times, places, and history.

It is within such a frame of philosophy and theology and their relationship that Lonergan situates his Catholic philosophy of education. It is a philosophy that accounts for what is new in one's time, and for how the human subject comes to know and understand in the context of philosophy. Furthermore, the shift from philosophy as a discipline, with no possibility for an applied philosophy, to a reframing of philosophy to include such applications is not problem-free, of course, but such a "shift in conception can be effected on a basis strictly in harmony with the tradition." Lonergan proceeds then to reflect on the relationship between philosophy and theology and upon their mutual relationship to the particular and existential dimensions of living.[42]

Lonergan devotes the rest of his work on education to developing such a philosophy. And while reference will be made to this work in subsequent chapters, it is helpful to have a general understanding of how he plans to proceed as he closes his first chapter. He says that while he could begin with human intelligence in relation to the new learning, thus enabling him to elaborate on what is meant by a Catholic philosophy of education, he will proceed in a different way. He will pursue such a philosophy by beginning with a reflection on the good, how it develops, changes, and grows over historical periods. Such a discovery will enable him to understand the good in specific terms. Since schools exist in historical periods, they are always in relation to society, and so he inquires into the nature of society. He says, "Your idea of the school will be a function of your idea of society, and your idea of society is connected with your notion of the good."[43] Lonergan sees the good as related to history, for it is within history that the subject chooses the good. In concluding his first chapter, he returns to the issue of Catholic education. He also returns to philosophy in the context of a particular age and history, and asks how the good is understood for the living of one's life.

In conclusion, Lonergan raises the pressing question of the nature of philosophy of education, and the possibility of a Catholic philosophy of education. His philosophical and theological method, like that of any philosopher who has written widely, is spread across his writings, and is not contained, as a self-sufficient entity, in any one work. The same is the case for his philosophy of education. He elaborates on the tension between timeless and eternal truths, a perennial philosophy, and an existential philosophy that grapples with being and becoming, the shaping of the self through choice, decision, and judgment, as understood in the context of human development and history. As we shall see, his understanding of existential philosophy is linked to broader themes such as authenticity, conversion, the relationship between authentic subjectivity and authentic objectivity, and personal levels of transcendence. In such a philosophy, it is the knowing, deliberating, judging, and choosing subject who remains at the centre.

IV Maritain and Lonergan: Catholic Philosophers of Education

Maritain's philosophy of education was composed before the Council, and it shows evidence of its historical context and limitations, but how could it be otherwise? Some maintain that Maritain's works on the philosophy of education lack the depth of his other philosophical works such as *Distinguish to Unite; or, The Degrees of Knowledge* or *Creative Intuition in Art and Poetry*. His philosophy of education stems from "lectures in pedagogy," which does not lessen its philosophical worth; the brevity with which he treats his educational themes, however, is a drawback.[44] This brevity is noticeable when one compares the complexity of educational questions and the length of Maritain's educational works.

Responses to his educational theory depend upon one's philosophical school. Some say that Maritain sees the object of education, the student, with a penetrating clarity, and that he understands what is needed at each level of the student's growth.[45] Maritain, it is noted, has a compact philosophical style, and does not make for easily accessible reading.[46] And while he bases his educational theory upon philosophical categories, even his own age was not sympathetic to the universality of metaphysical theories.[47] Others maintain that his educational theory is "exasperating to a degree. Time and again, in *Education at the Crossroads*, one feels the voice is the voice of Jacob, the hand that put in the crossheads (in the most bizarre places) is the hand of a journalist."[48] This criticism is inaccurate and unfair, and it could not have been made if the critic had known of the interconnectedness and interdependence of Maritain's writings. Some claim that Maritain, along with other notable educators such as Mortimer Adler and Robert Hutchins, had to present the "fundamental problems of education half-heartedly and offer half truths for their solutions, because they were addressing audiences that could not stand the whole truth."[49] On reading and rereading *Education at the Crossroads* and *The Education of Man*, it is difficult to reconcile Maritain's prophetic style with half-truths. Certainly Maritain's philosophy depends upon perennial and universal Thomistic categories.[50] However, what is attractive and convincing about his position is his applied style; it is not a calcified position, nor culturally or historically insensitive. His is truly a philosophy of education applied to his time, but in spite of his Thomistic stance, it is not uncompromisingly tied to his time or to a yearning for some golden age. Educators in our day continue to see the relevance of Maritain, especially his themes such as the distinction between the person and the individual, integral humanism, and the nature of knowledge.[51] Other prominent educators, while recognizing that Maritain's educational theory is practically forgotten today, see the relevance of his Thomistic approach.[52]

Lonergan's philosophy of education takes a different approach from Maritain's. *Topics in Education* is far more theoretical, and while he gives examples of educational implications, he approaches the philosophy of education by examining what that field is in itself – that is, the possibility of an applied philosophy. He also examines what he sees to be the distinguishing features and components of philosophy of education, particularly the possibility of a Catholic philosophy of education. Given the shift from a classicist and conceptual position to one of historical-mindedness, Lonergan begins from human knowing and understanding. He asks three questions: "What am I doing when I am knowing? Why is doing that knowing? What do I know when I do it?" The questions relate to cognitional theory, to epistemology, and to metaphysics.[53]

It is too obvious to state that education is concerned with knowing, but Lonergan's philosophical method would suggest that the relationship between knowing and understanding is often not clear, particularly when confused with looking and seeing. He notes that while people know what seeing is, they are perplexed when asked to elaborate on the nature of understanding.[54] Lonergan's philosophy of education attends to the relationship between knowing, understanding, and the implications for decision, choice, and action. "The art and science of education intends the development of the human subject as a knowing and acting being. Little wonder then that it is Lonergan's theory on cognition and the related fields of consciousness that holds out most promise for those working in the classroom and lecture hall."[55] However, given the obvious educational connection between knowing, understanding, and decision and choice, it is surprising that his educational thought has not found wider application.[56]

Parallels have been drawn between John Dewey and Lonergan. Dewey's reliance upon experimentalism limits his method, and consequently his understanding of philosophy. For Lonergan, "philosophy is self-criticism, self-knowledge, and self-appropriation." What also distinguishes Lonergan and Dewey is their understanding of transcendence: for the former, "transcendence is a realm of human meaning (i.e., a realm meant by human beings) and is real ... For Dewey, transcendence is a realm of human meaning and is ideal and not real."[57] These distinctions have important implications for education. Parallels have also been drawn between Lonergan and the scientist and philosopher Michael Polanyi on their understanding of subjectivity and objectivity and personal knowledge.[58] Again, the implications for personal knowledge, particularly as framed in the distinction between subjectivity and objectivity, have important educational implications.

Why are Maritain and Lonergan's educational philosophies being employed here side by side? After all, they represent two different and, some say, conflicting interpretations of Thomistic philosophy. Are these differences insurmountable, or can they both contribute to a Catholic philosophy of education? Indeed, a thesis has been written on Maritain and Lonergan's understanding of critical realism. While the author recognizes the similarities of their positions, particularly on how knowing attains reality and how it is inextricably bound to the senses, Maritain and Lonergan, it is maintained, also differ in what is involved with human knowing and how that knowing is arrived at. There are also differences around their understanding of concepts and conceptualization. The conclusion of the thesis is that it is Lonergan who has the more convincing appreciation of the philosophy of St Thomas.[59] Whether this is a correct reading of Maritain's texts and position remains another matter. However, some of the conclusions of this thesis must be responded to.

The two main concerns of this author's thesis are the formation of concepts, and knowing as looking and seeing versus understanding. First, an erroneous understanding of concepts and how they are formed leads to what Lonergan considers the error of conceptualism, which is the opposite of understanding, without which education does not occur. What then is conceptualism? It is the acceptance of concepts without understanding; conceptualism gives priority to conception over understanding.[60] While understanding is personal, concepts are abstract. It is by attending to the "data of consciousness that one can discover insights, acts of understanding with the triple role of responding to inquiry, grasping intelligible form in sensible representation, and grounding the formation of concepts."[61] Concepts are formed in a particular time and intellectual age, but as human beings change over time, as does their understanding, concepts change as well, and they fail to be educational if they do not culminate in understanding.[62] Conceptualism is the opposite of both insight and understanding. Thus the conceptualist thinks only about concepts without sufficient attention to understanding those concepts.[63]

The other concern is with equating knowing with looking. Lonergan distinguishes between the world of immediacy, that of the infant and the immediacy of the senses and sense knowledge, and the shift to meaning for the world of adults.[64] The mediation of meaning involves understanding, which, while initially dependent upon sense knowledge, moves beyond sense knowledge. Understanding is one part of a complex of operations, which includes smelling, inquiring, imagining, conceiving, reflecting, etc.[65] Thus, knowing is more than just looking, objectivity is more than seeing the external, material world, and reality is much more than what is constituted through the immediacy of experience and the senses.[66] This more comprehensive outline of knowing enables Lonergan to avoid the error of Platonism, on the one hand – which is essentially knowledge as "confrontation; it supposes a duality between the knower and the known"[67] – and Kantianism on the other – the distinction between phenomena, things as they appear to us, and noumena, things as they are in themselves. For Kant, human knowing is confined to phenomena; the noumenon is unknowable.[68] The critique is that Maritain's philosophy, since it begins with being and with metaphysics rather than with cognitional theory, epistemology, and metaphysics – recall Lonergan's three questions: what am I doing when I am knowing? why is doing that knowing? what do I know when I do it? – makes him a conceptualist and limits understanding and knowing to looking and seeing, to picture thinking.[69]

What is of interest here, of course, is not Maritain and Lonergan's metaphysics and epistemology per se, but how these philosophers can assist in explicating a Catholic philosophy of education for our time in relation to the documents from the CCE. Nonetheless, in spite of the specificity of the purpose here, the question remains whether their differing primary philosophic positions render their philosophies of education to be radically different and irreconcilable. Maritain and Lonergan are realists, and while there are differences between them, the commonalities in their educational theories are more than sufficient to contribute to a Catholic philosophy of education. While Maritain does not employ the method of *Insight*, he speaks of insight in the educational context, and insight in relation to truth, and that thinking is not confined to difficulties but applies also to gaining and acquiring insights. Furthermore, Maritain emphasizes understanding and preparing students to think for themselves. Both Maritain and Lonergan see students as the principal and active agents in their understanding and learning. Education is not about endless inquiry and searching without set goals, nor about raising doubts, objections, and obstacles without providing solutions and answers. While Lonergan stresses the importance of students asking questions, he would confirm that they are questions that seek solutions and answers, not spiralling into relentless doubt and scepticism. Maritain's position confirms that he does not subscribe to conceptualism, nor believe that knowing is like looking:

> What is learned should never be passively or mechanically received, as dead information which weighs down and dulls the mind. It must rather be actively transformed by understanding into the very life of the mind, and thus strengthen the latter, as wood thrown into the fire and transformed into flame makes the fire stronger. But a big mass of damp wood thrown into the fire only puts it out. Reason which receives knowledge in a servile manner does not really know and is only depressed by a knowledge which is not its own but that of others. On the contrary, reason which receives knowledge by assimilating it vitally, that is, in a free and liberating manner, really knows, and is exalted in its very activity by this knowledge which henceforth is its own. Then it is that reason really masters the things learned.[70]

This extensive quotation should set the critic's mind at rest. Maritain sees understanding and the appropriation of knowledge to be vital and central to the educational enterprise, in a similar way that Lonergan did. There is elasticity to Maritain's thought, which shows that there is more than one way for a person's cognitional method and process to express itself. Lonergan's approach is to give an account of the cognitional process, and how this is identified and actualized. Another way, admittedly less direct but equally trustworthy, is to see what a person does with regard to this cognitional process, the process of knowing and understanding; that is Maritain's approach. Indeed, he says that the curriculum of a Christian educational institution should be concerned with all of human culture, and should be inspired by a sense of "enlargement, Christian-inspired enlargement, not narrowing, even Christian-centered narrowing, of the humanities."[71] In addition, how Maritain envisages understanding in the student, the errors of what he terms as the *misconceptions of education*, and education for wisdom are all examples of his non-conceptualist and non-picture-thinking approach to education.

Operationally, Maritain is illustrating a cognitional process that is, in fact, highly insightful, and his philosophy of education shows a human appreciation of how understanding occurs. In his philosophy of educa- tion, Maritain is operating in a similar way to what Lonergan refers to as forming concepts via insights, even though he does not formulate the issue in the philosophical language of *Insight* or *Method in Theology*. Mari- tain's philosophy of education gives real lived meaning to the Christian adage: "by their fruits you shall know them." The large quotation above from *Education at the Crossroads* (and there are other examples, particu- larly regarding the purpose of the liberal arts and the humanities) shows that Maritain's educational philosophy is not guilty of conceptualism, nor is he reducing knowing to simply looking, to picture thinking. Even his broader understanding of the purpose of philosophy confirms this: "It is true, of course, that philosophy is a human thing; it is in time by the subject wherein it resides — in the philosopher, that is. It must, then, be of the present moment, *by its application to the real and by the use made of it*. If it is not ... it will have no hold upon men."[72]

V Conclusion

The purpose of this chapter was to highlight the distinguishing features of Maritain's and Lonergan's philosophies of education, and to address their differences, but also to see what unites them, in spite of their dif- ferent Thomistic approaches. While Maritain's philosophy of educa- tion is largely in keeping with some of the philosophers who flourished before the Council, Lonergan represents the tradition after the Council, even though his work on education was written beforehand. In addition, it would appear that Lonergan's educational philosophy does not have a corresponding following to Maritain's. Understanding and the appro- priation of knowledge and learning are important for both Maritain and Lonergan. Lonergan establishes this more overtly in his writings. Maritain's thought, through a school of Thomism that Lonergan did not subscribe to, presents a philosophy of education that is versatile and dy- namic; it is a helpful, other side of the coin for a contemporary Catholic philosophy of education.

It is useful to employ Maritain and Lonergan's Catholic philoso- phies of education side by side for a few reasons. First, they represent positions on education prior to and after the Council, and in this they demonstrate the continuity of Catholic thought. Second, while Lonergan writes on the new learning, such as in mathematics and science, Maritain deals, however briefly, with the kinds of subjects that a Catholic educational institution should include. Third, while Maritain does not elaborate a great deal on the practicalities of education, he sees his role as elucidating the nature of the student as a person and clarifying why knowledge and learning are crucial to the development and growth of personhood. Lonergan is also interested in such matters, and pursues them through themes such as authenticity, conversion, and the primacy of the person as subject in the quest for objectivity in knowing. Fourth, the Catholic educational documents from the CCE recognize the importance of an educational philosophy, though they do not express a preference for the philosophers one should turn to in developing such a philosophy. However, while the intellectual position since the Council would be more receptive to different kinds of philosophies, the school of philosophy that the CCE would have in mind is undoubtedly more in keeping with the broader, more inclusive, and holistic approach of Thomism. For Thomism, as for Maritain and Lonergan, students are the active agents of their learning. Finally, both men present two traditions of Catholic philosophy of education that are represented in the documents. One is a tradition that stresses the place of the liberal arts and the humanities as integral to education and education as wisdom; this would be the tradition that Maritain represents. The documents also recognize that students now live in a world that is not unified in the sense of Christian culture in the way that it was envisioned prior to the Council. Today students must grow as persons and subjects, the foundation for their authenticity and integrity, and their integral subjectivity. This is the tradition that Lonergan represents. Together, Maritain and Lonergan provide ways of understanding what the *philosophic* aspect of a *Catholic philosophy of education* involves for our time.

3

The Aim and End of the Catholic School: The Role of Knowledge and Learning

I Introduction

The Catholic school must first aim to be a good school, though its aims and end may differ from those of other schools.[1] An aim relates to what is intended, where one seeks to be at the conclusion of a process. An aim is usually expansive in scope and related to action. Here, *end* is broader than *goal*. While a *goal* is a long-term aim, an *end* has a greater breadth, but given human contingency, is unpredictable. The final *end* of the Christian life is union with God. Human beings are strengthened by God's grace and providential love to journey towards that end; however, it is an end that is neither certain nor uncertain. It is not certain as human choice and freedom can opt to choose evil and sin, nor is it uncertain given the promises of Christ and the faith of the Christian community in the resurrection of Jesus Christ from the dead. The Christian faith echoes the promises of Christ, but acknowledges that the certainty of those promises is precarious, and depends upon living a life worthy of one's baptismal call; they are not independent of, nor do they supersede, human choice and action.

Any school must be founded on certain aims and possess the means of attaining them, as education is an intentional, purposeful, planned activity, attending to the stages of mental, moral, intellectual, emotional, and spiritual growth.[2] It is obvious why a Catholic school requires clarity regarding its aims and means. The *end* of a Catholic school, however, is broader than the *goal*, because its end, unlike a goal, is never achieved, neither at the conclusion of schooling nor during some other stage of life. The Catholic school in educating the student, a person called to a divine destiny, shares in the broader and pastoral end of the Church: that final end, union with God. In that sense, the end of the Christian life is never achieved, in any complete sense, in this life. Given that the Catholic school is an arm of the Church, its *end*, even though not attained in this life, must remain central, particularly in relation to its aims and objectives.

The educational documents are all written at a particular historical time, and reflect the political and ideological concerns, cultural context, and educational perspective of their age. A useful study could be made of the historical particularities of each of these documents. That, however, is not the intention here. The purpose here in examining the documents, rather, is to look at their philosophical cohesiveness as a whole. While each document is self-contained, their themes confirm that they continuously add to the Church's understanding of a Catholic philosophy of education.

There is also a change in perspective in the Roman educational documents, and it can be marked in three stages. The first is prior to the Council, between 1885 – *Spectata Fides / On Christian Education* – and 1962 – the opening of the Council. The second is the promulgation of the Council's document *Gravissimum Educationis*, and the third commences with the documents issued since the Council, the first being *The Catholic School*, in 1977. The third stage is open-ended as the cce continues to publish educational documents. Thus, in one sense, there is no complete Catholic philosophy of education contained in a single document. Prior to the Council, the emphasis was on the catechetical and religious dimension of the Catholic school, as Thomistic philosophy had highlighted hierarchies, divisions, and structures in knowing, and the implications thereof were set in the curriculum. It was a classical approach to education: one consulted a text in order to know what to learn, how to think, and how to proceed intellectually, religiously, morally, and socially; it was a classical approach, and to use Lonergan's terminology, it had classicist dimensions. That changed with the Council. Education now has to do with intention and active engagement; knowledge and learning are meant to raise questions and critical engagement, to aid students in thinking for themselves. Knowing and learning are communal activities, with social implications that go beyond the individual.

This chapter examines the aims and end of the Catholic school, and how knowledge and learning serve that end. The school's mandate is intellectual in nature, but that mandate serves all that happens during the school day, but also, and more importantly, the education of the student as a whole person. The documents, Maritain, and Lonergan each make their own contribution in specific ways. The documents emphasize the development of the personality of the student and their preparation for life, enhanced by the unity of the curriculum and the synthesis between faith, culture, and life. Maritain distinguishes between the various ends of education, and how the intellectual mandate serves the whole person. The liberal arts and the humanities enhance human unity, whereas early specialization hinders the gradual freedom that comes from knowledge and learning appropriate to the stages of mental and moral growth. Finally, Lonergan's contribution is through a detailed examination of knowing, the known, and insights, and the personal dimension of these processes. His transcendental method becomes the foundation for true knowing and for objectivity.

II The Documents of the CCE

II.1 CCE: THE AIM AND END OF THE CATHOLIC SCHOOL

While we shall not examine the documents in chronological order, it is worthwhile to make some brief comments on three educational documents between 1865 and the close of the Council in 1965, and to do so chronologically. Neither *Spectata Fides* (1885) nor *Acerbo Nimis* (1905) is an educational document in the strict sense. The former is concerned with Christian education as religious instruction, though it does see a relationship between the wider curriculum and religious knowledge, particularly catechetical instruction.[3] The latter concerns the teaching of Christian doctrine, particularly catechetical instruction, and notes with alarm the crude and damaging levels of ignorance in religious matters.[4]

However, there are no sharp educational distinctions between the parish and school. Priests are responsible for imparting Christian doctrine, and must not confuse homiletic erudition for religious instruction, nor must the homily become a substitute for catechetical instruction, meant for the young and adults.[5] Finally, *Divini Illius Magistri* (1929) is on Christian education. It is longer than the previous two and is unquestionably educational in nature. It refers to principles and relates them and the task of education to the final end of the Christian life, one that the school cannot ignore:

> It is therefore as important to make no mistake in education, as it is to make no mistake in the pursuit of the last end, with which the whole work of education is intimately and necessarily connected … since education consists essentially in preparing man for what he must be and for what he must do here below, in order to attain the sublime end for which he was created, it is clear that there can be no true education which is not wholly directed to man's last end for which he was created.[6]

While the end or goal of life, and its relationship to education, is central, it is an end that is outwardly directed, and points to social and communal responsibilities; education is social and not individualistic.[7] While there are diverse educational theories, given the end of the Christian life, education cannot ignore the perennial journey towards human perfection, thus the only adequate educational theory is one inspired by the Gospel. However, education is also considered philosophically, particularly the span of the various branches of knowledge and their relation to the journey of human perfection, and the methods and principles of the sciences.[8]

Gravissimum Educationis is the bridge for a Catholic philosophy of education between the pre- and post-conciliar Church, though it does not concentrate exclusively on the Catholic school, as later documents will. A single aim of education is identified: "For a true education aims at the formation of the human person in the pursuit of his ultimate end and of the good of the societies of which, as man, he is a member, and in whose obligations, as an adult, he will share."[9] The Council stressed the social and communal dimensions of the Christian life, and this document situates them in the context of knowledge and learning. The following sums up the document's educational philosophy:

> [Students are] to develop harmoniously their physical, moral and intellectual endowments so that they may gradually acquire a mature sense of responsibility in striving endlessly to form their own lives properly and in pursuing true freedom as they surmount the vicissitudes of life with courage and constancy. Let them be given also, as they advance in years, a positive and prudent sexual education. Moreover they should be so trained to take their part in social life that properly instructed in the necessary and opportune skills they can become actively involved in various community organizations, open to discourse with others and willing to do their best to promote the common good.[10]

This synopsis of a Catholic philosophy of education summarizes education for Christian maturity, given the invitation at baptism and the journey towards the Christian final end; it is more than just human maturity. So while education must engage with culture and provide human formation, it must also create a human community of persons whose personalities are transformed by baptism, the Gospel, and the mysteries of faith. Again, this transformation has broader civic and social implications: "So ... the Catholic school, while it is open, as it must be, to the situation of the contemporary world, leads its students to promote efficaciously the good of the earthly city and also prepares them for service in the spread of the Kingdom of God, so that by leading an exemplary apostolic life they become, as it were, a saving leaven in the human community."[11]

The aims and end of education are related to the student as a person, transformed in baptism. It is an education in communion with others, with implications for the common good. The ultimate end of Catholic education must serve the ultimate end of the Christian life. The more immediate aims of Catholic education, while in service of the ultimate aim of the Christian life, are realized in a particular time and age with its intellectual and social contexts, recognizing the contributions that strengthen this aim and the threats that diminish it. Sharing in the saving mission of the Church, the Catholic school identifies subsidiary aims: the aims of the teacher, the curriculum, and the school environment; but the aim of the school per se is singular: "the Catholic school has as its aim the critical communication of human culture and the total formation of the individual, it works towards this goal guided by its Christian vision of reality."[12] The dialogue with culture – consistently developed in the documents, particularly the *synthesis between faith and culture* and *faith and life* – and the formation of the student go together. Knowledge and learning, essential aims of the Catholic school, are related to lived values and a sense of truth. The efficacy of these virtues depends, ultimately, not on the subject matter or methodologies but on those who work in a Catholic school.[13]

A prominent theme is the human and Christian formation of the student, and while Christian formation has obvious links to faith, ecclesial life, the sacraments, religious instruction, etc., the formation envisaged is in relation to faith and religious belief, and in relation to society, culture, and the common good. Catholic education is framed as a communion of persons, and the relational dimensions of communion and communion are integral in the formation of authentic students. This communion of persons has an educational focus, which is the formation of integral persons through teaching and learning aimed at fostering good judgments, good thinking, growth in the virtues and values, and a sharing of personal interests. The student's formation is always in relation to freedom: "education to freedom is a humanizing action, because it aims at the full development of personality. In fact, education itself must be seen as the acquisition, growth and possession of freedom," integral for a mature personality.[14] Such formation is also grounded upon a Christian understanding of reality based on the spiritual nature of the person – *spiritual* understood broadly as the ability to know, to understand, and to transcend material reality and the senses. However, a Christian vision of reality is not an abstract and disengaged reflection on what does and does not constitute reality; this is the focus of advanced university study. Rather, a Christian understanding of reality depends on an integral education and all that happens during the school day, all that contributes in developing students' capacities and potentialities, preparing them for a profession, and encouraging growth in ethical and social awareness – all contributing to the religious and transcendent dimension of education.[15] This understanding includes civic and public life, and is ultimately secured upon an understanding of the world, human beings, and history, and responding to culture. All education is shaped by a concept of the person. And in spite of its religious foundation, Catholic education contributes to a pluralist society by educating students who will choose to transform culture through their integral humanity and their care and love for others.[16]

II.2 CCE: KNOWLEDGE AND LEARNING

A Catholic philosophy of education must be clear about the purpose of knowledge and learning, and the documents are clear on both. Knowledge and learning prepare students for life, including their professional lives and active citizenship.[17] The transformation from knowledge and learning is manifested in moral, ethical, social, and cultural choices. The religious response remains fundamental, but is contextualized by recognizing that the Catholic school is not for Catholics alone, but for all who believe in an integral education. This inclusive mandate of the Catholic school is more comprehensive than the differences of confessional affiliation.

The documents emphasize the roles of parents, the school, and the Church. All are agents of Catholic education, with interrelated but distinct roles. The school concentrates on pedagogical and cultural aims attained through an integral education that broadens one's understanding of culture and reality, though how culture and reality are distinguished is not clear.[18] What is clear is that integral formation is situated within a culture, and a Christian vision of reality forms and challenges culture. While reality is more than what is externally constituted, and the person is more than what culture makes them, culture is powerful and transformative, and the school must reflect on its aims in the context of culture.[19] The following is an impressive statement on the nature of education and knowledge:

> Education is not given for the purpose of gaining power but as an aid towards a fuller understanding of, and communion with man, events and things. Knowledge is not to be considered as a means

of material prosperity and success, but as a call to serve and to be responsible for others.[20]

This concise statement enables Catholic education to be envisaged as a spiritual process, spiritual not just as the particularities of religious practice or one's relationship with God, but as enabling persons to transcend the world of immediacy and their physical, material, and sensory environment. Persons transcend themselves through their choices and decisions; they can also be present to others in ways not confined by the immediacy of their external and material reality. The student is a spiritual being, and accordingly Catholic education is spiritual in the widest sense, and as an integral education it must elucidate the implications of this spiritual nature.

The distinction between the aims of catechesis and of the school has important educational implications. Catechesis, usually parish-based, is the handing down of the Christian message, particularly the spiritual, liturgical, and sacramental dimensions of faith. However, the aim of the school is imparting knowledge. So while the school has a role in catechesis, especially faith formation, its proper role is to transmit knowledge.[21] This focus on knowledge is comprehensively understood; it is nether neither bookish nor narrowly curriculum-based. Knowledge and learning are transformative, and are sources of freedom; education is more than a heady, intellectual acquisition of information, however orderly and systematic.

The documents lay out the role of knowledge and learning; here they will be considered under four categories. The first is how they shape an attitude towards life, particularly the virtues and values. The task of the school is "to draw out the ethical dimension for the precise purpose of arousing the individual's inner spiritual dynamism and to aid his achieving that moral freedom which complements the psychological."[22] Note the use of *spiritual* referring to moral and psychological freedom. Such freedom depends on enduring values giving meaning and purpose to life. A disposition and a way of looking at life are learned in different ways, particularly through the educational worldview, which extends, implicitly or explicitly, across the school day. The attitude to life is a common vision based on a hierarchy of values, which is the mandate giving teachers their authority to teach.[23] One example of students being knowledgeable about an attitude to life, and of knowledge as more than disengaged information, is in sex education and the influence of technology, media, and culture in general on sexual matters. Students must realize that the information they acquire through the immediacy of seeing, hearing, and reading must be transformed through under-standing, and with the teacher's help, they must learn to reach correct judgments.[24] The truths of the Catholic faith and an orderly introduction to Christian living, especially its ethical and moral dimensions, are the foundations for correct judgments.[25] Any criticism of indoctrination is thwarted by recognizing that such a systematic presentation must not be at the expense of the student's own personal critical inquiry, but rather that such inquiry should be assisted by the orderly presentation of the curriculum, enabling students to understand how to frame their ques-tions within the breadth of their knowledge.[26] Inquiry and questioning, however, are not endlessly open-ended, nor are they meant to encour-age doubt and relativism, leading to confusion. There is knowledge to be gained and truth to be acquired, and while a Christian vision of reality begins with inquiry, every stage of the student's growth is increasingly confirmed in the confidence of knowledge and truth. So questions and inquiry must be unified through conclusions and answers, as an integral education depends upon a commitment to truth, and the knowledge and learning that the teacher communicates should not be housed in non-committed neutrality.[27] So the school moves students to understanding and to thinking about how their knowledge must be transformed into wisdom, and how the immediacy of facts must be judged through their acquired values.[28]

Second, knowledge and learning are considered under the category of the subjects of the curriculum and their integration and relationship. The documents are consistent regarding the independence of each sub-ject in the curriculum and their unity, and ultimately their integration within the student. Knowledge and learning play a decisive role in the personal unity and the well-being of the student. The method of each subject is emphasized, as is the danger of artificially reducing sub-jects as supplements for faith, thereby also compromising the distinct values and truths of each subject. However, the autonomy of each sub-ject does not imply independence from spiritual and moral values.[29] A fragmented and unevenly balanced curriculum harms the unity of the student by presenting an incomplete picture of who the person is and the breadth and scope of the desire to know. Subjects such as anthropology, biology, psychology, sociology, and philosophy can assist in developing a holistic understanding of the person, including the religious aspect. Persons shape history, that stage of human becoming that records the great struggles between good and evil, so history must be prominent in the curriculum.[30] Further, science and technology must not eclipse the humanities, the arts, philosophy, or the breadth of the Christian intellectual tradition. The student's maturity depends upon the breadth of knowledge and learning to which they are exposed, and as they mature, knowledge and learning have broader implications for the relationship between faith and culture.[31]

While the Catholic school does not claim neutrality in religious truth, neither does it confuse neutrality with critical inquiry. An avowed neutrality not only turns the curriculum into a dispersion of unrelated and fragmented facts, but it also harms the personal, integral unity of the student, a unity that, while historically situated, has transcendental aspirations. What is noteworthy is that the documents see the subjects of the curriculum as each contributing to the ongoing growth of the student, perfecting them in encountering truth at different levels, different kinds of truths, and truth's implication in serving others.[32] Beyond imparting knowledge, education is also about experience and the relationship between knowledge and action. The diversity of the curriculum encompasses the different forms of human knowing, with its ethical, social, and communal dimensions. The documents emphasize that education is participatory and dialogical, cooperative, and calls for the giving of self.[33] The epistemological diversity of the curriculum and the methodology of each subject are united in the teacher's worldview, and are transformed into a unity of realized wisdom manifested in acting and choosing. It is because each subject teaches particular truths, each according to a particular methodology, that subjects are not independent fiefdoms.[34]

Finally, the Church's repeated call for a *synthesis between faith and culture* and *faith and life* is realized in the school through the unity and integration of the curriculum, enlightened by the Gospel and the Christian virtues. While the aim of the school is knowledge, it is a knowledge that heightens awareness, obligations, responsibilities, and communal implications. Religious education, far from a neutral account of religion, leads by elaborating on the relationship between faith and culture, and actualizing what knowledge of the Christian life entails. Catholic religious education, interdisciplinary in nature and broader than catechesis, relies upon theology, philosophy, the social sciences, and other disciplines, and must be prominent in the curriculum.[35]

The third category regarding knowledge and learning pertains to the personality of the student shaped by a Christian anthropology as a person created in the image and likeness of God, offered the freedom from sin that was won by Christ, and called to a virtuous life and an eternal destiny. Christian personality, then, is wider than a psychological category; so a well-rounded formation of the student must include the theological, philosophical, ethical, and social teachings of the Church.[36] A Christian concept of the person is the foundation for a Christian worldview, not abstract or conceptual, but related to the tonus of living and integrated into the student's life. Amidst diversity and plurality, the world and Christian reality are discovered through choice, meaning, decisions, and actions. The Christian personality is a unity, and knowledge and learning are essential in enhancing and revealing that personality.[37] Education is more than the acquisition of information, especially when that information eclipses the other dimensions of life that are essential to the integration of what is known and learned, an integration that depends upon knowledge and values. Knowledge and values also enable the student to acquire skills of communal and interpersonal engagement and life; and so the educational program of the school is meant to bring about a unity between study and living, crucial for the formation of the whole person.[38] Learning is meant to enable students to know how to live, and to understand what maturity means and entails, enabling human intelligence to serve an integral education and the ongoing growth of a mature personality.[39] The Christian personality is a harmonious development of one called to a new creation in baptism, amidst the dimensions of human formation that include the psychological, social, ethical, cultural, and sexual. These dimensions "are not separate and parallel paths; they are complementary forms of education which become one in the goal of the teacher and the willing reception of the student."[40] The curriculum is not simply in response to educational regulations; rather, the diversity of the curriculum progressively integrates and unifies the student, and the documents stress how the curriculum is integral for the development of Christian maturity.[41] Given this, education cannot be limited to the utilitarian, technical, and practical dimensions of knowledge. An unbalanced curriculum violates the integral unity of truth, which includes, but goes beyond, sensory truth. A balanced curriculum is indispensable for the maturing of the Christian personality.[42]

The fourth category is the Catholicity of the school, particularly amidst religious diversity. The documents stress the Catholic nature of the school and the necessity of enhancing the Catholic life of the students, and not just confined to their faith life; they stress the development of Catholic sensibilities. While Catholic religious instruction must be a distinct and systematic subject, religious awareness is not confined to that alone, and this furthers the synthesis between faith and culture and between faith and life by preventing artificial distortions between religious and general culture.[43] While cultural diversity can take its toll upon the educational distinctiveness of the Catholic school, the documents situates religious diversity under the principle of religious freedom and the rights of parents to educate their children as they see fit.[44] However, religious diversity among students is common in Catholic schools, and this diversity is viewed educationally as encompassing the different dimensions of knowledge and learning:

> On the cognitive level, schools develop the contents of the curriculum: areas of knowledge to be taught and skills to be promoted. On the relational-affective level, schools develop attitudes and ways of talking with others, teaching the students to respect diversity and taking different viewpoints into account, cultivating empathy and collaboration.[45]

The progression of a Catholic philosophy of education is especially noticeable in the context of religious diversity and the importance of dialogue, with dialogue and relationships viewed as educational.[46] And while the Catholicity of the school remains foundational, the school has many aims amidst religious diversity: it is a place of "evangelization, of complete formation, of inculturation, of apprenticeship in a lively dialogue between young people of different religions and social backgrounds."[47] The documents' understanding of the Christian vision of the

person has grown and expanded. There is greater awareness that diversity and difference, if handled correctly, can be educational. Students can
hardly be expected to be proficient in the technicalities and nuances of
religious dialogue. Rather, they must be introduced to the basic principles of dialogue in the context of education and learning in relating to
others, which includes non-believers.[48]

The documents are clear as to the expansive role of knowledge and
learning for the Catholic school. That understanding has undoubtedly
evolved, but the evolution has been built upon a basic principle in all
Catholic teaching: the dignity of the person. Catholics regularly refer to
this principle, but often it seems to be limited to a legal and juridical
sense. The documents lay out how knowledge and learning are related to
human dignity, how that dignity grows incrementally, and how one can
understand the dignity of knowledge and learning in educational terms.
Educators understandably concentrate on the scholastic aspects of the
school day. The broader Catholic vision of knowledge and learning, as
an essential means for human unity, goes beyond the obvious scholastic
nature of the school.

Another noteworthy feature of the documents is how knowledge and
learning about what is different, particularly religiously and culturally
different, are seen as educationally nourishing. Not only is there no hint
of accepting religious and cultural diversity reluctantly, on the contrary,
that very diversity is seen as rich with educational possibilities. While
the foundations of such a change are to be found in the documents of the
Council, what is remarkable is how the documents have interrelated
theological, ecclesial, cultural, and social themes with education and
pedagogy. While engaging with and relating to the religiously and culturally *other* are understood in educational terms, knowledge is seen in
relation to experience and action, and the different ways and kinds of
knowing reflected in the curriculum have a social and communal dimension that unifies the student. Institutional education is a participatory activity, and the diversity of the curriculum and the diversity of the
student body are mutually educational and humanly enriching.

The clarity of the documents on the nature of knowledge and learning is a substantial contribution to the ongoing task of formulating a
Catholic philosophy of education after the Council. What is remarkable
is the absence of a narrow, churchy language in relating knowledge and

learning to the Catholic mission of the school and the integral formation of the student. Knowledge and learning are understood philosophically, and thus the documents make a fundamental Catholic contribution to a philosophy of education. While the primacy of religious faith and belief are affirmed, there is not a whiff of indoctrination, an odour so repellent to philosophers of education. And this philosophical approach of the documents is a vital link to Maritain and Lonergan – who extend great attention to the philosophical understanding of what is known and learned in the context of education – and their transformative role.

III The Contribution of Jacques Maritain

III.1 AIMS OF EDUCATION

Maritain attends to the aims of education through addressing seven misconceptions, beginning with ignoring and overlooking the ends of education.[49] The confusion lies in failing to recognize that education is an *ethical art* aimed at an end. Today education has excellent means, but its educational efficacy is lost as the end is forgotten. The second misconception is false conceptions of the end, with three foci: the distinction between a scientific and a philosophic-religious anthropology; a Judeo-Christian anthropology; and personality, particularly the distinction between the person and the individual.[50] With these clarifications, the aim of education is to guide students to shape themselves through knowledge, sound judgment, the moral virtues, and the spiritual and religious dimensions of civilization.[51] However, as education is not for the repose and pleasure of a privileged class, the practical and utilitarian dimensions cannot be neglected.[52]

Maritain has been accused of an abstract educational theory; there is sufficient evidence to the contrary. Two points in particular: "the educational task is both greater and more mysterious and, in a sense, humbler than many imagine," and "educators must not expect too much from education."[53] The first conviction is founded upon the nature of the student as a person and the spiritual nature of an integral education. The mysterious nature of the educational task is exemplified in his seventh misconception "that everything can be learned," and countered by the realization that what is most important in education and learning lies beyond the task of educators and education.[54] The second conviction is hardly cynical. Educators must not expect too much from education, for in ultimate terms, given the final end of the student, education pertains to wisdom, which cannot be taught. This educational crescendo reaches its zenith: in "human life there is nothing greater than intuition and love ... yet neither ... is a matter of training and learning, they are gift and freedom. In spite of all that, education should be primarily concerned with them."[55] For our purposes, aesthetics, rather than metaphysics, provides a better understanding of what Maritain means by intuition. Intuition is that spiritual ability of persons, endowed with senses and passions, to reveal themselves and communicate with others. Intuition is the fruit of the relation between the subjectivity of the person and the objectivity of the world.[56] The intuitive power is released through what is acquired in knowledge. The intellect tends towards an object, not physically, but as the goal of knowing. Among its tasks, it frees experience and the imagination by interacting with what is seen and understanding the object of knowledge in its different dimensions and manifestations, beyond just the physical and material.[57]

III.2 THE END OF EDUCATION

While Maritain lays out a detailed plan for the curriculum, albeit a European model thereof, he establishes the philosophical underpinnings of the aims and end of education; thus the final end of education is framed succinctly as the "fulfillment of man as a human person."[58] His distinction between the person and the individual is not suggestive of dualism or Gnosticism. Though personality concentrates on the spiritual and individuality upon the material, they are united in the one human being, composed of material substance and the nonmaterial soul.[59] Personality is manifested through "knowledge and intelligence, good will and love."[60] Even though individuality renders a human being a small part of an immense material universe, knowledge and love render a person no longer a part, but a whole, opening up the wealth of the created order to be known. The person is mystery, and education ignores this at its peril.[61] The metaphysical integrity and unity of the student is preserved from positivist and pragmatic philosophies that overlook the nature of the student as a person and the primacy of truth.[62]

While the Catholic school contributes to preparing students for their final end, it has its own immediate ends pertaining to the nature of the school, and determined by an integral vision of the student. Maritain distinguishes between a natural and a supernatural ultimate end.[63] While intellectual and pedagogical progress necessitate a ceaseless examination of the means of education, the end of education is determined by virtue of the student as a person, particularly as "the prime goal of education is the conquest of internal and spiritual freedom to be achieved by the individual person," realized through the four characteristics of personality: knowledge and wisdom, good will and love.[64] Maritain turns to the aim of education, warning of the dangers when the means overpower the ends, noting that modern educational means have the student so well tested and analyzed that the purpose of the means is forgotten, and so is the end.[65] Education without an aim, which tends to growth for its own sake, leads to randomness and confusion.[66]

III.3 THE INTELLECTUAL TASK

The primary task of the school is intellectual: the enlightenment of the intellect; accordingly, the ultimate purpose of the school is knowledge and intellectual development. Even moral education, essential for the ultimate end of the student, is realized through such enlightenment.[67] Students grow as persons through their spiritual and intellectual personality, which remains the primary aim of education. Maritain acknowledges the social, civic, utilitarian, and family responsibilities that students will have to assume in adulthood, all of which constitute the secondary aims of education. However, the intellectual mandate of the school is realized though the acquisition of truth, the acquisition of knowledge, and thinking and making personal judgments.[68] Thus while the primary aim of education is not social in nature but relates rather to intelligence, there is an irreplaceable link between education and the social nature of the person. Society and social life are natural and essential for the flourishing of personality, and freedom and communication are the heart of life in society.[69]

In spite of Maritain's philosophical approach, he warns against the misconception of "intellectualism": education fails when it is reduced to skills of argument and oratory. Education is for freedom and human awakening, and the school performs part of this task.[70] While the school must concentrate on what can be taught, and concern itself with the education of intelligence rather than of the will, the shaping of the will, in ultimate terms, is far more important than shaping the intellect. It is better to be a good person than a learned one.[71] The following acts as the backdrop for the spiritual nature of knowledge and learning:

> [T]he spiritual activities of the human being are *intentional* activities, they tend by nature toward an object, an objective aim, which will measure and rule them, not materially and by means of bondage, but spiritually and by means of liberty, for the object of knowledge or of love is internalized by the activity itself of intelligence and the will, and becomes within them the very fire of their perfect spontaneity.[72]

III.4　KNOWLEDGE AND LEARNING

Knowledge and learning have curricular implications, manifested in the humanities and the liberal arts.[73] Knowledge and learning are considered broadly; they are not ends in themselves – though there is a value in knowledge and learning for their own sake – but as sources of transformation, liberation, and freedom. The ability to know can only develop step by step, and depends upon collective human experience; knowledge and learning are systematic and incremental.[74] However, everything cannot be learned, particularly all that constitutes personhood, not just in ultimate terms of one's relation with God, but also in the integral living of life. Love, intuition, wisdom, experience cannot be taught; they are the fruit borne by freeing the powers and abilities that constitute personhood:

> the chief aspirations of a person are aspirations to freedom ...
> [not] free will ... which is a gift of nature ... [but] freedom which
> is spontaneity, expansion, or autonomy, and which we have to gain
> through constant effort and struggle. And what is the more profound and essential form of such a desire? It is the desire for inner
> and spiritual freedom.[75]

Maritain warns against the futility of a bookish, pre-prepared knowledge, where answers are unaccompanied by personal understanding; to know for oneself is an essential source of liberation and freedom.[76] Knowledge and learning begin with sense knowledge, but the mind moves progressively away from sense knowledge and transforms it into intelligibility, understanding, and reasoning, vital for the increasing liberation of the student from other immediacies of the human environment. These stages are not to be viewed as incomplete, achieving perfection only in adult knowledge. School education is neither adult knowledge nor the mastery of university knowing. Knowledge in all its dimensions must be imparted according to the stages of mental and moral growth. Knowledge is perfected at each stage; it is complete, while continuously building, both naturally and cognitively, towards greater maturity. Knowledge is not to be viewed as a unified whole and then simply divided out. It is because knowledge and learning are complete at each stage of intellectual growth, that play is included as an educational category.[77]

What is learned is not theoretical nor unapplied nor disengaged from the student's humanity. Learning is the mastery of reason, and not reduced to a series of hurdles to be overcome, nor to mere memorization. Learning is transformed into freedom and its spiritual nature is realized when it is incorporated into the life and living of the student.[78] While Maritain secures his curriculum on the liberal arts and the humanities, a number of qualifications are necessary. First, he distinguishes between knowledge of "least worth" and "most worth." The latter emphasizes "knowledge value," the former "training." Play is part of the second category, including other examples, and both categories are essential to an integral education.[79] Second, in promoting the liberal arts and humanities, Maritain is not advocating a disengaged program of the great ideas and concepts. This is "dilettantism — and a dilettante has certainly [a] weak and not a well-trained mind."[80] Learning must always be in relation to truth and beauty. Third, university education is not the culmination and perfection of education; vocational and manual work are noble in themselves, and essential for the internal unity of the student. Accordingly, students will be internally free to choose their vocational or technical specialization to the extent that their education is liberal:

"youth has a right to education in the liberal arts, in order to be prepared for human work and for human leisure."[81] Finally, he calls for an
enlargement of the curriculum of the liberal arts and the humanities that
recognizes human achievement and knowledge in every age.[82]

School and university education are further distinguished. A school
educates "natural intelligence," whereas the university exalts the "intellectual virtues." Educating natural intelligence is in keeping with the
stages of mental and moral growth. It tends towards integration, to unity,
and to the general phases of knowledge that enable the student to see and
understand the diversity of truths. In every way, natural intelligence is
distinct from and opposed to early specialization. It is distinct in that
it encourages a breath and diversity of knowledge as a means of unifying the student's experience; it is opposed to early specialization, which
confuses and disrupts education if not secured upon the stages of growth
that depend on diverse forms of knowledge, peculiar to each stage.[83]
Undergraduate education is the final stage in the education of natural intelligence. Like the school, but in increasingly more concentrated form,
it is guided less by details and more by "intellectual enjoyment," and is
still general knowledge, according to each discipline. The intellectual
virtues, however, are specialized bodies of knowledge, and are the focus
of graduate studies, which are the completion of knowledge as science.[84]
Finally, graduate specialization, the development of a *habitus*, depends
upon the diversity of natural intelligence and enhances the freedom of
the adult student, enabling them to take their place within the diversity
of human living.

Maritain emphasizes universal knowledge, aware that its immensity
makes it impossible to acquire the intellectual virtue particular to every
sphere of such knowledge. Natural intelligence, if unified and ordered
according to the stages of mental and moral growth, depends upon unity
and integration and a "hierarchy of values."[85] Ultimately, human perfection is attained through knowledge and love.[86] And while the former can
be imparted, the latter cannot be taught, yet as regards the absolute ultimate end, it remains the preeminent virtue: that ultimately love has a
more unifying power than knowledge.[87]

Maritain's contribution to the aims and end of education is simple and
sophisticated, resting upon the nature of the student as a person and the
continued effort to ensure the unity of the student. The means of edu-

cation must adapt to intellectual and social progress, but the aims and end remain constant. This constancy should not be confused with being static, but seen as dynamic and open given the nature of the person. His list of seven misconceptions of education draws attention to how human unity is compromised when the aims and end are continually revised because of social, cultural, and ideological shifts that move in one direction and then another. His position is simple: the nature of the person, and the development and manifestation of that nature in the integral personality of the student, determines the aims and end of education. While the intellectual nature of the school is emphasized, the student, as a person, does not exist in a solitary intellectual and conceptual realm, a realm swirling with things known and varied information. The student is an integral person, and all that is required for growth towards personhood places demands upon education. The aims and end of a school must be in response to the development of personhood, as must the goal of knowledge and learning.

In the context of diversity and plurality, and the expansion of knowledge and learning, and the increasingly expansive understanding of culture, there is no doubt that today Maritain's curriculum in the liberal arts and the humanities would need to be expanded to include the diversity of cultural, intellectual, social, and religious expressions, and he would be the first to agree. However, including a broad intellectual diversity to represent the diversity of the school's population will not be easy. Maritain's emphasis is less on amounts taught or diversity represented than on the ability to think and to understand amidst diversity and plurality. He says that a Christian institution of learning must not be confined by European, Western, or Christian boundaries, but must be open to all expressions of human knowledge and learning, insofar as they continuously contribute to the internal and spiritual freedom of the student as a person.

Also noteworthy is Maritain's emphasis on how knowledge and learning, at the different stages of growth, and through the diversity of a curriculum, but not encumbered by early specialization, perfect human nature. Knowledge and learning are essential for students taking their place in community and society, and for enabling them to manifest themselves through their ability to communicate with others amidst diversity and plurality. Early specialization and the narrowness of the

specialized nature of professional education make this communication and manifestation of human personality ever more difficult. The
education of natural intelligence in schools cannot be overemphasized
today. University education, particularly with early professional education, seems to bypass the necessary link between the education of natural intelligence and the narrower focus of graduate studies, the realm of
the intellectual virtues. Maritain's distinctions between natural intelligence and the intellectual virtues emphasize the integrity of each phase:
school, undergraduate, and graduate. Without such integrity, the school
is then rendered incomplete in not attending to professional preparation. That, of course, is not its purpose, intellectual though its focus is.
All this, again, is secured upon Maritain's stress on the integrity of the
person and the relationship between individuality and personality. If, as
he says, education is ultimately for freedom, then the integrity and unity
of each phase of education needs to be protected and ensured.

IV The Contribution of Bernard Lonergan

IV.1 KNOWING AND KNOWLEDGE

While Maritain expands on the means, goals, and end of education,
Lonergan does not attend to them, per se; rather, in his view, knowing
becomes the foundation. Education is not about abstraction, and depends upon indirect communication as well. He emphasizes the place of
history, context, and the particularities of time and culture. Colonial rule
depended upon how one was trained and educated to make appropriate
responses in administration and amidst conflicts. Such administrators
could be relied upon as their responses could be anticipated. However,
passing a civil service examination and having the knowledge to administer are not interchangeable; education is broader than acquiring information and passing examinations.[88]

In *Insight*, Lonergan recognizes the great diversity and volume of
human knowledge, well beyond the capacity of libraries and books – true
then, and even more so today. His intent in *Insight* is not to determine
whether or not knowledge exists; he is concerned, rather, not with the
known but with the process of knowing and its "recurrent structure."[89]
Insight is a vast and complex book, and any attempt to synthesize it, how-

ever briefly, is beyond our scope here.[90] Lonergan uses Archimedes's enlightenment while investigating whether the king's crown was made of pure gold, and his coming to understand the principles of displacement and specific gravity, as an example of insight: Archimedes's insight was to make sense of his feeling lighter while in the bath. Lonergan details five steps that lead to an insight.[91] Insights, he warns, are common and plenty; they could be wrong, thus requiring doubting, checking, and confirmation.[92] Insights need to be tested with the question, "Is that so?"[93] To confirm it is so requires an act of judgment; without that, one is left guessing, but once further questions reveal it to be so, it is judged to be so. Archimedes grew in awareness that he had learned something new, but his understanding moved from the externals of the crown and water to an internal, personal understanding, to the intelligible, an understanding beyond sense knowledge, though initially dependent on such knowledge.[94] Insight is a process, and while in the process, one is still learning.[95] Insight is a step in the process of learning and understanding:

> Just as we move from the data of sense through inquiry, insight, reflection, judgment to statements about sensible things, so too we move from the data of consciousness through inquiry, understanding, reflection, judgment, to statements about conscious subjects and their operations.[96]

Knowing is radically diminished by a variety of narrow epistemological theories. For naïve realism, knowing "is a matter of taking a good look; objectivity is a matter of seeing what is there to be seen; reality is whatever is given in immediate experience." Accordingly, objectivity is not determined by examining the operations of one's knowing, but by simply looking, and objectivity is limited to what is seen, ignoring or being unaware of what is not seen. Knowing is limited to "picture thinking."[97] Empiricism, however, rejects everything that is not given in immediate experience, and it is empiricism that gives birth to naïve realism. For critical idealism, understanding is again limited to sense knowledge. Human knowing is confined to the phenomenal world, to what is seen and sensed. Critical idealism, represented by Kant, is superseded by Hegelian absolute idealism where there is an identity between thought

and what exists – being. And finally there is "subjectivism," which leads
to relativism.[98]

Lonergan's transcendental method is the foundation of knowing and objectivity, and begins, as described above, by asking three foundational
questions. The first is "what am I doing when I am knowing?" and it concerns "cognitional theory"; and as knowing is not the result of a single act
or activity, one must attend to the operations of one's consciousness. He
thus elaborates on the basic patterns of consciousness, such as seeing,
inquiring, understanding, reflecting, all of which intend an object.[99]
His transcendental principles – be attentive, be intelligent, be reasonable, and be responsible – are the foundation for cognitional theory.[100]
In addition, intending, intelligence, reasonableness, and responsibility
are all vital in knowing and confirming the objectivity of one's knowing.[101] Questions of intelligence that culminate in acts of understanding
(that is, insight) are questions such as: What is it? Why is this happen-
ing? They cannot be answered by a yes or a no. Questions of reflection,
however, culminate in a judgment that something is or is not, and are
answered by yes or no.[102]

The second question pertains to epistemology, "why is doing that
knowing?" and seeks to establish the objectivity of knowing. Such objectivity depends ultimately upon subjects asking whether their knowing
is correct and true.[103] Looking and seeing, picture thinking, do not confirm the objectivity of knowing, nor, on the other hand, do they confirm
truth by identifying something external to the self. Rather, truth is confirmed through acts of judgment. While the subject's knowing is limited,
the subject's desire to know, the questions that seek to know, stretch into
infinity; they are unlimited.[104]

The third question, "what do I know when I do it?"[105] pertains to
metaphysics, with cognitional theory and epistemology as its foundation; it seeks what is to be known. Lonergan rejects reducing *being* as
simply outside, external to the subject, reducing being to knowing by
looking. Knowing is not confirmed by gazing outward, resulting in variations of empiricism, nor is it confined to the subject, thus leading to
idealism, rationalism, and ultimately to subjectivism. Rather the real is

understood and confirmed through a series of operations, noted above, and through the dynamic structure of knowing that Lonergan lays out in his transcendental method of inquiry, understanding, reflection, and judgment. He consistently warns against knowing as looking and seeing, thus compromising judgment and understanding. "For man observes, understands, and judges, but he fancies that what he knows in judgment is not known in judgment and does not suppose an exercise of understanding but simply is attained by taking a good look at the real that is already out there now."[106]

IV.3 CONCEPTUALISM AND CLASSICISM

An important implication of Lonergan's rejection of conceptualism and classicism for education is the rejection of the premise that knowing is simply the possession of knowledge and information. Rather, coming to know is a human process, involving the whole person. Lonergan acknowledges the Augustinian approach to knowledge. For St Augustine, truth is known by looking within the self.[107] For Plato, knowledge is acquired confrontationally; the culmination is not who one becomes as a result of knowing, but what is seen. The known is known through contact, physical or spiritual, and through confrontation.[108] The foundational shift of Lonergan's theory, with enormous implications for education as knowing and understanding together, is realized when he states that "the ultimate validation of knowledge is not something that we know but in something that we are." And additionally, the validation of knowledge is not in what is known, per se, but in who the subject is.[109]

The errors of conceptualism and classicism are avoided by understanding what it means to know. While knowledge of the real, in all its diversity and various forms, begins with sense experience, what constitutes the real "cannot be other than what is affirmed by true judgments." Lonergan outlines the characteristics of the mind, and one of the fundamental characteristics is that the intellect, as is confirmed in what is intelligible, is not limited to empirical knowledge; knowledge is not simply the acquisition of facts without understanding the why of the facts. Again, the intellect is more than just a confrontational faculty and capacity.[110] Knowledge, then, is more than just a correspondence between the knowing and the known; if that were so, one would never know anything. In order to know, to reach knowledge of something and to acquire the meaning of something that is meant – that is, to acquire understanding for oneself – one looks to true judgments.[111] What one knows, one knows from the senses, but what comes to be known has been internalized through recurrent patterns of the intellect; knowledge is a unity and depends upon the progression and confirmation of true judgments of the concrete, not just in a physical sense but, of being, of what actually is in all dimensions and manifestations. This is all essential to the unity of the knowing process.[112]

IV.4 KNOWING AS DYNAMIC

Knowing forms a dynamic structure, comprising experience, understanding, reflection, and judgment. It is a series of operations, and to reduce knowing to empirical fact is to submit to unbalanced epistemologies that harm the integral process of human knowing. Both the purely empirical and the purely rational trap human knowing. Reducing knowing to seeing imprisons it, as knowledge is more than just the sum of the immediacy of the senses – that is, knowing is not just "immediate but mediate." Human knowing is not limited to seeing, but is a complex of many operations, and the confirmation of the objectivity of knowing requires more than just seeing. The converse is to be trapped by idealism, where what appears to the senses can only be confirmed, once again, by referring to appearances alone.[113] For Lonergan's critical realism, knowing is not a single operation like seeing, but a combination of different operations; it has a structure.[114] Similarly, objectivity is a combination of various operations and not just a single operation, like seeing what is out there.[115] The operations of the intellect and the senses are distinct, though complementary.

The knower must reflect on his or her operations of knowing in order to possess knowledge. Again, the educational implications depend upon students reflecting on what they are doing when they know, and what they are trying to do. Asking questions leads to understanding what is known.[116] This leads to another theme: "the differentiation of consciousness" and the distinction between "a world of immediacy and one mediated by meaning." The differentiation of consciousness begins in the basic thrust of consciousness, "consciousness as dominated by the desire to understand and by the reflectiveness that follows from under-standing."[117] Education enables students to construct their own world. Not a series of individually constructed solipsistic worlds. Creating a world means broadening one's own horizons as well as acknowledging one's concerns, but also broadening and widening one's concerns. How-ever, subjects never see their horizons or their world in isolation. One's world includes many horizons, different forms of understanding and different realities understood, one's interests, concerns, and experien-ces, and one's biases.[118]

The construction of the student's and the teacher's worlds will be re-ferred to in later chapters. However, regarding the primacy of knowing and knowledge, the construction of one's world depends upon "four terms, four movements in concrete existence: subject, concern, hori-zon, world. The subject's concern determines his horizon, and his horizon selects his world."[119] The history of the world shows that going beyond one's horizon or collective horizons is never easy, for such a movement requires the "reorganization of the subject, a reorganization of his modes of living feeling, thinking, judging, desiring, fearing, will-ing deliberating, choosing."[120] Subjects, of course, do not live exclusively in their own worlds, so education must attend to the intersection of their communal worlds, and their development of the ability to relate their individual worlds to the communal.[121] The differentiation of conscious-ness is a progressive process. As the student learns and knows in greater depth, the distinction between the subject and the object increases, as does the differentiation of consciousness. The school curriculum is an example of such differentiation as the student progresses in knowing and learning. The differentiation of consciousness is exemplified in graduate studies, as distinct from a general undergraduate education. Increasingly, consciousness is differentiated as university study ne-cessarily becomes more specialized; often, however, this happens too quickly, and in that sense does not envelop the whole person as a general education is meant to do.[122]

The differentiation of consciousness is complex and technical. For our purposes, differentiation is the ability of subjects to take possession of themselves through their knowing, and to adapt to their environment through the different operations in coming to know. However, all the differentiations are developments that occur in a student by virtue of the student's own agency. Learning is occasioned by one's own questions, emerges through one's own answers, and is grounded upon one's own choices. The first category in such consciousness is the distinction between the infant's world of immediacy and the sensory, and the adult's world revealed through the mediation of meaning.[123] As the child grows, learns, and matures, that immediacy is put into a wider context of time and space, and the child is introduced to a larger world mediated by meaning. And while such a world includes immediate experience, its diversity shows that it is no longer confined to and revealed only through what is immediate and sensory. Understanding and correct judgments are essential in order to reveal the world mediated by meaning.[124] A world mediated by meaning is not given in the same way that an object is encountered, as perceived by the senses. Rather, the objects of a world mediated by meaning are part of a "universe that is intended by questions, that is organized by intelligence, that is described by language, that is enriched by tradition. It is an enormous world far beyond the comprehension of a nursery."[125]

Making true judgments and progressively learning from the diversity and variety of what constitutes the real and the varieties of the real depend upon the differentiation of consciousness. As subjects mature and grow, and as their consciousness continues to be differentiated, they depend more and more on a world mediated by meaning.[126] The movement away from a world of immediacy towards a world mediated by meaning reveals the responsibilities that accompany such meaning. A recurrent theme in Lonergan's work is the "existential discovery ... where one finds out for oneself that one has to decide for oneself what one is going to make of oneself."[127] This movement from immediacy to meaning, however, is grounded upon the primacy of feelings, and essential to human knowing. However, being attentive, intelligent, reasonable, and responsible relates feeling to broader cognitional structures and questions, particularly questions that lead to "deliberation, evaluations, and decisions"; and feelings are part of the level of decisions.[128] Once one understands the real in terms wider than just seeing and looking, beyond what one perceives through the senses, when the diversity of reality (particularly through meaning) is affirmed, questions of decision emerge regarding the good and right thing one must do as a result of one's knowing and understanding, in order to avoid an existential contradiction.[129]

At first blush it may seem that Lonergan's contribution to the aims and end of education is not as apparent as those of the documents or Maritain. This is not so. His philosophical contribution broadens the personal agency of the student and the teacher. The primacy of understanding and knowing frames his approach regarding the aims and end of the Catholic school. This is a foundational contribution to a Catholic philosophy of education. Too often in that discipline, knowing and understanding become too abstract and technical, and are at a level of philosophical analysis that makes little contribution to knowing and understanding in the context of education, which is both a theoretical and a practical field. What one learns and how one learns relate to Lonergan's three fundamental and foundational questions, which have enormous implications for the school: What am I doing when I am knowing? Why is doing that knowing? And what do I know when I do it? Integral knowing is reached neither through the immediacy of the senses nor through some form of introspection, of thought reposing in upon itself. Knowing is active engagement, and because knowing is composed of different operations, all foundationally and initially dependent upon the senses, thus it cannot be confined either to the senses, to seeing, or to a form of Cartesian isolationism.

While it may seem straightforward to say what is meant in knowing by seeing, it often appears to be more demanding to say how one knows by understanding, and in this Lonergan's cognitional theory, epistemology, and metaphysics, as revealed through his three questions, make an enormous contribution to the theoretical and practical discipline of education, particularly in the school. University education proceeds to get more and more specialized, and thus there is concentration of knowing and understanding in particular fields, to an increased differentiation of consciousness. However, Lonergan's contribution to what is meant by knowing and understanding, and his expansion of them beyond the immediacy of the first, sensory level, provides a structure not only for the aims and end of the Catholic school, but also for an integral education. When knowing moves beyond the immediacy of the senses to meaning, other existential questions emerge. Themes that are central to how Lonergan conceives knowledge include the subject, conversion, authenticity, and the good, and will be pursued in subsequent chapters. Knowing is active and dynamic, and it reveals intellectual, moral, and religious dimensions, which require conversion at each level. Lonergan's exposition of the nature of insight and its relation to knowing clarifies the relation of insight to knowing. Also, the question of why insights are a process in the act of understanding, and the understanding that they need to be stamped by judgments, has vital educational implications.

Lonergan's detailed attention to knowing, understanding, and the nature of true judgments makes an enormous contribution to a Catholic philosophy of education, for the structure of knowing, understanding, and judgments serves not only the diversity of the school curriculum, but also makes clear how this diversity is unified in the knowing and understanding of the student, the subject – that is, the unity of the student. It is because the school performs a primarily intellectual task, that clarity on how knowledge and understanding are appropriated serves the aims and end of the school, and avoids the errors of intellectualism.

V Conclusion

It was stated earlier that as the documents from the CCE continue to be published, each publication adds to or elaborates on a particular dimension of a Catholic philosophy of education. Thus more recent documents have focused on education in a pluralist society and the role of dialogue in such a society. The addition of newer documents renders Catholic philosophy of education an open-ended and heuristic process. However, the wisdom of philosophers such as Maritain and Lonergan enables the reading of the documents through the lenses of foundational questions. Both philosophers take different approaches, and future Catholic philosophers of education will likely take still different ones. However, Maritain and Lonergan contribute to the perennial and foundational matters, and their contribution remains fresh and adaptive precisely because of their attention to these foundational principles.

The documents lay out the role of the Catholic school and its particular mission through intellectual education. They qualify this with the realization that such an education is only partial, in concert with other agencies, and continues through life. The aims and end of the school, and the transformation and liberation that come from an integral education, are secured upon a Christian vision of reality and a philosophical and theological anthropology. Thus while the means of education must adapt and change according to the times and to intellectual and social progress, the end of education, which may seem settled and unchanging, must, on the contrary, be dynamically engaged with the constancy of this vision of reality, secured upon an integral understanding of the person amidst change and progress. This vision and anthropology also provide a foundation upon which to respond to all that enslaves and compromises the internal and spiritual freedom of the student and the teacher.

One matter that remains of perennial importance is the spiritual nature of education, and as explained previously, the spiritual is understood philosophically – that is, while knowing begins in the senses, there is an increasing movement away from the senses to knowing through the intelligible and through intelligibility. Maritain's philosophy of personhood and Lonergan's understanding of the person as subject are elaborations of a Christian anthropology, particularly the spiritual nature of the student, and both philosophers can assist Catholic educators in situating this spiritual nature within a wider Christian anthropology. Maritain's distinction between the person and the individual, and Lonergan's elaboration of how the human person can be understood at various stages – ranging from the subject as asleep to the subject as critically engaged through the transcendental method and asking questions – point to the spiritual nature of a Catholic education and the spiritual process inherent in how the student comes to know. Knowing and learning cannot be confined to what Lonergan calls picture thinking, and neither, as Maritain points out, can institutional education promise to educate the student about everything. Both perspectives are linked where education is reduced to what is observable and experienced through the senses. But as Maritain reminds us, wisdom and love cannot be taught, but in every way – recognizing the role of the two other educational agencies, parents and the Church, regarding wisdom and love – how the student is taught and what they are taught will have enormous influence on how they will continue to grow in wisdom and love.

The documents ground the aims and end of Catholic education upon a Christian vision of reality and an integral anthropology. However, while the ultimate aim of the Christian life is union with God, the educational aims of the school are not rendered subservient to this ultimate aim, as these aims serve in actualizing the freedom and liberation of the student. The documents understand the place and the role of the curriculum, but the curriculum is not reduced to an instrument serving that last end in a narrow manner. Rather, the distinctiveness and the methodology of each subject and body of inquiry is preserved, and such preservation becomes essential to the search for truth in diverse bodies of knowledge, but all secured in the one knowing, understanding, choosing, and deliberating individual student. Maritain's distinction between natural intelligence and the intellectual virtues, and his distinction between subjects of most worth and least worth, widen the curriculum in relation to the student as a person. What one knows and how one comes to know it are essential for education; knowing has intrinsic hierarchies precisely because the living of life is hierarchically arranged. Lonergan's three questions of cognitional theory, epistemology, and metaphysics have important implications for the curriculum and for the spiritual nature of knowing. While Lonergan does not frame his philosophy of education in term of the aims and end of education, the way that Maritain does, he does make an essential and significant contribution to these themes by his distinctions and relationships in all that goes into making the educational claim: I understand; I know. While the documents elaborate on the aims and end of education, Lonergan's contribution is invaluable in showing why a judgment is necessary before one can make a claim to know. His distinction between the world of immediacy and the world mediated by meaning, and the differentiation of consciousness, provides great clarity, particularly in our age when the visual and what can be sensed are deemed the ultimate foundation and confirmation of reality. Neither meaning nor the various operations that constitute knowing can be satisfactorily responded to by reducing knowing just to seeing and to the other senses. In turn, Maritain's distinctions between natural intelligence and the intellectual virtues contribute to the progressive development of knowledge; the diversity of knowledge related to natural intelligence is another way of understanding why such diversity cannot be limited to picture thinking or sense knowledge. Intelligibility depends upon the senses, but what is intelligible increasingly sheds sensory knowledge, and that shedding is essential to the spiritual nature of knowing and the student's mastery of things learned. The documents, Maritain, and Lonergan all warn against reducing knowing or learning to bookish knowledge, and thus they prevent an integral education becoming the exclusive domain of the intellectually gifted and the academically strong. The purpose of knowledge and education, the documents state, is much more than gaining power and control; they are for communion and understanding, and knowledge is not a means to material prosperity so much as it is a path to service and responsibility for others. Maritain and Lonergan contribute to an integral understanding of knowledge and learning by deliberating on what one learns and the intrinsic hierarchies thereof, and how one learns by taking ownership though acts of judgment and the decisions and choices that follow each judgment when claiming to know, with implications for living.

Finally, the documents, Maritain, and Lonergan all make a great contribution to understanding the aims and end of education, and the purpose of knowledge and learning, in the context of religious diversity. The documents recognize that Catholic schools have a sizeable number of non-Catholic students, particularly in countries outside the Western world. All those who share in the educational mission of the Catholic school are welcome. And though such a school is foundationally inspired by a Christian vision of reality and an anthropology that is based upon the Gospels, the educational mission of the Catholic school neither compromises the faith tradition and beliefs of non-Catholics, nor narrows the knowing and learning in such a school to *a churchy Catholic knowing and learning*. The documents continually underscore the spiritual dimension of knowing; education is not limited to the senses nor confined to the immediacy of one's environment. Knowing and learning pursue truth, in all its forms and diversity. Maritain's expansive understanding of the student as a person – characterized by knowledge and intelligence, good will and love – is foundational in realizing what the documents identify as a civilization marked by love, and respecting the other, and seeing, understanding, and relating to the other as important moments in one's own education. Lonergan's cognitional theory is hardly for Catholics alone. His three questions and four transcendental principles provide a philosophical anthropology, and enable educators to communicate what is entailed in personal responsibility. To apply Aristotle's opening conviction in his *Metaphysics*, all students desire to know. In fact, a more recent translation chooses *understanding* over *knowing*.[130] One desires to know whatever one's religious affiliation. Lonergan's cognitional method contributes to understanding how a Catholic school can recognize the dignity of religious diversity, the unity that knowing and learning provide, and the personal responsibility of each student to themselves, to their fellow students, and to society. The Church recognizes religious plurality existing under God's providence. The aims and end of a Catholic school, precisely because of the width of its understanding of knowing and learning, and assisted by Maritain and Lonergan, can show how its epistemology and cognitional theory are neither compromised by religious diversity, nor claim to find their perfection in religious supremacy.

4

The Unity of the Student

I Introduction

The focus of the educational documents is the student. While they cover a variety of topics, from the role of the laity to religious education, and from sex education to the challenges and opportunities of religious and cultural diversity, the focus remains the student, and particularly their internal and spiritual unity. And while this theme of unity is not as prominent in the earlier documents, its importance grows in an increasingly complex and diverse religious and cultural world, amid all that compromises the student's unity. It is this unity that becomes the focus of the Catholic school. Indeed, the internal unity of the Catholic school, the unity of its mission and purpose, is essential for the unity of the individual student.

From its earliest document, *The Catholic School* (1982), the Congregation focuses on students, Catholic and non-Catholic. And while the Catholic nature of the school is central, the unity of the student is addressed amidst increasing cultural complexity and religious diversity. The later documents, *Education to Intercultural Dialogue in Catholic Schools* (2013) and *Education for Today and Tomorrow: A Renewing Passion* (2014), recognize the educational challenges, both personally as students search for their individual place and role in the world and communally as they engage with one another, growing from this engagement and contributing to and building up society and the common good.

The documents realize that the Catholic school is only one agent of Catholic education, parents and the Church being the other two, with parents being the primary educators of their children. All three educate in their distinct ways, but all are interdependent. The challenge of parents in educating their children, and the complexity of diversity and plurality that the Church encounters, necessitate a response beyond these two agents. These matters now spill into the life of the school, and the school may now be assuming responsibilities that are beyond its scope and mandate. In recognizing the complexity of life in the school,[1] the documents emphasize the role of all three agents in ensuring the unity of the student by carrying out their distinct roles and responsibilities.

This chapter focuses on the unity of the student. In ultimate terms, the documents, Maritain, and Lonergan all see an integral education as essential for the student's personal unity. The documents call attention to the relationship between the school's environment and the development of an integral personality, all within the wider context of a Christian anthropology and worldview. The education of the whole person depends, primarily, on the internal and spiritual freedom of the student, and has implications for their social and moral life. Human unity is an integral part of Maritain's philosophy, and he provides a philosophical structure of human unity though such pillars as freedom and integration, all with implications for the moral and spiritual life. Finally, Lonergan provides another philosophical structure to secure human unity and grounds this structure on the four transcendental principles – experience, understanding, judging, and deciding – and their relationship to human development.

II The Documents of the CCE

II.1 CCE: CHRISTIAN ANTHROPOLOGY AND THE STUDENT

The Christian environment of the school must be immersed in the Gospel's call to freedom and love. The student is a person composed of body and spirit, possessing an immortal soul and needing redemption. And so the student "experiences his dignity as a person before he knows its definition."[2] Older students will benefit from anthropology, biology, psychology, sociology, and philosophy, enabling them to have a more complete understanding of the person, including the religious aspect. These contribute to a growing and systematic understanding of who they are as persons, the power of the intellect and will, the nature of freedom

and feelings, and their status as active agents in their own becoming, responding to rights and duties: relational beings, each called to a special
vocation in the world.³ This conception of the person stands in relation
to freedom. So education, personal freedom, and the developing personality of the student are interrelated.

> Education to freedom is a humanizing action, because it aims at
> the full development of personality. In fact, education itself must
> be seen as the acquisition, growth and possession of freedom. It
> is a matter of educating each student to free him/herself from the
> conditionings that prevent him/her from fully living as a person,
> to form him/herself into a strong and responsible personality,
> capable of making free and consistent choices.⁴

The integral development of students reveals their divine call and
destiny. The documents are grounded upon a Christian vision of the
person and an attitude to life, a worldview, a *Weltanschauung*, a unified
vision and understanding of life, secured upon a hierarchy of values culminating in the salvation won by Christ. This worldview is presented in
the context of cultural pluralism; hence the emphasis on a well-formed
character and the school's role in integral human formation.⁵ The elements of a Christian view of the world or reality are not outlined in any
one document; each contributes to what is entailed, and the whole develops thematically under the documents' titles: religious education, the
role of lay Catholic teachers, intercultural dialogue, sex education, etc.
The climate of the school must be considered as a whole, made up of persons, relational beings, teaching and learning, and the other activities
that make up the school day.⁶ This worldview also depends upon a correct understanding of choice and choosing, which are vital in expanding
the student's understanding of reality and the purpose and end of life.⁷
Like Lonergan, the documents confirm that reality is wide, not limited
to something already existing out there, but emerges though good, free,
and correct choices.⁸

Later documents attend to Christian anthropology in more pronounced ways, based on the Gospels and at the service of the student and
society.⁹ Relationships amidst diversity are described as a *communion*,
enabling the anthropological and theological vision to have an outward

thrust. The complexity of modern living requires us to guard against strains of individualism, and dialogue and service give flesh to the cultural, spiritual, and religious identity of the student as a relational and communal being. The breadth of a Christian anthropology for the school is clear:

> First of all, we must express the anthropology underpinning our educational vision for the 21st century in different terms: it is a philosophical anthropology that must also be an anthropology of truth, i.e. a social anthropology whereby man is seen in his relations and way of being; an anthropology of recollection and promise; an anthropology that refers to the cosmos and cares about sustainable development; and, even more, an anthropology that refers to God. The gaze of faith and hope, which is its foundation, looks at reality to discover God's plan hidden therein. Thus, starting from a profound reflection on modern man and the contemporary world, we must redefine our vision regarding education.[10]

There is no doubt that this anthropology is decidedly Christian. It is because of the divine destiny to which each person is called, that culture is essential for human becoming, particularly as it is a human creation and depends on the relational nature of the person. What is emphasized is the universality of this anthropology, in the service of all students, uniting by distinguishing the essentials, enabling the growth of an integral personality — a universality bringing together individuals amidst diversity.[11] One important example of the evolution of the documents concerns how a Christian anthropology serves the school. Earlier documents see human formation in entirely Christian terms, thus distinguishing the Catholic school from other schools. Later documents have a wider understanding of Christian anthropology, and while not diminishing Christian formation, see it in the context of relationships, communion, and fellowship, and encountering the other amidst religious and cultural plurality.[12] Thus a Christian anthropology becomes more comprehensive.

The Religious Dimension of Education in a Catholic School (1988) elaborates on the relationship between religious education and catechesis. The

Christian life is a journey, an invitation from God, and an experience of learning to understand the ways that God is present in the world. While parents and the Church have their roles to play in religious development, the school ensures its educational atmosphere through the values contained in each subject and activity, all dependent upon the teacher's care for students and love of the truth. "The Christian process of formation is, therefore, the result of a constant interaction involving the expert labour of the teachers, the free cooperation of the students, and the help of grace."[13] Faith is vital for education as it strengthens values, which in turn enables a Christian worldview, particularly in the areas of culture and history. The Christian ethos of the school, and a faithful presentation of the Christian faith and growth in one's relationship to Christ, are clearly outlined.[14] Religious instruction cannot be marginalized; it is essential for personal development; it is a bridge between faith and culture; the Church has a role in its content. Religious education is interdisciplinary; it is distinct from catechesis; and it must take its rightful place in the school's curriculum, and be taught as rigorously and systematically as other disciplines.[15]

Religious education is essential for the integral development of the student, thus giving rise to the question of similar instruction for non-Catholic students. While this is not addressed directly by the documents, the claim that an integral education is offered to all students, some of whom are not offered religious instruction in their own traditions, is surely open to criticism today. Religious instruction is essential for the personal formation of students, and moral formation and religious formation are closely linked, with implications for the social and civic dimensions of life and the common good.[16] In an interreligious world, the religious identity of each student must be recognized and protected. They must also become knowledgeable of other religions, and see in other contexts the relationship between religion and culture.[17] While an older document sees the religious education of non-Christians in the traditional ways of catechesis and the proclamation of the Gospel, later documents, while not compromising the primacy of religious education, emphasize religious and personal identity.[18] Could this be interpreted as an invitation for Catholic educators to think of the place of *religion* and *religions* in the Catholic school, inspired by a Christian anthropology?

The young people we are educating today will become the leaders of the 2050s. What will religion's contribution be to educating younger generations to peace, development, fraternity in the universal human community? How are we going to educate them to faith and in faith? How will we establish the preliminary conditions to accept this gift, to educate them to gratitude, to a sense of awe, to asking themselves questions, to develop a sense of justice and consistency? How will we educate them to prayer?[19]

II.2 THE STUDENT AS A WHOLE PERSON

All the educational documents refer to the *education of the whole person*, with one making sixty references.[20] The permanence of Christian formation is an education of the whole person, in human, professional, and religious dimensions.[21] The education of the whole person is vital for sex education, for sexual maturity is personal, encompassing the totality of body, soul, and emotions. This complexity of the person is important to recall today, when sexuality is devoid of its mystery and associated mainly with pleasure, leading to selfishness. Sexuality impacts the whole person.[22] The invitation to personal relationship with Christ is made to the whole person, thus the need for an integral education, which depends both on the distinctiveness and autonomy of each subject of the curriculum and on the irreplaceable role of the teacher.[23] The education of the whole person is especially urgent in the context of diversity. The school imparts more than instruction and narrow learning, and the document on intercultural dialogue is an invitation to widen the education of the whole person amidst diversity, and to build society through solidarity. This is important given the integral role of religion in the education of the whole person, and hence its centrality to human dignity.[24] While the documents distinguish between catechesis and religious education, they repeatedly draw attention to the school's mandate, which is knowledge.[25] Hence religious knowledge, both of one's own tradition and those of others, is framed in the context of knowledge in general.

The documents are concerned about the young, and while the issues that face them vary according to local situations and historical contexts, there is a commonality to the concerns: a milieu lacking human relationship, wherein young people worry about the future, escape loneliness by turning to drugs, alcohol, and sex, and hold an attitude, common in society today, that is critical of the Christian life.[26] While new concerns will be added to this list, which was compiled in 1988, sadly many of the listed concerns still prevail. A pressing matter for today is the immensity of undifferentiated information on the Internet. Truth, goodness, and beauty have been so relativized and narrowly conceived that seeking direction and help itself becomes difficult, all of which adds to the challenge of a chaste sexuality.[27] The role of truly liberating knowledge is all the more pressing:

> These young people absorb a wide and varied assortment of knowledge from all kinds of sources, including the school. But they are not yet capable of ordering or prioritizing what they have learned. Often enough, they do not yet have the critical ability needed to distinguish the true and good from their opposites; they have not yet acquired the necessary religious and moral criteria that will enable them to remain objective and independent when faced with the prevailing attitudes and habits of society.[28]

The school has a formative role in handing down an intellectual tradition. While imparting knowledge remains the aim of the school, and while the education of the intellect is the focus of the school, the education of the whole person is not limited to the intellect, but includes the affective dimensions, such as the will, feelings, and emotions.[29] Students remain active agents in their own education, learning, and formation, which include intelligence and freedom: "it is impossible for education to be genuine without the active involvement of the one being educated."[30] The expression of the Christian faith is expansive, and is not content with shallow knowledge or with judgments unaccompanied by critical awareness and uncritical acceptance. It relies upon personal responsibility, sacrifice, and intellectual rigour, and a love for the truth. Ensuring that students are active learners means trusting them and giving them the responsibility to realize the contribution that their thinking and decisions make in shaping who they are and become, and in shaping the common good. Thus, loving and doing God's will have intellectual dimensions as well.[31]

Today much is said about freedom, but this is often freedom limited to free choice and the absence of constraints, while respecting laws. The documents situate freedom in terms of responsibility and its proper human expression. Freedom needs to be cultivated; it is the fruit of education. The illusion that one may do as one wills, within the limits of the law, is not freedom, nor does it enhance personhood, which is manifested in the will, but also through intelligence. The active and creative agency of the person, protected by rights and responsible for corresponding duties, a relational being with a specific vocation in the world, and inspired by the values of the Gospel – such is the context of personal freedom.[32] In a Catholic school, truth and freedom are never apart. An education for freedom – a dominant theme in Maritain's educational philosophy – is essential for the integral development of personality, when students are made aware of their own horizons and conditioning, and grow and strengthen their personalities through responsible choices that are truly free.[33] A correct understanding and exercise of freedom is integral for the education of the whole person. While knowledge and learning are ends in themselves, they are not disengaged ends, so Catholic education must guard against "the temptation to a knowledge which yields to pragmatism or which loses itself in the endless meanderings of erudition. Such knowledge is incapable of giving meaning to life."[34] Such meaning is personally learned, with communal and social implications, especially as the Catholic school is concerned with personal and interpersonal development.[35] The education of the whole person is demanding, particularly as it is a unified process, founded upon the integral, ontological unity of the individual student. The student's personal liberation grows in the measure of fighting the temptations of evil and the desire for an unaccountable and boundless freedom. The education of the whole person guards against the student's "loss of serenity."[36] It is a serenity compromised by concentrating on future professional identity, skills, and technical knowledge at the expense of the humanity and personal development of the student.[37] The greatest responsibility that Catholic educators face in the education of the whole person is to "make human beings more human."[38]

II.3. THE SOCIAL AND THE MORAL DIMENSIONS

Catholic education is personal and communal, and dependent upon the moral and social life of the student. Indeed, the education of the whole person would be incomplete, and grossly deficient, without these dimensions, calling into question the development and formation of the student. Two aspects are emphasized: that students must be introduced to a systematic and complete sense of values for living, and that their progress and development are intrinsically social and communal, best exemplified in the Council's understanding of the Church as the People of God.[39] Both aspects depend on personal contact and a relationship between the teacher and the student as a "dialogue and not a monologue." Even though the teacher is the secondary agent, the student being primary, students need the teacher's committed, clear, and systematic agency to guide them, enabling them to deal with doubt, uncertainty, and confusion. The efforts of the Catholic teacher are rooted in the primacy and the dignity of students as persons, particularly their moral dignity.[40] The values that are learned are not heady or theoretical, but pertain to the actual, concrete living of life. The moral life depends upon the integration of values, and both are necessary for the life of faith. And education and teaching are inextricably concerned with the living communication of values.[41] While the documents underscore the intellectual mandate of the school and the education of the intellect, they warn against reducing that mandate to filling the mind with information disengaged from life. Under the Catholic anthropological vision, the student is a knowing and relational being, whose freedom is realized in responsible judgments, decisions, and choices. The student's unity depends upon the relationship between their rational and relational natures, integral to personality, and realized in ethical choices and actions.[42]

The student's personality is a combination of different facets, and in a Catholic school the life of faith and belief, the intellectual, social, and moral values, and other capacities acquired through the curriculum and other educational means are all formative for this integral personality. In the face of the challenges of religious and cultural pluralism, the later documents are particularly strong in highlighting the communal and relational aspects of the social and moral life. In the context of diversity, students' interpersonal relationships shape their being, and are manifested in their choices and actions. Not only are they relational beings called to care for the other, but this relational nature, and the ensuing responsibility to others, is framed in the language of a *spirituality of communion*, and the unifying awareness of all persons having been created in the image and likeness of God.[43] Accordingly, dialogue occupies a prominent place in later documents, where students understand and become knowledgeable about the differences and similarities in religious and cultural traditions; but dialogue also as presence to the other, friendship with the other, openness in the face of difference and diversity, all as a human encounter with the other, marked by openness and the gift of the self.[44]

Education is called to unify a world torn by conflict and division, frequently in the name of religion. The school is called to promote a humanism for its time with a "vision of society centered on the human person and his inalienable rights, on the values of justice and peace, on a correct relationship between individual, society and the State, on the logic of solidarity and subsidiarity."[45] Such a vision of society is served by a Christian anthropology where the relational, responsible, and loving nature of the person is prominent. The opportunities and challenges of globalization necessitate the protection of personal, religious, and cultural identity, and enable all to see that the suffering and the despair of so much of the world is a call to service and solidarity. This is challenging in an environment where the person is seen as an isolated being in pursuit of goals and ends that are defined only in relation to oneself. This rise of contemporary individualism, and of the apparent conviction that reality is now contained in an electronic device held in one's hand, threatens the social and communal dimensions of the education of the whole person. The young face challenges to their personal unity when sensation, the sensory, and the fleeting are confused with the real. The notion of experience today is itself compromised, where the understanding of what constitutes experience is ever constricted. Thus, the young "consider themselves and their lives as a series of sensations to be experienced rather than as a work to be accomplished."[46]

The Catholic school is positioned to make its contribution in the context of religious and cultural diversity and plurality, and its strength lies in its Catholic identity and nature. It is that identity and nature, shown in its vision of the world, its anthropology, and its understanding of the student as a person, as well as its growing understanding of the anthropological and personal implications of communion and solidarity, that enable it to be at the service of more than just Catholic and Christian students. It is precisely the school's emphasis on the human person that enables it to be of service in context of plurality and diversity.[47] The call to dialogue was set down in the documents of the Council, including its document on education. The Council saw the student as one called to transform and renew the world, the social order, from within, through their own conversion and authenticity, thus being a living witness to their faith.[48]

The educational documents of the Church are well aware of all that makes up the complexity of the person, and why the personal and internal unity of the person is a delicate and demanding responsibility. What is noteworthy is that while the contribution of each subject in the curriculum and of the other components of the day are given due recognition, the unity of the student as a person becomes the foundation that gives meaning and significance to everything that happens and should happen in the school. Human unity is seen as progressive and cumulative, never occurring in a straight line, and always in need of the higher integrative help of grace, faith, love, forgiveness, and other Christian virtues. In our age when the notion of personality has been so narrowly psychologized as to deprive it of its capacity to become a means of manifesting an integral person, the documents' understanding of personality and why human unity is integral to a flourishing and Christian personality is a great contribution to a Catholic philosophy of education. Like Maritain and Lonergan, the documents return to key principles and fundamental themes, and show why these form the foundation and how they enable one to return to what holds the Catholic educational project together.

Diversity and plurality have the potential to draw the best and noblest responses from persons who are willing to see them as ultimately mysterious, and not as a puzzle to be solved by statistics. The documents frame the unity of the student, and the Christian anthropology that is at the foundation of such unity, as a means to appreciate that the mysterious identity of the other is better encountered, and that more is revealed, through dialogue, selflessness, and the willingness to learn from differences. This, of course, is not to disregard the dangers of subjectivism and relativism. Such dangers, however, are challenged by a Christian anthropology, and both Maritain and Lonergan show how a Christian anthropology can reveal the dangers of subjectivism and relativism. The emphasis on the education of the whole person is another means of ensuring the vitality and the freedom that come from a Christian anthropology. When freedom and responsibility become the measure of the full and mature growth into one's personal humanity, then the education of the whole person is enhanced.

However, a Christian anthropology also teaches that freedom and responsibility are never just self-referential. The social and communal nature of the individual person necessitates the recognition that freedom and responsibility have social and communal dimensions as well. Diversity and plurality can often be reduced to the exotic and the unusual, and thus can render the public square little more than a jumble of differences, with no source of unity. Students as increasingly unified beings will eventually take their place in society as citizens. It is this community of unified beings that contributes to the unity of society and culture, where differences are unified on a more primordial foundation: the nature of the person, created by God. While the Catholic identity of the school stems from the Christian tradition, it is at the service of the student as a person by virtue of intelligence, understanding, and the desire for society, community, and fellowship. In this, the documents present a universal understanding of the student as a person, one that arises above the particularities of creed and culture. For Maritain, like for the documents, even though the primary aim of the school is intellectual, it must attend to the important secondary aims that are communal and social.

III   The Contribution of Jacques Maritain

III.1   UNITY

For Maritain, all levels of education are based on a Christian vision of the world and the anthropological distinctions and relationships between the person and the individual.[49] His is a traditional understanding of liberal education and the humanities, and these have undergone significant change since his time. However, his thought is perennial as to how students are active agents in their own learning, assisted by the secondary agency of the teacher, an agency of service.[50] As in the Church's documents, the unity of the student is prominent in Maritain's philosophy of education: *the internal and spiritual unity of the student* is one of its main themes. He rejects the Platonic conviction that knowledge already exists in the soul. Also rejected is the premise that human beings have the power to engender knowledge in a completed form. Rather, the truth is that knowledge proceeds from the known to the unknown.[51] Conscious of the progressive and incremental nature of knowledge and learning, Maritain establishes a principle of teaching, with the unity of the student in mind: "the whole work of education and teaching must tend to unify, not to spread out; it must strive to foster internal unity in man."[52] The unity of the individual student arises internally from a previous metaphysical and ontological structure, a being composed of matter and spirit, growing through the spiritual distinctiveness of personality and possessing the material uniqueness of individuality, and both of these dimensions forming one knowing and loving whole, and both essential for and realized in human unity.[53] So teachers must never forget their unifying role, nor the fact that the mind and the ability to think depend upon the unity of what is presented. The freedom to think depends upon a prior unity.[54] The inspiring agent of the student's unity is the teacher and the truths taught.[55] Unifying students through their educational experience can never be forced; unification is the fruit of the active and cooperative engagement of the student and the guidance of the teacher. Knowledge unifies through the values imparted, and in the mind's capacity to free itself from the senses, moving towards intelligibility. Human unity is also presupposed in personality, and the development of personality depends upon the ability to communicate, through the knowledge gained and the ability to love.[56] Thus the inner unity of the person is manifested when their spiritual nature and freedom master the life of the senses and the passions. For Maritain, personality is a spiritual concept, thus furthering his understanding of unity. And in spite of their material individuality, persons are complete unto themselves, and in this sense independent. While the needs of the individual prevent total independence in practice, the freedom of the person is marked by a spiritual and ontological independence.[57]

III.2 FREEDOM

Freedom and unity are closely related for Maritain, and his thought on freedom is demanding and complex.[58] Freedom of choice, associated with free will, is meant to grow and culminate into an expansion of the autonomy of the person. It is never easy, and requires constant vigilance.[59] Freedom is an internal and spiritual disposition, one of the prime ends of education, and is manifested through four characteristics: knowledge and intelligence, good will and love. Freedom of choice and free will are given as a means to attain the true nature of freedom, which is internal and spiritual.[60] Freedom of choice by itself is not what distinguishes a person, but rather freedom as culminating in a spiritual independence; personality and freedom advance and grow together.[61] And while education appeals to the student's freedom of will and intelligence, growth in personality depends upon the transformation of the freedom of the will into the autonomy and independence of the student as a person.

The school regulates the freedom of the student, absolute though that freedom is in ultimate terms, because human beings are never born free; freedom must be earned and struggled for, especially in the social realm.[62] Education is a unified activity for a unified being, a spiritual being with a mysterious identity.[63] It is in the context of freedom as an internal and spiritual disposition that Maritain warns against the kind of educational snobbery which depicts intellectual activity as the only worthy dimension of education. He says this would be to miss a vital unifying principle that comes from the Christian dignity of labour and work, outside of what is narrowly intellectual. Genuine manual labour is neither the work of a "beast of burden nor that of a robot, but human work in which both body and mind are at play." Both intellectual and manual works are human, and play an equal role in the attainment of personal freedom.[64] Growth in freedom as a spiritual and internal disposition, beginning in the freedom of choice, depends upon students submitting themselves to their teacher in order to learn about true human freedom:

> It is not true that the autonomy of an intelligent creature consists
> in not receiving any rule or objective measure from a being other
> than itself. It consists in conforming to such rules voluntarily
> because they are known to be just and true, and because of a love
> for truth and justice.[65]

The mastery of the self is realized to the extent of making free choices that contribute to and enhance one's personal liberty and internal freedom.[66] Like Lonergan, Maritain says that freedom is at the service of persons who know what they must do and choose, given the end that they are called to. The metaphysical and ontological structure of personhood is realized in the moral and psychological orders, which in turn depend upon choice and action actualizing and giving flesh to the metaphysical and ontological nature of persons. The metaphysical and ontological structure that lies beyond the senses is realized and made concrete in the moral and psychological orders.[67] In the end, freedom of choice is neither achieved nor acquired; it is part of the very structure of human freedom.[68] What is more important is the ultimate aim of that freedom of choice. Growth and maturity in freedom are meant to make the human person less self-conscious in the very act of freedom: "Thus we understand that freedom of choice is not an end in itself, but that one chooses in order, finally, not to choose."[69]

III.3 INTEGRATION

The unity of the student grows through what is learned and how it is learned. Learning is a contemplative experience, an experience of self-reflection; it is opposed to the narrowly practical and utilitarian. The spiritual dimension of knowledge means that less emphasis is placed on the factual and more on personal understanding. Like Lonergan, Maritain says that thinking is not reserved for difficulties, but for insights whose worth is judged by the verification of reason.[70] He says that the truc value of reading a book is when the student encounters the world of the author and enters that world in a personal and spiritual way, rather than limiting what one learns to thought, opinion, or the soulless task of acquiring information.[71]

Regarding the liberal arts and the humanities: first, they aim at enabling the student to think and to enjoy truth and beauty for their own sake, and in this they are truly an education for personal freedom. Second, they are meant for all students, including those who will choose a vocational and practical professional field over an intellectual and academic one. Indeed, given that such an education is for wisdom, it can hardly be restricted to a particular social class, nor confined, given the advances in knowledge. Third, a broad education in the liberal arts and the humanities defeats the narrowing of premature specialization.[72] The specialist is blinkered, unable to pass judgment beyond a narrow field, leading to "a progressive animalization of the human mind and life."[73] Fourth, mathematics and the sciences are an integral part of education, and less emphasis should be placed on their practicalities and more on their place within a broader understanding of the created order and a sense of what is sacred. These subjects should be taught in a philosophical manner concerned with human nature and the functioning of the human mind.[74] Fifth, the school must prepare students for adulthood and life in community and society; being an active and engaged citizen requires one to think beyond the confines of work.[75] Sixth, Christian education recognizes the role of the senses and their relationship to the intellect and knowing, and education must therefore free the senses and integrate them into the totality of personhood, along with the imagination and feelings.[76] Maritain's emphasis on the liberal arts and the humanities, whatever the student's vocation, is summed up with the appeal: "popular education must become liberal and liberal education must become popular. Is it not clear that liberal education for all means liberal education for prospective manual workers as well as for prospective intellectual workers?"[77] Manual work must not be reduced to "doing something," nor treated as something extraneous to human unity and the education of the whole person.

"La vie chrétienne est à base d'intelligence – intelligence is the very basis of the Christian life," the foundation of Christian education.[78] In spite of this prominence, Maritain's seventh misconception of education cautions against *intellectualism*, which takes two forms. First, education is reduced to rhetoric or abstract reasoning, or to bourgeois knowledge, and reserved for the select few. The modern form of this error forsakes universal values and culminates in specialization and technical knowledge, leading to educational dangers from early specialization.[79] Second, the will and character formation are glorified, thus compromising the unifying role of intelligence. And while ultimately one will be judged on loving rather than knowing (thus the importance of the education of the will), nonetheless in the context of the school, "intelligence is in and by itself nobler than the will of man, for its activity is more immaterial and universal."[80] The immateriality and universality of the intellect are vital for the unity of the student, as sources of freedom to rise above contingencies.[81] The other misconception with implications for intelligence is *sociologism*. Maritain applauds the progress of modern education in its concern for the social and communal dimensions; preparation for social life and civic obligations is part of the secondary aims of education.[82] However, such preparation begins by attending to the spiritual nature of the student:

> [T]o be a good citizen and a man of civilization what matters above all is the inner center, the living source of personal conscience in which originate idealism and generosity, and the sense of law and the sense of friendship, respect for others, but at the same time deep-rooted independence with regard to common opinion.[83]

The education of intelligence is an education for freedom, and freeing the mind is a spiritual task and is achieved through the liberation of the transcendentals: truth and beauty, rather than factual accumulation or refinement.[84] Education is a progressive process of integration; it is an integrated knowledge growing towards wisdom.[85]

III.4 MORAL AND SOCIAL LIFE

Parents are the primary educators of their children, and are irreplaceable in integrating children's experiences and forming them in their individual unity, particularly in the moral and spiritual life, assisted by the Church. However, physical, psychological, and emotional abuse can compromise that formative role, and the history of families is as fractured as is history in general. And so schools may be called on to compensate for what is lacking in the family's role in moral formation. While recognizing the primary role of the family, the school and the university enjoy their own autonomy from the family and the state.[86]

One of Maritain's aphorisms captures a variety of concerns regarding the student's freedom, the autonomy of the school, the student's responsibilities regarding what they have learned, and the formative role of the teacher: "education and teaching must start with experience, but in order to complete themselves with reason."[87] The history of reason and rationality is also hardly unblemished – Maritain notes how fascism, Nazism, and Stalinism thwarted reason and rationality.[88] Healthy reason is essential for personal unity, and students' command over what they have learned and the appropriation of their learning is essential for their

knowing and their freedom.[89] The experience of the student is personal,
but with moral and social implications. However, the completion of experience in reason has both speculative and practical dimensions.[90] And
like Lonergan, Maritain confirms that it is the personal act of judgment
that is necessary for appropriating and internalizing knowledge.[91] The
relation between knowledge and virtue goes back to Plato. Knowledge
is a precondition of virtue in that it provides both a vision of the world
and the convictions and decisions to appropriate such a vision. And
apart from its own curricular integrity, religious education informs the
moral life.[92]

Institutional education is personal and communal, and these dimensions intersect across the school. Social ties and society are natural to
human beings for a variety of reasons, but mainly because of reason
and freedom.[93] And while more will be said on the social implications
in chapter 6, the relationship between the life of reason and social life
has important implications for education. In his conviction that liberal
education and the humanities are formative in the unity and freedom of
the student, freeing them from the burden and the narrowing of premature specialization, Maritain sees such education as vital preparation
for social and civic life, and as a personal and communal preparation for
morality and the moral life. An integral democratic education enables
persons to be able "to shape themselves, judge by themselves, discipline
themselves, to love and to prize the high truths which are the very root
and safeguard of their dignity, to respect in themselves and in others
human nature and conscience, and to conquer themselves in order
to win their liberty."[94] A democratic education is a social education of
human persons living in society, and given the advances in human
knowledge and the pluralist nature of modern democratic societies, the
liberal arts and the humanities must be expanded beyond the Western
canon. Christianity is not a sect, and Christians are thus called "to confront the world and to take risks at every stage or degree of human existence and human culture."[95] The moral foundation of social life is at the
foundation of Maritain's political and social philosophy and his philosophy of freedom. A religiously and culturally diverse student body must
be united in a way that rises above their obvious differences. That unity,
growing from reason and intelligence, is the human desire for life in
society that stems from personhood. For pluralist societies, such unity

is more natural and more unifying than the differences of religion and culture. It is "good will and a relation of respect and love between person and between the person and the community [that] can alone give to the life of the social body a truly human character."[96] Thus, a purely intellectual life is neither sufficient nor satisfying. It is care and love for the other that brings about real unity.[97] While the dignity of persons might be legally ensured, growth in personhood is perennial and heuristic. For the Catholic school, such growth involves knowledge and love, those fundamental anthropological traits of the person.

Maritain's contribution to the unity of the student is significant and substantial, and this is possible because of the unified nature of his overall philosophical thought and his writings. This emphasis on the unity of the student undoubtedly stems from his Christian convictions, and from the unity of the Christian message and its elaboration of why such unity is essential for living and being a Christian as invited by Christ, the Gospels, and the Church. But what is striking is how this understanding of unity is then further secured upon philosophical and anthropological pillars, and in this his elaboration on the unity of the student serves all human beings, and transcends the immediacies of cultures, castes, and creeds.

Maritain saw much progress in educational means and methods, and the advancement of a deeper understanding of what human nature means in the context of education, as well as how that nature can easily be compromised. But again, he approaches human nature (and in this context, the nature of the student) from a dynamic, active, engaged, and heuristic perspective: the student as the primary agent in education, and the causal agent in his or her own learning. And while this conviction is not Maritain's exclusively, and there are other educators who also hold it, it is how he places this active and dynamic agency where students are the agents of their own learning that makes a unique contribution to a philosophy of education, but more particularly, to a Catholic philosophy of education. Even writing before the pedagogical, educational, and methodological changes that have occurred over the fifty years since the Council, Maritain understands and elaborates on why rote learning as a means to pass examinations is never educational, and more fundamentally, how it strikes at the heart of the unity of the student, where learning, knowledge, and understanding are crucial to their freedom and liberation, and to the progressive pilgrimage to their last end. However, that pilgrimage is hardly framed as a dreary trudge to a promised and unknowable heavenly bliss. The fulfillment of human living as increasingly emerging from human unity is a source of joy and happiness itself.

Maritain thus in many ways sets out a structure and edifice that later Lonergan comes to fill out with additional philosophical colour and flair. Maritain's seven misconceptions of education are all an essential part of that structure in securing the unity of the student as a person. Particularly noteworthy among those misconceptions is that of intellectualism. Like the Church's documents, and like Lonergan, Maritain repeatedly reminds the reader of the primarily intellectual nature, mission, and aim of the school, and his elaboration of the misconception of intellectualism shows how this intellectual focus of the school could easily be abused, thus warping the very unity of the student. Again, the nature of the intellectual mission of the school is seen as one essential and irreplaceable element in the education of the student as a unified being. Intellectualism could easily transform the school into a false panacea of freedom. However, Maritain's theory of freedom is an adequate bulwark against such an illusory panacea. Lonergan's elaboration on the nature of insight, responsible and correct judgments, and the forms of human development takes over in elaborating on the unity of the student.

IV The Contribution of Bernard Lonergan

IV.1 THE STUDENT AND THE ACCUMULATION OF INSIGHTS

For Lonergan, as for Maritain, students are active agents in their education, and the three questions of cognitional theory and epistemology (discussed in chapter 3) are essential for education and learning. Human unity is realized through the transcendental principles, experiencing, understanding, judging, and deciding, and intellectual, moral, and spiritual conversion, leading to self-transcendence. The subject's self-transcendence depends upon a world mediated by meaning, what constitutes "the real world," realized through experiencing, understanding, and judging.[98] However, self-transcendence is uncertain and changeable, involving a tension between the subject who has achieved self-transcendence and the same subject who must continue to seek transcendence through regular, contingent acts. So the authenticity of the subject is never possessed in any one act.[99] Self-transcendence is conscious and intentional, relying upon the transcendental principles. The subject's operations of knowing reveal objects of knowledge, and they become aware of their operations and of the fact of their operating, and the objects of their knowledge are thus revealed not as object but as subject.[100]

Learning is a "spontaneous process ... It is an accumulation of insights in which each successive act complements the accuracy and covers over the deficiency of those that went before." Learning happens gradually; it is the progressive store of insights, and judgment of those insights is initially withheld, as the student has not reached the maturity needed for its autonomous realization.[101] The questions that arise are, first, questions of intelligence, reflection, and deliberation, such as why and how. Second, questions of reflection seek certainty: is that so; is one sure. Third, questions of deliberation arise that are practical and existential; they are questions of commitment: "for commitment is a personal act, a free and responsible act, a very opened-eyed act in which we would settle what we are to become."[102] Thus consciousness is empirical, intelligent, reflective, and rational.[103] The inquiring subject is driven by the thrust of intelligence: a seeking that satisfies their intellectual nature. In the search to know, and once the evidence has been gathered, the subject must make a judgment: "Judgment proceeds rationally from a grasp of the virtually unconditioned. By an unconditioned is meant any x that has no conditions. By a virtually unconditioned is meant any x that has no unfulfilled conditions." The virtually unconditioned "is a conditioned whose conditions are all fulfilled. To marshal all the evidence is to ascertain whether all the conditions are fulfilled." Whereas the "the virtually unconditioned has no unfulfilled conditions. The strictly unconditioned has no conditions whatever. In traditional terms, the former is a contingent being, and the latter is necessary being. In more contemporary terms the former pertains to this world, to the world of possible experience, while the latter transcends this world in the sense that its reality is of a totally different order. But in either case we come to the question of God."[104] To make a judgment means the conditions have been met; understanding culminates in a judgment, based upon a previous insight. To make a judgment is to claim to understand, which, in turn, is

the cessation of reasoning, as "reasoning in its essence is simply the development of insight."[105] How does one know whether there are further
relevant questions before making a judgment? Here is where teachers
are crucial, for they give students a sense of the totality and comprehensiveness of knowledge and learning.[106] Teachers possess a cumulative
understanding, coupled with prudence, wisdom, and the experience
of the living of life. The comprehensiveness of the experience of life
characterizes a wise person, who, being self-transcending, has moved
from the immediacy of pleasure and gratification to an appreciation of
and the appropriation of values: one who has moved from "satisfaction
to values."[107] A wise person has good judgment, and knows when there
are no further relevant questions to be asked – a skill that comes with
age, experience, and maturity. It is this cumulative experience that the
student is being introduced to.

> So wisdom is something that we acquire … we connect degrees
> of wisdom with age. So wisdom, while it is necessary for good
> judgment, for knowing whether or not there are any further rel-
> evant questions, still is a foundation that lies ahead. It is not the
> sort of foundation that we have at the start and on which we build;
> it is the goal towards which we move. And we can always grow
> in wisdom.[108]

Learning is a self-correcting process where the inadequacy and deficiency of an insight leads to further questions for further insight.[109]
Thus, while students reach insight for themselves, it is not solitary but
occurs within a learning community. "Learning is not without teaching,"
and teachers assist in enabling the students to reach insight for themselves. To be able to make a correct judgment requires the accumulation
of correct insights.[110] To know what it means for students to be the active
and principal agents of their learning is to realize that a "teacher cannot
undertake to make a pupil understand. All he can do is to present the
sensible elements in the issue in a suggestive order and with a proper
emphasis. It is up to the pupils themselves to reach understanding, and
they do so in varying measures of pace and rapidity."[111] Teaching is indispensable to learning, in spite of the primacy of the student's own
understanding. The teacher's comprehensive understanding "throws

out the clues, the pointed hints, that lead to insights; it cajoles attention to removing the distracting images that obstructs them; it puts the
further questions that reveal the need of further insights to complement
and modify and transform the acquired store."[112]

The phantasm is essential to understanding and learning. A phantasm is an image, a mental image, dependent upon the imagination,
and teachers help students to acquire a correct image, a correct phantasm, through the process of good teaching.[113] This mental image has
the same relationship to the intellect as perceptible objects have to the
senses.[114] Lonergan uses the example of understanding what a circle
is. A dictionary could be consulted and definitions professed, but this
would not necessarily lead to understanding. On the other hand, drawing a circle, an image, and explaining the relation of the radii to the
curvature of the circle could be more helpful in assisting the student to
understand the circle's nature.[115] Quoting Aristotle, Lonergan says, "a
person without sense perception would never learn anything or understand anything … phantasms play the role taken by sensible objects in
sense perception … Phantasm is the object of the intellect. It is also the
mover of the intellect."[116] Accordingly, there is a primacy of the senses
in human knowing, but a primacy of the intellect in knowledge of the intelligible. "Understanding" always means understanding something in
particular, and what is understood depends upon the image, the phantasm, transformed through the intelligibility of the mind.[117] Lonergan's
example of geometry should not be taken to suggest that the phantasm
is of material or visual objects alone. The phantasm would be realized
analogously in different forms of knowing and understanding. Technical
as this is (and this summary hardly does justice to what Lonergan devotes his work Verbum to), two points are being made here: first, students
are the principal agents in their own understanding, a dynamic process;
and second, understanding stems from the senses, but, through the abstractive nature of the intellect and the power of intelligibility, moves to
intelligibility and abstraction.[118]

A few matters are worth stressing. First, Lonergan is also aware that
specialization, while inevitable, makes integration difficult.[119] Second,
adolescents experience the demands of intelligence, but education prepares them to reach independence and self-mastery through their learning, and moral and religious education exerts a special role.[120] Third,

Lonergan's sense of objectivity avoids the imprisonment of pragmatism, and opts for the objectivity of "intentional self-transcendence." An authentic objectivity is based upon the authentic subjectivity of one who is attentive, intelligent, reasonable, and responsible; authentic subjectivity is the source of authentic objectivity.[121] Fourth, a general education is the best preparation for the human sciences, for it provides a foundation that enables a specialization to be situated in a broader discourse of knowledge and understanding. After all, human beings live their lives on the artistic, symbolic level.[122] And fifth, being is not an abstract concept but is known through correct judgment; it is specific – what is known.[123]

IV.2 THE STUDENT AND HUMAN DEVELOPMENT

Human development has an upward and a downward movement. Development upwards begins with experience, understanding, judging, and decision (or values), while development downward begins with values to beliefs, moving to understanding and appropriating into one's experience the tradition and values handed down:

> Development may be described … as from below upwards: it
> begins from experience, is enriched by full understanding, is
> accepted by sound judgment, is directed not to satisfactions, but
> to values. [From above downwards] it begins in the affectivity
> of the infant … the pupil. On the affectivity rests the appre-
> hension of values. On the apprehension of values rests belief.
> On belief follows the growth in understanding of one who has
> found a genuine teacher and has been initiated into the study of
> the masters of the past. Then to confirm one's growth in under-
> standing comes experience made mature and perceptive by one's
> developed understanding.[124]

Frederick Crowe's work on these forms of development is very helpful.[125] He refers to the developments as *vectors*, calling the development from below, beginning with experience, *education as achievement*, and development from above, from values, *education as heritage*. Both are essential for the education and unity of the student, and "a single structure of consciousness guides each process, the way of progress moving from experience through understanding and judgment to values, [and] the way of tradition moving in the reverse direction from values through judgment and understanding to mature experience."[126] The two developments, upwards from experience and downwards from affectivity and values, depend on each other and begin at infancy. The development downwards cumulatively moves the subject away from a more primitive state, while development upwards ensures a personal appropriation and understanding of what is learned.[127] Development from above comes through the family where the child is born and raised into a tradition, and it is through education that the young are moved to values and away from the gratification of the immediate. This development begins with the child trusting its parents, but as it grows, its own questions and intellectual curiosity and even dissatisfaction are manifested in questions, and it is here that teaching and learning begin their active and dynamic role.[128]

Lonergan's magnum opus, *Insight*, is written from the perspective of development from below, and so he says more on that than he does on development from above.[129] Obviously development from below must be attentive to the stages of mental, moral, and other forms of psychological, social, and physiological growth. Thus the school will differ considerably from the university, particularly regarding the role of experience, understanding, judging, and deciding, or values. Given Lonergan's conviction that teachers provide invaluable assistance to the student in reaching insight and understanding, these developments occur side by side, especially during the early stages of education, with development from above given priority. The child is born into a family, with values and beliefs communicated by parents, where love and tradition are formative.[130] The school educates by imparting an intellectual tradition, set in a particular worldview. Nonetheless, and in spite of this priority of development from above, the school must give prominence to personal understanding, particularly as understanding cannot be communicated, since it is personal to the individual pupil.[131] The teacher helps form the judgment of the young, but it is a living and dynamic process; it is not pouring information into the mind without personal appropriation. To teach students to judge wisely is to enable them to move away from the immediacy of new and fresh ideas and insights to the permanence of these ideas and insights being validated in good and correct judgments.[132] Theoretical as this sounds, education must be attentive to values, moral feelings, and the authentic construction of the self through choice and judgment:

> The judgment of value presupposes knowledge of human life, of human possibilities proximate and remote, of the probable consequences of projected courses of action ... But knowledge alone is not enough ... moral feelings have to be cultivated ... Finally, [there is] the existential discovery ... that one not only chooses ... but also thereby makes oneself an authentic human being or an unauthentic human being.[133]

There is a danger of being hasty in leading the young to decisions, thus failing to recognize their stages of growth and development. Further, while experiencing and understanding come prior to commitment, making a decision has a finality to it.[134] Crowe's reading of Lonergan leads him to emphasize development as heritage or tradition, particularly in the context of education.[135] Education is the communication of an intellectual heritage, and what that heritage is, and how it is constructed, evaluated, critiqued, and finally appropriated, are all crucial to the unity of the student. There is a dynamism and complementarity between these two developments: "just as the upward development was powered by the capacity and for the drive toward intelligibility, truth and the good, so the downward development is powered by the love and responsibility of the educator for the child, and the corresponding love for, and ensuing trust in, the educator on the part of the child."[136] In this context, recalling Lonergan's three kinds of love shows how love unifies both forms of development: the love for God in religion; the love for family; and a wider love beyond the immediacies of one's family and country for humanity as a whole.[137]

Communicating values is an integral part of downward development, and communicating the values held by the family or nation is a natural part of who human beings are: it involves coming to an understanding of human nature not as a social scientist but as an artist, where values, attitudes, and possibilities of greatness and weakness are recounted in stories and poetry. Stories and poetry are accounts of behaviour, values, attitudes; they record the possibilities of greatness and weakness, of pride and humility.[138] However, Lonergan warns against reliance on abstract theories of human nature, applicable universally whether one is awake or asleep, as good or evil. On the contrary, human nature is in relation to particular conscious subjects becoming and growing through their intentionality, choice, judgment, and values.[139]

The arts are a powerful educational means of actualizing the potential of the human subject. While artists withdraw from the world of daily living in pursuit of inspiration, they do so in order to return to the living of life, its demands and opportunities. Experience strengthens this conviction; while everyday life may seem mundane because it entails so many purely practical functions, it is the task of the artist to probe the possibilities inherent in those selfsame necessities of life.[140] Perhaps what might seem an abstract account of insight, a seemingly passionless movement towards truth and judgment, is countered by Lonergan's trust in art as conveying inspiration for human living and the analogous approach to insight:

> Art is a twofold freedom. As it liberates experience from the drag of biological purposiveness, so it liberates intelligence from the wearing constraints of mathematical proofs, scientific verifications, and common sense factualness ... The artist establishes his insights, not by proof or verification, but by skilfully embodying them in colours and shapes, in sounds and movements, in the unfolding situations and actions of fiction.[141]

If the tradition handed down is a source of the student's unity and freedom, then even though the values being handed down may not be generated individually, the tradition can be transformed into personal judgments, without neglecting the truth that while understanding cannot be taught, the judgments and values of a tradition can be communicated. Transforming values and judgments into part of one's experience depends on personal understanding.[142] The communication of beliefs and traditions is similar. After all, human knowledge relies upon trust and upon beliefs that are not each, individually, confirmed by personal verification.[143]

Education is the harmony that emerges from these two forms of development. And while such harmony seems particularly unattainable during the turbulent years of adolescence, the experience of life in the years following is marked by an increasing merging of the two forms of development, resulting in their greater equanimity and peace with each other.[144] These developments, vectors, occur side by side, neither claiming greater importance, though one can recognize that the way of tradition is chronologically prior, and that for students to bring to bear their own experience and understanding and judgment, they must be introduced to a tradition and a worldview. However, life is never always smooth or consistent, and the integration of these developments is found neither in textbooks nor in a directionless and uncritical freedom. Rather, the fullness and unity of life depend upon the integral structures of the knowing and understanding human subject where these two developments are united within human consciousness. Averting a war between these developments entails maintaining a peaceful coexistence wherein human operations of knowing are each assigned their particular role.[145]

Lonergan's contribution picks up where Maritain's concludes. Maritain spends much attention on the curriculum, the diversity of knowledge, and the distinction between natural intelligence and the intellectual virtues to shore up the student's unity. Lonergan's approach to the unity of the student, however, is based on his understanding of cognitional structure and the two forms of development. Of course, this is all prefaced by the foundational concept of students being active agents of their learning, confirmed by the place of insight and the nature of human understanding. What is deceptive is Lonergan's Aristotelian style – that is, one devoid of as many examples and colourful stories as one encounters in a more Platonic approach – not that Maritain's style is Platonic. However, Lonergan's cognitional structure, and the subsequent questions of epistemology and metaphysics, are all at the service of the unity of the student. It is through such a framework that human freedom and unity are to be understood. Lonergan's theory also provides a complementary approach to understanding what is entailed in the education of the whole person. Being secured upon a philosophical anthropological foundation, his approach to human unity and the education of the whole person, or what he might have called the *education of the subject*, is offered through a universally applied philosophical theory, rather than through theological distinctions and creedal distinctiveness.

Lonergan's demanding analysis of the nature of insight and under-standing, and the importance of personal and correct judgments for the appropriation of what one has learned and been taught, are foundational pillars for a Catholic philosophy of education. Knowing by looking and seeing is all too apparent, and requires little explanation. However, Lonergan painstakingly elaborates upon the empirical trap of such a limited form of knowing as he unfurls the place and role of understanding. It would not be fair to say that the Church's educational documents and Maritain do not attend to the nature of understanding sufficiently. Rather, they use different language and a different way of approaching the same question. Lonergan's steely precision regarding understanding, devoid of too many distracting examples, is an essential contribution on how understanding is essential for the unity of the student as a conscious, intentional, and self-appropriating subject. Catholic philosophers of education have rightly called for continued studies and scholarship in this field, and often that call seems to be interpreted as a call to address the field's regional and continental particularities. Important as such scholarship is, Lonergan's philosophical method as to how the subject understands makes a significant, and significantly different, contribution to a universal approach for a Catholic philosophy of education.

V Conclusion

This chapter shows how the educational documents and Maritain's and Lonergan's philosophical theories focus on the student. All see students as the primary and active agents in their learning. The documents situate their attention in the context of the Council, and not just of the Council's document on education. Living the Christian vocation amidst religious diversity and cultural plurality is challenging. However, this challenge gives new meaning to living and embodying the Christian message actively and concretely. The Catholic school faces that challenge by enhancing the internal unity of the student as a person, a subject, and strengthening that unity amidst diversity and plurality.

What is noteworthy is the progression in the understanding and role of a Christian anthropology in the documents. While the earlier documents focus on the development of Christian students, the more recent ones widen this understanding, without compromising the fundamental reason for the existence of the Catholic school: the education of Catholic students. However, the progressive understanding of the documents on the role of a Christian anthropology and worldview is not so much a *change* in focus or emphasis as it is a *widening* of that focus and emphasis. The watchwords in this widening are: *persons* (or subjects); *relational*, especially in the relation to rationality; *communion*; *service*; and *opening oneself to others*. And this widening is not fundamentally sociological. Rather, society and community are where persons encounter each other in all their depth and diversity. Society and community are necessary for the life of persons. In the context of the Catholic school, Christian anthropology has the ability for such widening as it is based on an integral understanding of the student as a person, a subject, whose education and learning are personal, communal, and relational. Such an anthropology serves all students, as it is based upon an integral understanding of personality. Perhaps one of the most significant implications of the widening of Christian anthropology for Catholic education is emphasizing the primacy of religious education for Catholic students and the primacy of religious education for all students. Indeed, an integral education, which is what Catholic education is, would be incomplete without students receiving an adequate religious education, particularly as such an education has essential moral, social, and civic implications for the education of the whole person.

The *education of the whole person* should be of interest and concern to teachers and educators of all stripes and religious affiliations, but often what this implies and entails is left to vague generalizations and tired platitudes. The documents are very attentive to the education of the whole person, and are secured on a Christian anthropology and the social and communal responsibilities that comprise an integral education. Important to note is how the documents emphasize the challenges and opportunities of the education of the student as a whole person amidst diversity and plurality. Catholic educators are charged with the responsibility of making human beings more human, a responsibility seen as formation, rather than a narrow focus on knowledge and information alone. The relationship between what is learned and how it is appropriated and assimilated through choices and actions is essential for the education of the whole person. Also important to that education is the understanding of freedom. Freedom is a source of maturity, which includes one's relationships in society and community. In all this, the unity of the student is front and centre.

Maritain and Lonergan make significant contributions to the unity of the student, the moral, social, and civic implications of education, and the education of the whole person. Maritain's emphasis on the personal, internal, and spiritual unity of the student is underlined in many ways. He sees the humanities and liberal arts as unifying the student, a unity that is essential for their future role as active citizens. The cult of specialization, which creeps ever closer, is halted when a student is introduced to diverse knowledge in preparing for the diversity of living. Lonergan is also concerned with the cult of specialization, and how premature specialization imprisons one if it is devoid of a human context and a vision of the whole of life. Indeed, the place and role that art occupies in his educational theory confirms the analogous nature of human learning and living, and how it is grounded on the freedom for living made possible by the arts. Both philosophers also contribute to the unity of the student through their understanding of the place and role of human freedom: Maritain in seeing free will as a springboard for autonomy and an integral independence, and Lonergan in showing how the four transcendental principles, the three forms of conversion, and the relationship of subjectivity to objectivity all contribute to freedom and hence to human unity.

The spiritual and personal nature of learning is another dimension contributing to the unity of the student. Maritain's broadening of the humanities and his offering of them to all students, whatever their future occupations, have implications for how students experience their own unity, and how it is manifested socially and communally. Lonergan's cognitional theory and his elaboration of the relationship between understanding, insight, and judgment are another approach to freedom, the spiritual and personal nature of learning, and hence human unity.

Amidst a religiously diverse school population, the Catholic school plays a decisive role in the upward and downward forms of development: education as achievement and education as heritage or tradition, as understood by Lonergan and Crowe. In this context, Maritain's belief that the school enjoys autonomy with regard to the family and the state

focuses the attention of the student's unity on what is learned, how it is
learned, and the personal responsibility of learning that must be revealed
through understanding and judgment. Lonergan's compact conviction
that intelligence is driven towards intellectually satisfying answers is not
cerebral, but is based upon a broader philosophy of the human subject
in the quest to know, to understand, and to judge. Both philosophers
share the call of the documents in putting a Christian anthropology and
vision of the world at the service of the unity of the student amidst diversity: Maritain through his emphasis on the unifying role of the humanities and the liberal arts, and the social implications for freedom
and life in society; and Lonergan in his expression of the freedom that
comes from understanding, which is always personal but never private,
and in this has implications for one's freedom and becoming and for
one's relations with others. Both philosophers, therefore, contribute
to how Catholic schools can educate a diverse student body. And while
grounded upon a Christian anthropology and worldview, the intellectual mandate of the Catholic school is focused on educating the student
as a person or subject, and in assisting them to know, to understand,
to judge, to decide, and to appropriate values, it prepares them for life
amidst diversity, whatever their religious affiliation.

5

The Vocation of the Teacher

I Introduction

While the focus of the educational documents is unquestionably the student, they also note that an integral education depends upon the teacher's Christian witness and artistic instrumentality. In addition, the personal presence, engagement, and intentional interaction of the teacher are essential for the education of the student as a whole person. As noted previously, while students are active agents in their learning, and move through the stages of growth by progressing from the known to the unknown, a process that is dynamic and cumulative, it is the teacher who is essential in guiding this process, for it is the teacher who has a comprehensive vision of the subject matter, of the wider educational process, and of life. The teacher's encouragement enables students to be agents of their own learning by supporting and enabling them to see and understand all that is involved in the appropriation of their knowledge and learning, and the implications thereof. Institutional education must be an engagement of persons. While technology provides enormous amounts of information swiftly, it can never replace the teacher. Learning and understanding are dynamic human processes, and what is fundamental is for students to learn *why* and *how* the appropriation of learning and knowledge is manifested through their convictions, commitments, authenticity, choice, and freedom; this requires the ministerial guidance of the teacher, who embodies these ideals. While *what* is learned is undoubtedly important, equally important are *how* and *why* it is learned, which depend upon the witness of teachers in multiple ways. While Christian witness is primary, the documents' repeated call for a synthesis between *faith and culture* and *faith and life* confirms that the teacher's convictions and beliefs, rooted in a Christian anthropology and worldview, must be comprehensively educational if this synthesis is to be realized in all that happens during the school day, rather than confined to a class in religious instruction. Technology cannot replace the teacher in witnessing and living out what this synthesis means and entails.

This chapter focuses on the vocation of the teacher. In ultimate terms, who the teacher is remains more important than what is taught. The teacher's lay, secular vocation is instrumental in the synthesis of faith, culture, and life, and hence the documents emphasize the pastoral and educational formation of the teacher. The teacher is essential for the unity of the student. Maritain's contribution on the vocation of the teacher begins with the artistic dimension of teaching and how teachers help shape the student's worldview. In enhancing the student's freedom, the teacher exercises influence in their moral and social life, and thus contributes to the student's personal unity. The teacher must be a unified whole person in order to carry out the liberating task of education. The intellectual dimensions of the teacher's personality and worldview are fundamentally formative. For Lonergan, teachers make the most important contribution as self-reflective, authentic, and self-transcending subjects. Knowledge and understanding have a public and formative role, and the personal appropriation of the teacher's knowledge, and their authentic witness, enable students to see what a unified life looks like and how it is lived. Thus, for Lonergan, the good is in relation to who the human subject is and chooses to be, and here again, the teacher's witness is vital.

II The Documents of the CCE

II.1 CCE: CATHOLIC IDENTITY AND WITNESS

The witness of the teacher to all dimensions of the truth is fundamentally educational: "For the Catholic educator, whatever is true is a participation in Him who is the Truth; the communication of truth, therefore, as a professional activity, is thus fundamentally transformed into a unique participation in the prophetic mission of Christ, carried on through one's teaching."[1] Such an appeal is educationally focused when teachers

communicate truth across the curriculum. However, truth is not a cerebral possession; teachers accompany students in the search for truth and
beauty, and a sense of right and wrong is indispensible.[2] Teachers are
forming whole persons, not just their minds but also their behaviour,
their language, their expressions, the very heart of their being. Freedom
is an internal disposition, and teachers must be aware of all that hinders
this disposition from being realized in the integral development of the
student as a person.[3] The documents emphasize the place of religious
education, and underline that it must be rigorous and take its place in
the curriculum; as noted in *Gravissimum Educationis*,[4] there is no educational substitute for the life and witness of the teacher of religion: "faith
is principally assimilated through contact with people whose daily lives
bear witness to it. Christian faith ... is born and grows inside a community."[5] Religious education is a living and whole presentation of Christian
faith and morality, and depends on the lived, existential witness of the
teacher. Teachers of religious education are leaders; it is their effectiveness that helps realize the integral mission of the school. They witness
through their lives, through their personal integration of the Christian
invitation and message, and through their professional and educational
training; and their openness enables them to be recognized as authentic
witnesses and teachers.[6] Authentic education and Christian witness are
repeatedly stressed, especially in matters of faith. However, while teachers of religious education are leaders, they do not shoulder the entire
responsibility of ensuring the religious climate of the school; this rests
with all teachers, individually and as a teaching community.[7]

The document *Lay Catholics in Schools* is important for many reasons.
The change in the demographics of Catholic religious orders, particularly in the West, means that now a majority of lay men and women teach
and administer in Catholic schools. This fact is not accepted grudgingly;
rather it is celebrated in recalling the theological and ecclesial changes
of the Council calling all to service as the *people of God*.[8] It is hoped that
men and women from religious orders – consecrated persons – will continue their educational involvement. However, they come with a prior
religious formation; thus there is a parallel need for the comprehensive education of lay teachers, particularly in religious education. Thus
a teacher of religion who is not adequately and systematically prepared
compromises the mission of the school and the unity and integrity of

the student.[9] Nonetheless, the lay teacher has a formative role to play in
Catholic education: "the special task of those educators who are lay persons is to offer to their students a concrete example of the fact that people
deeply immersed in the world, living fully the same secular life as the
vast majority of the human family, possess this same exalted dignity."[10]

The identity of the lay teacher is formative in witnessing to faith and
the transformative nature of knowledge and learning; this witness of the
appropriation of knowledge, beliefs, and values has no educational equal.
But teachers are not simply transmitters of knowledge and information;
they are educators who form and shape integral persons.[11] Amidst rapid
changes in society, that witness of the secular vocation of lay teachers
becomes all the more urgent. The vocational identity of an educator is
the identity of the whole person, one that can inspire students to elevate
and influence the cultural and moral dimensions of life. The documents
clearly understand the identity of the Catholic educator.[12] A distinction
is made between the influence of *secularization* and a *secularized* worldview that characterizes modern society, and the *secular* vocation of Catholic lay teachers. They exercise a specific role within the overall mission
of the Church, a role that is realized in the school as a community.[13] This
secular vocation is developed in *Lumen Gentium*:

[T]he laity, by their very vocation, seek the kingdom of God by
engaging in temporal affairs and by ordering them according to
the plan of God. They live in the world, that is, in each and all of
the secular professions and occupations. They live in the ordinary
circumstances of family and social life, from which the very web of
existence is woven. They are called there by God that by exercising
their proper function and led by the spirit of the Gospel they may
work for the sanctification of the world from within as a leaven. In
this way they may make Christ known to others, especially by the
testimony of a life resplendent in faith, hope, and charity.[14]

However, the facts on the ground depict a different reality. The
number of teachers who continue to profess the faith is dropping, which,
in turn, wears heavily on the importance of the witness of teachers.[15]
Thus there is a renewed call for the educational witness of consecrated
persons, especially those from religious congregations that profess an

educational charism, making their witness all the more important in assisting students to mature in their identity. Consecrated religious seek
to follow Christ, and they seek happiness and fullness of life in varied
ways: through the evangelical counsels of poverty, chastity, and obedience; their commitment and dedication to their congregational charism;
their search for the truth and an authentic life; and their desire to love
and care for others – all integral aspects in the pilgrimage of encountering the living God.[16] And while their presence in Catholic schools is
vital, lay teachers will be in the majority. Though the Church's educational mission would be wanting without the participation of lay Catholics, the preparation of Catholic teachers, particularly those who teach
religion, takes on an urgency, as they do not teach on their own authority
but through the authority of the teachings of Christ.[17] Their preparation
must be systematic and theological, and they must refrain from upset-
ting the minds of the young "with outlandish theories, useless questions
and unproductive discussions."[18]

The ongoing intellectual and pastoral formation of teachers depends
on a Christian way of seeing and understanding the world. The religious
formation of Catholic teachers is often seriously deficient compared to
their expected professional and academic competence.[19] The lay teacher
must also be formed and educated as a whole person, and care must be
taken in integrating their knowledge and learning, enabling them to
critically draw on and learn from their social, cultural, and intellectual milieu.[20] Teachers who do not receive a just salary are distracted
by seeking additional employment, and that, along with an insufficient
personal, religious, professional, and academic formation, compromises the integral education of the student and the teacher's ability to situate their Christian witness within a wider context. Catholic teachers, by
virtue of their mission, are called to make human beings more human.
All that is entailed in the Christian life must profoundly shape their personality and witness, making their ongoing intellectual, cultural, social,
and moral formation all the more vital.[21]

While emphasizing the formation and ongoing intellectual and pastoral care of teachers, the documents realize that the school cannot help
but be one of the intersecting points where the problems and challenges
of society are encountered. The young lack role models; often families
are found wanting in religious and moral life, resulting in a negligent

and, often, at best a lukewarm religious environment and example. This makes the task of even committed teachers difficult. All this contributes towards a "pedagogical tiredness that intensifies the ever increasing difficulty of conciliating roles of the teacher with that of the educator in today's context."[22] The school's environment amidst cultural, economic, and social pressures, the breakdown of families, and moral, ethical, and religious indifference and relativism can leave teachers feeling isolated and misunderstood, wondering about the viability and effectiveness of their teaching vocation.[23] The individualism that marks contemporary life makes the communal and personal relationships between teachers and students all the more necessary.[24] The demands and discipline required in being a teacher and administrator extend beyond the classroom and the school.[25] All this is tempered by the realization that the teacher pursues an ideal that "is always beyond one's grasp. Every educator needs a firm hope, because the teacher is never the one who truly reaps the fruits of the labour expended on the students."[26]

II.2 CCE: SYNTHESIS OF FAITH, LIFE, AND CULTURE

Underscoring the Catholic identity of the teacher does not compromise the overall educational mission of the school amidst religious diversity. It is a Christian anthropology and worldview, a scale of values, and a social and cultural philosophy that makes Catholic education distinct and depends upon the dynamic and intentional agency of the teacher for its realization. All these specific features embody the broad and inclusive mission of the school. The creative and personal contribution of teachers must stem from their personal unity. The teacher's disposition towards life – their worldview, whether implicit or explicit – unavoidably shapes and influences whatever happens in the school.[27] It is not uncommon that the Catholicity of the school is relegated to religious educators and the school chaplain. The documents reject such a reduction. Catholic teachers are called to adopt a common worldview and attitude to life, secured on a hierarchy of values.[28] This broader Catholic vision unifies the individual teacher within themselves and unites them communally in their common vocation; but it also enables them to understand the contribution of individual subjects in the integral development of the student towards an increasingly unified Christian personality.[29]

The formation and education of the Christian personality of the student has many dimensions, and is framed in a comprehensive manner that relies upon teachers and educators communicating a systematic and ordered hierarchy of values. In a world fascinated by methods and techniques, the Catholic school depends less on methodologies and subject matter, and far more on those who teach and work there.[30] The personal contact of teachers is far more important than educational methodologies. To educate and teach is to engage in human formation, and today the difference between generations, and the variety of influences upon each generation, makes personal contact all the more crucial.[31] Teachers are irreplaceable in the integral formation of their students, a formation that is grounded on the nature of the person, the purpose and end of life, and the meaning of history and the world. Teachers enable students to develop their critical faculties in distinguishing values that contribute to their integral growth and the maturation of their personality from those choices that hinders and imprisons it. The values that are learned are to be appropriated, thus shaping and influencing life. Indeed, they become the lenses for life.[32] In an age of instant and often undifferentiated information, such witness to values and their integration is all the more challenging:

> As far as educators are concerned, deculturation is limiting their knowledge of cultural heritage. Easy access to information, which nowadays is broadly available, when it is not selected with critical awareness, ultimately favours widespread superficiality among both students and teachers, not only impoverishing reason, but also imagination and creative thinking.[33]

The teacher's personal contact is imperative in providing the human face and personal dimension of education. It might appear anomalous that the documents are engaged in a hesitation waltz between the *way* students learn and *what* they learn, but it is less a hesitation and more a change of emphasis; now on one aspect, the *way*, and the reasons, and then on the *what*, and the reasons. The *way* is emphasized to avoid an uncritical and unengaged education, ensuring the active participation of students. The *what* highlights the teacher's role in communicating the various inherited traditions to students. This back-and-forth emphasis has the future in mind, the contribution of future citizens to society and the common good, as opposed to a narrow utilitarian vision of education. In spite of the demands of a society eager to equate education with material gains and tangible results, education and teaching must first provide all that is required for the integral growth of the student as a person.[34] The interior dispositions of the teacher are preeminent, precisely because education and teaching are demanding when shaping and forming human persons. Thus the personal integration, the pastoral formation, and the intellectual, cultural, and religious enlightenment of the teacher are important areas of concern.[35]

A distinctive feature today of how the Catholic school is conceived as dynamic and heuristic, in a cautious and qualified open-ended way, is the conviction that teachers, staff, and students continue to discover and shape the school, without of course compromising its religious, moral, intellectual, social, and cultural traditions. This seemingly bold suggestion is secured on the dynamic and living nature of knowledge and learning; the school is ever growing and developing, and teachers play a significant role in that evolution.[36] Such openness is impressive, and attests to the depth of the CCE's understanding of the nature of the Catholic school, and to a confidence that such a heuristic conception of the school, if understood carefully, would not weaken or compromise its nature and mission. However, this conviction is also laid as the foundation for what the Church refers to as the synthesis between *faith and culture* and *faith and life*.[37] Such a synthesis is vital in the context of *"New Age* religiosity," which, while responding to a spiritual hunger, attracts Christians due to a "lack of serious attention in their own communities for themes which are actually part of the Catholic synthesis such as the importance of man's spiritual dimension and its integration with the whole of life, the search for life's meaning, the link between human beings and the rest of creation, the desire for personal and social transformation, and the rejection of a rationalistic and materialistic view of humanity."[38]

Lay teachers play a special role in this synthesis in communicating the relationship between truth and knowledge and the ongoing dialogue between faith and culture.[39] This synthesis and dialogue is dynamic, living, and active, it is essential for the personal unity of students, and to grow it must be realized in the living witness of the teacher's life. While the specifics of the Catholic faith are essential for such synthesis, the other subjects will also be brought together in an organic unity.[40] For this reason, too, the education of Catholic teachers is especially noted:

> [A] close relationship ... exists between the way a discipline (especially in the humanities) is taught, and the teacher's basic concept of the human person, of life, and of the world. If the ideo-logical orientation of a center for teacher formation is pluralist, it can easily happen that the future Catholic educator will have to do supplementary work in order to make a personal synthesis of faith and culture in the different disciplines that are being studied. It must never be forgotten, during the days of formation, that the role of a teacher is to present the class materials in such a way that students can easily discover a dialogue between faith and culture, and gradually be led to a personal synthesis of these.[41]

The synthesis between faith and culture and faith and life emphasizes the incarnational nature of Christianity, and while this synthesis has the maturity of faith in its sight, it also provides a broader vision in as-sisting in distinguishing between what enhances personhood and what compromises it. The synthesis begins with the conviction that the truths of human tradition and its various expressions require critical engage-ment and choice.[42] This synthesis has a decidedly educational purpose, and stretches across the curriculum and life outside the classroom. And though the root of the synthesis between faith and culture depends on what is known in the environment of faith, it is meant to mature into a disposition for Christian living that shapes a vision of the world, culture, and history.[43] One of the most foundational statements about the school, formation, learning, and wisdom is made in the context of this synthesis:

> In the Catholic school's educational project there is no separa-tion between time for learning and time for formation, between acquiring notions and growing in wisdom. The various school subjects do not present only knowledge to be attained, but also values to be acquired and truths to be discovered. All of which demands an atmosphere characterized by the search for truth, in which competent, convinced and coherent educators, teachers of learning and of life, may be a reflection, albeit imperfect but still

vivid, of the one Teacher. In this perspective, in the Christian educational project all subjects collaborate, each with its own specific content, to the formation of mature personalities.[44]

The Catholic school is founded on the person of Jesus Christ and the Gospel, and this foundation places the student's personhood at the centre of Catholic education. This foundation is all the more crucial in a world where human beings experience fragmentation, not only from societal and cultural forces but also in their personal lives, that challenges their unity and spiritual tranquility. In the midst of religious diversity, the Catholic school places its educational tradition at the service of all. This contribution shows how "the person is not only the sum total of his horizontal dimensions, but also the harmonious composition of the ethical, spiritual and religious aspects of human reality."[45] The synthesis between faith, culture, and life situates the broader questions for an integral life. Such a synthesis is formational for society, for it widens education and learning, and protects them from individualism, and from schooling reduced to professional formation.[46] The teacher exercises an instrumental role in this synthesis, so the initial formation acquired at the start of a teaching career will be insufficient. The synthesis requires an ongoing formation for the integration of human knowledge in all its dimensions in the curriculum, realized through the light of the Gospels and Christian virtue. Teaching is more than imparting knowledge; it is instrumental in cultivating the integral humanity of the student.[47]

An essential aim of this synthesis is the personal unity of the student, particularly in sex education and its implications for Christian personality. Modesty, temperance, respect for one's body, openness to others, controlling instincts, all contribute to an affective maturation. The virtue of prudence is crucial, exemplified through the example of Christian lives, such as the saints'. Measured language, a sense of beauty and the beautiful, and modulated modes of expression are crucial in teaching and educating on the sensitive matter of sexuality.[48] And while students may object that society is far from these ideals, they "may need to be convinced that it is better to know the positive picture of personal Christian ethics rather than to get lost in an analysis of human misery. In practice, this means respect for oneself and for others."[49]

Teachers must be sensitive to how doubt and indifference desensitize the human spirit. Teaching has social implications that prepare students to take their rightful place in society as engaged and contributing citizens. The school provides lay teachers the environment to live and express their vocation in an integrated and unified manner amidst diversity and plurality. Teachers have a special role in welcoming non-Catholic students, where dialogue and interpersonal relations depict the dignity of each student and confirm that education is not limited to the dissemination of knowledge.[50] The educational value of true and genuine friendship shapes the personal and social dimensions of personality.[51]

The social challenges that teachers encounter are much more than the separation between culture and Christianity; that is a separation experienced by all who profess religious belief. Christian morality and the social teachings of the Church enable teachers to shed light on other aspects of learning, such as law, economics, politics, and sociology, all of which make demands on living an honest and truly free life in society. The social doctrine of the Church serves all students, as it is based on the primacy, dignity, and freedom of the human person.[52] All this is situated within a community dimension of schooling and learning, one that aims at the integral education of students in their personhood. Teachers form persons to realize their social responsibilities as future active citizens who will shape and influence society, and in this, the teachers' own witness and lives are irreplaceable.[53]

Students must be educated how to respond to a religiously diverse and culturally plural society. The ability to listen to others and enter into an open spirit of dialogue is fundamentally educational. Unity amidst diversity and differences requires teachers and administrators to be leaders in dialogue and reconciliation. One way is to identity what unites persons in their common experience of living and manifesting themselves in the world.[54] The challenges of multi-religious and multicultural societies cannot be glossed over by good will alone. Neither can difficulties be ignored, resulting in ghettoization, or in religious differences defining and dominating the public square. Teachers must be open and welcoming, witnessing to the mission of the school and sharing their own commitments and values. They must be knowledgeable of other religions and cultures, and accompany students in their search for truth, in distinguishing right from wrong, and in contributing to the good of society. The school must also be mindful of the poor, both in and outside the school.[55] Finally, while education is broader than academic and intellectual pursuits, given the intellectual nature of the school and teaching, educators must attend to the power and precision of words.[56]

The teaching vocation is a noble one, and therefore it is difficult, demanding, and entails great responsibility. While the documents are aware of the many factors that add to this demanding vocation, they continually call attention to the spiritual nature of teaching without which education and schooling run the risk of becoming conveyer belts of information and unappropriated knowledge. The vocation of the teacher is spiritual because education is ultimately a spiritual act, a communion of persons who are engaged in human transformation. In ultimate terms, such transformation depends upon personal understanding and appropriation; it depends upon the intangibles: the virtues, strength of character, good judgment, love, and generosity. And it is teachers who show, through their lives and witness, how the tangibility of sense knowledge is transformed into the spiritually intangible convictions and certitudes that guide and shape personal life and one's relations with others.

The rapid pace of educational change and innovation, and the voluminous research in that field, understandably overwhelms educators and teachers. The documents are sympathetic, and while they recognize that those who teach and administer must keep abreast of these developments as best they can, they provide the anthropological and philosophical lenses through which teachers may judge and discern the implications of educational innovation in serving the student. The emphasis on the lay vocation of the majority of Catholic teachers and administrators is particularly striking, and is not a consequence of a reluctant acceptance of demographics; it is much more than the recognition of a changed sociological reality. What the documents provide is the theological framework for a Catholic secular vocation in the world. The followers of this secular vocation are charged with the responsibility of understanding how the transformation of the social and communal orders and the common good depend upon the Catholic laity continuing to grow in their understanding of their baptismal call, and taking their rightful place in the Church as the People of God. This secular vocation is also vital in the synthesis between faith and culture and faith and life, a call that has been made with repeated and increasing intensity by the teaching Church. Perhaps this can be framed in educational terms as the personal and communal understanding and appropriation of what one knows and learns. And towards such understanding and appropriation, the teacher's role is essential and indispensable. Apart from their religious witness, Catholic teachers have a wide moral, social, cultural, and intellectual role to play under the broad synthesis between faith, life, and culture.

From this context, moving to Maritain's contribution is really a philosophical continuity regarding the spiritual vocation of the teacher. Maritain too is clear about the personal responsibility of teachers and their intellectual mandate in shaping integral persons, guided by the intellect and realized in a spiritual transformation. However, such transformation has social and communal dimensions, and again, Maritain stresses those dimensions, not out of deference to a narrow sociological conception of society or human needs, but because human beings manifest themselves through their social and communal natures, and the teacher assists in expanding on the rights and responsibilities of that revelation.

III The Contribution of Jacques Maritain

III.1 THE TEACHER AS ARTIST

Saying that the teacher is an artist is not to suggest that the student is fashioned in any way the teacher chooses. The teacher's art is likened to a doctor's, as a causal agent cooperating with nature.[57] Teaching concerns truth, and the teacher respects truth by respecting the dynamic nature of the student's personal knowing and understanding, and the independence that comes with thinking for oneself. Thus education is open-ended, ongoing, and lifelong.[58] Teachers have knowledge that students do not yet possess, but teaching is not enabling students to remember or recall pre-existing knowledge, in a manner such as Plato envisaged. Rather, the teacher cooperates with the dynamic and self-propelling nature of the student's own knowing and understanding.[59] Students move from the known to the unknown. Teachers assist by being attentive to the natural energy and dynamism of the mind by using examples from the student's experiences and the facts or truths that they have acquired, enabling them to increase their knowledge, offering clues and hints in making connections and reaching conclusions that, given their stages of growth, they may not reach on their own. Students are the primary agents in their own learning and understanding, and while the teacher's role is secondary, it is vital.[60]

Teaching is concerned with thinking.[61] The teacher's task is assisting students to think, and to experience the freedom and autonomy that depends upon thinking and understanding for themselves, and to encourage their growing precision, particularly in their speech and expression. Students cannot give themselves what they do not possess; they need guidance and teaching. However, their ability to think and to come to their own insights and make judgments must always be respected, as must the student's personal mysterious identity, one that is hidden and beyond the purview of techniques.[62] Like Lonergan, Maritain confirms the educational role of insight, whereby one engages with reality through the questions asked.[63] The implications of thinking are always beyond the individual subject, which is what unifies the student through the diversity of the curriculum:

> [The teacher] teaches an object – mathematics or grammar – and has primarily to make the human subject capable of freely and eagerly submitting to the object and the requirements of the object; he has to teach his pupils the exacting ways through which to prepare for an adult life where they will be obliged to make the best of situations *not* of their own choosing and to do not as they please but as they ought.[64]

The teacher plays a prominent role in enhancing the student's freedom. Memorizing without understanding compromises freedom, and similarly the growth of the imagination is hindered by premature specialization. While there is a certain personal and collective discipline in learning and knowledge, education is ultimately concerned with freeing the mind to enable students to think and express themselves. The broad activity that is education is ultimately concerned with personal and internal freedom.[65] While technique and method have their place, it is this personal growth and freedom of the intellect that is foundational and must be respected. The power of personal expression is emphasized:

Education ... calls for an intellectual sympathy and intuition on the part of the teacher, concern for the questions and difficulties with which the mind of the youth may be entangled without being able to give expression to them, a readiness to be at hand with the lessons of logic and reasoning that invite to action the unexercised reason of the youth. No tricks can do that, no set of techniques, but only personal attention to the inner blossoming of the rational nature and then confronting that budding reason with a system of rational knowledge.[66]

It is the quest for truth that must be kept alive, and grasping truth and reality is part of the process of personal freedom and integration that comes from education. Maritain cautions teachers against posing and raising difficulties, problems, or challenges without also providing students with ways to respond to and answer these challenges. All this is essential in protecting the unity and integrity of the student as well as what is known and learned.[67] Teaching is not simply conveying information; its greater task is liberating the student, a liberation that stems from the moral authority of the one who teaches.[68] The student's expectation, by virtue of being a person, means teaching is more than listening and being instructed. The teacher's convictions are equally educative; they are the convictions of a concrete person, not the impersonal truths in books.

[Thus teachers present] a carefully and objectively prepared picture of incompatible opinions between which only subjective taste or feeling appears apt to chose. What is the effect of such teaching? To blunt or kill [the] sacred attention from the teacher and to make the student grope from pit to pit. The first duty of the teacher is to develop within himself, for the sake of truth, deep rooted convictions, and frankly to manifest them, while taking pleasure, of course, in having the student develop, possibly against them, his own personal convictions.[69]

The student's knowledge is progressive and in process, and as it is always growing and cumulative, and thus incomplete, the student believes the teacher in order to know. However, this desire and need to know are conditional, and the student may well reject the truth that has been taught.[70] Students are impressionable; their personality and character can easily be harmed and warped; thus their formation and education carries a great responsibility. And it is precisely because education and learning are more than the inert banking of information, that the teacher's responsibility is always a moral one: "the right of the child to be educated requires that the educator will have moral authority over him, and this authority is nothing else than the duty of the adult to the freedom of the youth."[71] However, the active nature of the teaching vocation needs to be qualified:

> Teaching ... belongs to the sphere of the active life, and it must
> be confessed that one finds too often in teaching the burdens and
> encumbrances peculiar to action; there is even a certain danger
> for the life of the spirit in the ponderous handling of concepts
> which constitutes the labour of teaching and which always runs the
> risk if you are not constantly on your guard, of becoming material
> and mechanical.[72]

What of the teacher's disposition? Teaching is primarily about developing a worldview – a way and manner of looking at the world; it is primarily an internal and spiritual disposition, as opposed to the narrow dissemination of facts and information. Teaching is encountering reality in its widest sense.[73] Teaching must be concerned with discernment, and Maritain elaborates, with poetic beauty, how difficult this task of discernment really is.[74] The teacher's commitment is vital, but is compromised by bureaucracy, demanding teaching schedules, or worldviews and convictions contrary to the integral education of persons: "it is preposterous to ask people who lead an enslaved life to perform a task of liberation, which the educational task is by essence."[75] Teachers are part of their society and culture, and to expect them to possess higher levels of freedom and transcendence from the influences and biases of their environment is unrealistic.[76] This is certainly a challenge, and puts further emphasis and a renewed urgency today on the pastoral, moral, theological, social, and overall intellectual development and formation of Catholic teachers. For without the personal transcendence and freedom of the teacher, education for the freedom and liberation of the student is compromised, as is the purpose and goal of the Catholic school.

III.2 THE INTELLECTUAL AND MORAL DIMENSIONS OF TEACHING

Teaching is an art, and "the intellect has primacy in the work of art ... *the first principle of all human works is reason.*"[77] Intellect and reason protect the integrity and primacy of the curriculum, and save education from the awkward and artificial speculation positing a Christian mathematics or physics. Enough has also been said previously regarding knowledge and learning in a Catholic education, how they reveal the diversity of reality, and how that engagement transforms the student as an integral being. Christian mathematics or physics are intellectual figments. What is required, rather, is first showing where mathematics and physics, and other subjects of the curriculum, are placed within the overall hierarchy of knowledge and learning, and second, developing an appreciation of truth in each discipline, and the unifying nature of truth.[78] The love that teachers have for their students is also essential for this intellectual and internal unity.[79]

The enlightening and freeing of the intellect is the school's primary concern, without compromising the primacy of the will, to which reference has been previously made. Education is human formation, and while the school does not form the will directly, neither can it be ignored. In moral education, the practical dimension of reason takes precedence over the speculative. An education of the whole person depends upon the intellect and the will. The ability to think, reason, and make sound judgments is vital for the education of the will, for moral education, which, while indirect, is crucial.[80] In spite of the primacy of the intellectual dimension, the moral authority of the teacher is indispensable. This back-and-forth emphasis on the intellect and will finds its foundation in Maritain's distinction between person and individual. Individuality must be protected as one grows in one's personality, and care must be taken in students' developing their individuality in the quest for personality, while not letting them become the centre of everything where the "ego is in reality scattered among cheap desires or overwhelming passions, and finally submitted to the determinism of matter."[81] The balance between individuality and personality, and the freedom of the person, also depend upon personal discipline, striving for holiness, and the continued Christian journey toward perfection, all essential for personal and spiritual unity.[82] Teachers and education depend on nature *and* grace, for the entire art of education "consists in inspiring, schooling,

and pruning, teaching, enlightening, so that in the intimacy of man's activities the weight of the egoistic tendencies diminishes, and the weight
of the aspirations proper to personality and its spiritual generosity increases."[83] This reveals that the person is perfected through love – not
by the actualization of a predetermined perfection, but by God's call to
realize one's personal vocation.[84] Lonergan makes a similar observation.

Moral education is also related to religion, and it is never a purely
rational speculation. In spite of this, moral education is not simply religious expression per se, nor a mere expansion thereof.[85] Persons grow
insofar as their internal and spiritual freedom directs their passions and
senses.[86] Maritain concludes his essay on moral education by calling for
attention to the morality found in the humanities and liberal arts. While
he saw the place of religious faith, he emphasized the moral influence of
reason, for he diagnosed his war-torn world as a "a disease of human intelligence and conscience" whose "special remedies [include the] revival
of religious faith, but also ... a revival of the moral power of reason."[87]

The prior unity and hierarchies of knowledge unify teaching.[88] Maritain's philosophy of knowledge has been referred to previously; his magnum opus is dedicated to the degrees of knowledge.[89] Teachers must
be familiar with a philosophy of knowledge and with the degrees and
hierarchies of knowledge for many practical reasons, and though wisdom can never be taught, ultimately teaching concerns wisdom.[90] Once
again the key lies in Maritain's emphasis. The school does not aim at
making students wise, but rather at equipping them through hierarchical and "ordered knowledge," enabling them to advance toward wisdom
in adulthood.[91] Such preparation introduces students to learning in its
diversity, vital in situating their future particular, specialized, and professional lives in a broader and unified context.[92]

III.3 THE SOCIAL DIMENSION OF TEACHING

Maritain places great emphasis on teaching the *democratic charter* as a
crucial step in preparation for adulthood and active citizenship.[93] Such
preparation is particularly vital today when the secular state is no longer
charged with bringing about a philosophic, religious, or doctrinal unity.
In spite of the absence of religious unity, there is a human and secular unity and cooperation that is based upon human freedom.[94] The

separation of Church and state means that "civil society has become grounded on a common good and a common task which are of earthly, temporal, or secular order, and in which citizens belonging to diverse spiritual groups or linages share equally." This unity now depends upon "a *civic* or *secular* faith, not a religious one. Nor is it that philosophic substitute for religious faith."[95]

While our modern democracy was born of Christian convictions, such inspiration solidifies this *secular faith* and contributes to the growth of a "common secular consciousness," and it is education that helps to elaborate the secular nature of the charter.[96] A free society depends upon persons who find common agreement, but such agreement is of a strictly practical and temporal nature; it does not suppose any philosophic, religious, or theoretical unity, nor indeed any common conception of the purpose of life.[97] Practical as the charter is, it is not conceived as a set of impersonal and conceptual ideas. Rather, those who teach the charter must do so based upon their personal, moral, and intellectual convictions, and also based upon the religious faith that they profess; this is elaborated upon in one of Maritain's works on political philosophy.[98] Teaching from the basis of one's own religious and philosophic convictions strengthens pluralism, giving it a human and lived context.[99] Teaching the charter from other theoretical perspectives enables students who are in a religious minority not to feel excluded or marginalized.[100] Some practical suggestions are offered in teaching the charter in homogeneous and heterogeneous communities, and how it can be embodied in the curriculum, particularly in history, the humanities (especially the great thinkers), and the social sciences.[101] One way of teaching the charter in order to engender freedom and responsibility is dividing students into teams who must then account for the discipline of their team members and their working towards a common goal. The charter would aim to instill civic and political virtues for life in community, secured through a sense of self-worth, discipline, and personal and collective freedom.[102]

The more that education and teaching are considered as professions, with the accompanying and obligatory need for qualifications and checks and balances, the more teaching as a vocation comes to be overshadowed. Even though Maritain's philosophy of education was formulated more than fifty years ago, he recognized the professional side of teaching and the need to benefit from the social sciences and other advances in better understanding the student. However, his fundamental contribution to the education and formation of the teacher is his understanding of teaching and learning as a fundamentally human engagement. As Maritain explains, unless teachers appreciate the spiritual and mysterious task that is teaching, they will run the risk of focusing on the professional dimensions of their work at the expense of teaching as a vocation.

Maritain's emphasis on the moral authority of the teacher and the vocation of teaching ties in with the documents and anticipates Lonergan's attention to the authentic subjectivity of the teacher and the act of teaching. The moral authority of the teacher can hardly be the subject of their professional education, and while it must undoubtedly be part of their vocational formation, that authority, like wisdom and goodness, cannot be taught – and yet that moral authority is imperative for the integral education of the student and for the integrity of the teacher's life and the art of teaching. Diversity and plurality can make that moral authority difficult, and limit its scope. Maritain's contribution sees such authority as arising from the nature of truth and the natural power and dynamism of the mind to organize reality, and to situate what is learned and understood within the hierarchies of knowledge and values. In pluralist societies, there is an understandable apprehension and suspicion when the language of hierarchies of knowledge and values is introduced. What Maritain shows is that such hierarchies are part of the natural yearning of the mind and its role in unifying the human person.

Lonergan says a great deal about the role that the teacher plays in the student's insight, learning, understanding, judgment, and decision. Maritain approaches these matters by accentuating the artistic role of the teacher and their intellectual and moral witness to their students. Perhaps in the midst of diversity and plurality, and the myriad ways that students can access information today, teachers may feel less like artists and more like packers along a conveyer belt, simply adding bits and pieces towards an end where the student is envisaged as a finished product. Today's ready access to electronic information challenges the communal nature of intellectual and moral knowledge, and the teacher's indispensable task is in showing why knowledge and learning that are tainted by individualism compromise the social and communal nature of the student as a person. Maritain realized that looking on teaching as a vocation will require the leisure time for contemplation – in its widest sense – and reflection. The pace of our society makes that invitation doubly difficult.

We move next to Lonergan's contribution to the vocation of the teacher, wherein he emphasizes attending to authenticity and subjectivity and the transcendental principles. Given the absence of communally unifying worldviews and metanarratives, the teaching vocation, more than ever, must be grounded in personal convictions, but united in the community of authentic and transcending subjects.

IV The Contribution of Bernard Lonergan

IV.1 THE TEACHER AS SUBJECT

For Lonergan, the primary influence of teachers is as authentic subjects, manifesting themselves through self-transcendence, pursuing truth and the good, seeking intellectual, moral, and religious conversion, and reflecting on their intending and intentionality, with the transcendental principles as their framework. His essay "The Subject" may be described as an anthropology for adulthood: how it is confined and diminished by historical circumstances, the social environment, personal traits, and one's worldview.[103] Teachers who are fragmented and estranged from their subjectivity will have an adverse effect on education, as their freedom is compromised. The relationship between authentic subjects and the world means that the world is much more than what is encountered externally; it is realized through active engagement, judgment, choice, freedom, and personal responsibility. Here existential subjects actualize those values that they have freely sought.[104] Authentic subjectivity is open-ended and heuristic, but subjects are present to themselves precisely as subjects, not as objects: "objects are present by being attended to; but subjects are present as subjects, not by being attended to but by intending."[105] Self-knowledge, then, is gained not through introspection but by presence to self, and increasing this level of self-presence is not attained by further introspection but by increasing one's activity – not as action per se, but as one who deliberates and chooses, thus moving to a level where free and responsible subjects make themselves through their choices and actions, and as a result construct and shape the world.[106] The subject and the world grow authentically insofar as the subject moves progressively away from what is self-serving and selfish toward an intelligibly ordered world where he or she grows in authenticity through an unbiased "detached and disinterested desire to know."[107]

Self-knowledge is dynamic; it reveals personal confusion, but it also moves towards redirecting and unifying the self.[108] The distinction between self-consciousness and self-knowledge is that self-knowledge, like knowledge itself, is a compound of different activities. Whereas consciousness is at the level of experience, the first of the four transcendental levels, "it is the experience of the subject, the subject's presence to himself; and everyone has that presence to himself. But not everyone understands himself. Not everyone knows himself. To understand oneself, one must go beyond the data of consciousness [and] perform acts of understanding."[109] Lonergan consistently warns of the dangers in reducing knowing to picture thinking, confining knowing at the sensory level, and thus limiting the subject and knowing. Subjects are intrinsically involved with their knowing and understanding:

> By person we mean a subject that not merely knows, but in knowing is aware that he is knowing; that wills, and in willing is aware of his willing; that chooses, and in choosing is aware of himself choosing; that speaks, and in speaking is aware that he is speaking; that promises and threatens, and in promising and threatening is aware that he is doing so; that is faithful, just and merciful, and in being so is aware of his own fidelity, of his own justice, his own mercy. This is the person as a subject.[110]

Subjects know and understand, and they are aware of their knowing and understanding and its appropriation, and the implications for ethical living; the subject moves from the level of knowing to a level of both knowing and doing. This relationship between knowing and doing has fundamental educational implications. Knowing something does not necessarily establish what one will do, or whether one will do it. Possessing knowledge leaves the knower with different courses of action or inaction.[111] Choosing a course of action involves freedom of the will. However, freedom to choose moves the subject beyond reasoning and deciding the best course of action, though it is always important to remember that one cannot show what a course of action will look like in the future or what its implications will be.[112] The subject moves deliberation to the fourth level of consciousness – empirical, intellectual, and rational being the first three – to the moral level, rational self-consciousness, when faced with the question of what to do.[113] The subject is confronted by a decision, the possession of a choice of agreeing or disagreeing, of seeing the implications of a judgment and acting, or ignoring the implications and not acting. However, there is a fundamental difference: making a judgment is an "act of rational consciousness," while actually making a decision is an "act of rational self-consciousness." The rationality of judgment responds to the "detached and disinterested desire to know." And in deciding, the rationally conscious subject seeks harmony between their knowledge, decision, and action.[114] Knowing, choosing, and doing can be tainted by bias.[115] Teachers must uncover bias, first within themselves and then by assisting students to become aware of their biases and how they influence their judgments and actions. Being attentive, intelligent, reasonable, and responsible enables the subject to achieve transcendence, precisely by recognizing and overcoming their bias. The subject encounters personal bias, then the bias of a community or society, and then a more universal bias.[116]

Subjects know through their authentic subjectivity, and authentic knowing reveals more than knowledge; it reveals the knower: "since we know by what we are, so also we know that we know by knowing what we are."[117] But most transformative is the realization that knowledge of truth and knowledge of oneself are inseparable, and in order to know the truth, subjects must come to know themselves, what their knowledge is, and the relationship between their knowledge and self-reflection.[118] This requires that the subject move to the third level of self-knowledge: the act of judgment.[119] The teacher's vocation is to enable students to understand how the judgments that they make are also their own commitment to seeking to know and act upon what is true, and how in this they encounter the real.[120] Subjects are characterized by their autonomy and freedom, and by their knowing and doing.[121] Authentic knowing depends upon the continual conversion of the subject, their intellectual, moral, and religious conversion, all part of the self-transcendence of the subject who moves to the truly good, that which possesses objective value and is judged to be so, as opposed to what seems to be the good and is judged to be so by subjects who have not achieved self-transcendence.[122] Lonergan contrasts the freedom and autonomy of the authentic subject with the drifter who simply follows the crowd. Drifters are not differentiated by their own reflective self-consciousness. The drifter's thinking, doing, saying, and choosing are no different from those of the similarly unreflective crowd.[123] Education, rather, is widening the context within which students make judgments and decisions for themselves. This process is progressive, dynamic, and cumulative, and it reaches a high point in self-reflection when students realize that it is their attentive, intelligent, reasonable, and responsible judgments and decisions that are progressively fashioning and shaping them, and that the opposite diminish and imprison them. And this realization is enhanced by students' remaining faithful to the truths and commitments that they have chosen and made. This is what distinguishes the truly autonomous and integral subject from the drifter.[124] Deciding and choosing, however, are one thing; carrying out a decision is another. Even deciding not to be a drifter is not enough; one may still drift: "making oneself is never finished in this life. One never knows how one's going to end up."[125]

IV.2 THE TEACHER AND THE GOOD AS THE DEVELOPING SUBJECT

While Lonergan's contribution to the vocation of the teacher is vast, particularly through their witness of authenticity, conversion, self-transcendence, and authentic subjectivity as the basis for authentic objectivity, it is worthwhile to focus on the teacher and the "human good as the developing subject."[126] Lonergan's definition of the good is lengthy, but given its educational implications, it is worth quoting in its entirety:

> The definition of the good that has been current since Aristotle is
> ... what everything seeks or runs after. However, it is not only *what*
> is sought or desired that is good; the capacity to desire is also good,
> and the desiring itself is good; and having the concrete situation
> in which the desiring can go to the operations through which one
> obtains the good is also good; and having the cooperation neces-
> sary to get there is also good. So one can see that not only what is
> sought is good, but also the seeking, the capacity to seek, skills
> that go into the process of fulfillment, and the fulfillment itself are

good. The definition of the good as what everything seeks does not exhaust the notion of the good. What everyone seeks is certainly good, but there is a whole set of other elements that are related to it, and they are good too.[127]

The teacher is witness to the good as developing subject, a good that is discovered by knowing and choosing what is true, and to know what is true requires one to be good.[128] The subject develops, but it is a precarious development: it involves a decision and the exercise of one's freedom, but the choosing is uncertain and unpredictable as the subject's knowledge is incomplete; one never fully knows the implications of one's decisions.[129] Choice and decision go beyond goals; they form habits and tendencies shaping the subject. While these habits enable one to act in the immediacy of a moment, they become ingrained and habitual. Decisions and choices shape the subject, and the shaping in turn depends upon previous decisions and choices.[130]

Human beings grow as subjects through their freedom and decisions. However, decisions are never free of uncertainty, as the subject does not know everything; knowing involves the risk of objects, the self, and others.[131] Being human is precarious; it includes progress today and failure tomorrow. Lonergan says that if the *rational* is simply understood as a pre-existing potency, it does not help explain how the rational dimension is necessary for the progress and growth of the authentic subject. In this sense, one is a rational being whether one is good or bad, wise or selfish.[132] As opposed to a general notion of rationality as a potential, there is the specific application that each person faces as to who one is, both individually and collectively. The awareness of such becoming is consciousness, "and not to be thought of as thinking about oneself. One is conscious no matter what one is thinking about. Consciousness means that one is *doing* the thinking."[133] There are different levels of consciousness – empirical, intellectual, rational – and while all of them ask different kinds of questions, knowing is related to doing, and it is the subject who does, chooses, and wills; the choice is personal, and this moves to a fourth level of consciousness, self-consciousness through willing and choosing.[134]

People see what they want to see and ignore the rest; they see what fits into their own horizons. Individually and collectively, horizons can be

limited, thus limiting and narrowing reality as it actually is.[135] Education includes acknowledging one's own world, and involves one's entry
into and participation in the wider world of community. Human beings
decide and choose with their own world as the background, shaped by
their experience, concerns, and interests, but these personal dimensions fall into the background through those intellectual traits of authentic and personal objectivity.[136] Education includes moving students
from their *worlds* to the *world*, but moving beyond a personal horizon,
circumscribed by the narrowness of one's own perspective, is never easy,
for moving to a wider horizon involves an expansion and reconstruction
of the self.[137] And while the increase and change of one's horizon may not
necessarily lead to personal growth, real growth is cumulative, building
on what one has learned, rejecting what is bad and compromises authenticity, and moving towards deeper growth.[138] As subjects develop,
their world changes, a world revealed in three ways. First is the world of
immediacy as revealed by the senses, a small aspect of the real. Next is
the world mediated by meaning, and third is a world not only mediated
but also embodied by meaning. This is the world of the subject, as the
first two are not freely chosen but given: "the free and responsible self-
constituting subject can exist only in a freely constituted world."[139]
Human beings engage in acts of transformation, and in this sense
meaning is essential for the cumulative constitution of the subject, and
it is here that human freedom makes its distinguishing mark.[140] Later,
Lonergan develops this understanding of meaning to include a fourth
level, above meaning, as constitutive to meaning as communicative.
Such communication is personal, artistic, symbolic, incarnational,
and rooted in one's subjectivity. As a result of this personal dimension,
meaning also becomes common, and education is one essential method
of communicating common meaning.[141]

The human good as developing subject means subjects moving from
the good understood narrowly in relation to the self to a broader, more
ordered good, which includes values, and values are realized in acts of
self-transcendence. The school prepares students, particularly adolescents, to come to self-possession as self-mastery, and to realize and
achieve this through their freedom. Lonergan concludes on the role of
the teacher in the context of a philosophy of education:

[T]he fundamental problem is the horizon of the educationalist
... and the horizon of the teacher. Insofar as their horizons are
insufficiently enlarged, there will be difficulties all along the line.
So the genuine function of a philosophy of education is to bring
the horizon of the educationalist to the point where he is not
living in some private world of educationalists, but in the universe
of being.[142]

Lonergan distinguishes between the universe of being and the real
world. If by the real world one means the sum of judgments that are true,
"then by definition the universe of being and the real world are identical
in all respects." However, Lonergan contrasts this with a world shaped
and defined by one's own particularities and biases, where judgments
and decisions are made from that narrow perspective; in that context,
the real world and the world of being are at odds. The universe of being is
concrete in that it is known through true judgments. For Lonergan, *being*
is not an abstract concept; it is known through true judgments. And to
know all there is to know about something in concrete terms is to know
being. Knowledge of being is not simply at the level of experience but
involves experience, understanding, and judgment.[143] For the student,
geometry exists in a book, but their study is meant to develop into an intellectual engagement with geometry that goes beyond a textbook. While
the textbook helps in the formality of communicating and expressing the
structures of geometry, the learning of geometry, or any other learning,
is situated in the student as a subject.[144] In an enlightening passage,
Lonergan contrasts the fixed principles and reasons in a manual outlining established procedures, definitions, and other terms that are set
in advance, with the internalized worldview of a person whose intelligence is freed by knowledge of the book, but whose understanding is
not bound to the book. Such a person knows how to adapt and to apply
what has been learned and understood to situations and contexts as they
change. What is required is the appropriation of what is contained in the
book, and thus knowing for oneself, but not being confined to the book.
In order to learn to do this, one needs a teacher: one who has understood
and is able to apply what is learned from a book by grasping what is essential and central.[145]

However, important as the cognitional dimension is to knowing, "to be authentically human is not just knowing; one has to deliberate, evaluate, decide, commit oneself; without motivation there is no commitment, and without commitment one just drifts."[146] And in this education is much more than simply a "matter of advancing in knowledge; it is also a matter of the refinement of one's feelings, creating a climate of discernment in which one can respond to values more fully, more exactly, more precisely."[147] However, authentic knowing and freedom have broader implications, for self-transcendence is not just individual nor unrelated to others. The subject also falls in love, and while falling in love is different for each subject and has different constituent parts, it forms a totality, a dynamic whole, which in turn influences the subject's judgments and choices and their thoughts and feelings.[148] Love is at the heart of conversion, for love leads and enables both the subject and the world to be transformed.[149] Through their knowing, seeking the good through authenticity, conversion, and self-transcendence, teachers are witnesses to a living and dynamic authenticity, without compromising the objectivity of truth.[150] The good, therefore, is not so external and so objectified that it lies independent of the transcendental principles. A catchy phrase reveals the error that "truth is so objective as to get along without minds."[151] This applies in equal measure to the good as developing subject, which is never independent of minds knowing and choosing and being converted through authentic judgments.

It is because Lonergan's contribution to the education and formation of the teacher is not conventional that it is demanding and challenging. In emphasizing the many complexities of the teaching profession, teacher education and formation are often easily forgotten. While both the documents and Maritain emphasize why it is that who the teacher is as a person is ultimately more important than what is taught (a conviction that requires delicate qualification), Lonergan's singular contribution to the vocation of the teacher is made through his detailed structure of the psychology, philosophy, and spirituality of what it means to be a truly self-conscious subject, and why and how this understanding of self-consciousness is so much wider than the narrow reduction of self-consciousness to introspection and the psychological trap of simply turning inwards. While such a structure is an invitation to enormous personal responsibility, it is also the source of a perennial and cumulative freedom.

Lonergan's call to conversion, transcendence, and an authentic subjectivity not only restores the vocational aspect of teaching to its rightful centre, but it also demystifies the view that teacher education is essentially confined to and completed in teachers' college, with the possibility of taking some additional professional courses over a teaching career. Important as this is, of course, Lonergan shifts the emphasis from teacher training that can be externally measured and accessed through a transcript or a certificate, to a much more demanding, but ultimately more rewarding, structure of authentic personal reflection and self-evaluation. Such an understanding not only defines teacher training as the education and formation of teachers, but it places a cyclical and perennial responsibility on the individual teacher and on the community of teachers regarding who they are, who they are becoming, and how that is ultimately far more influential and formative for their students and for the true purpose of education.

The professionalization of education can suggest that the teacher's decisions, choices, judgments, and actions can be easily identified through what is specified in the curriculum, school rules and regulations, and other legal, social, and cultural expectations made by school boards and the government. Again, the necessity of adhering to such practicalities can hardly be disputed or questioned. However, while the documents and Maritain certainly emphasize the being and the becoming of the teacher, Lonergan's contribution fills out not only why that being and becoming of the teacher as one who leads and guides is essential, but also how that being and becoming must be carried out in relation to knowledge and truth, and to encountering the world and what is real beyond the confines of a narrow empirical and material understanding of reality. The structure and process that he offers seem, at first glance, highly theoretical and seemingly abstract – quite the contrary. Educating teachers, either initially or though the course of their careers, according to Lonergan's structure, is certainly demanding, given its philosophical and theological nature. However, his contribution is especially important given the cultural diversity and religious plurality of today, and the accompanying inability to unify that diversity and plurality through a single consolidated narrative or worldview. In this context, the perennial being and becoming of authentic subjects offers a source of such unity, not through agreed-upon theoretical statements or creeds, but through the personal unity of the authentic teacher, and how that authenticity shapes and inspires the authenticity of the student.

V Conclusion

In our age when so much emphasis is placed upon teacher education and teacher training, it is refreshing to note that while the documents, Maritain, and Lonergan all understand the importance of professional and academic training, their emphasis is made from an anthropological and philosophical perspective, first in relation to the student as a person or as a subject, and second in relation to the unifying nature of the teacher's knowledge. The documents' claim that educators form persons is echoed, in its own way, by both Maritain and Lonergan, the former through the distinctions between the person and the individual, and how knowledge and learning are fundamental to the internal unity of the student, and the latter through his emphasis on authentic subjectivity, and on how such meaning is integral to the teacher with an eye to the future: students as future adults.

The witness of teachers is a theme that is found in the documents, Maritain, and Lonergan, and again each contributes to a Catholic philosophy of education by emphasizing different aspects of such witness. The documents keep the Catholic witness of the teacher clearly in mind, but increasingly the elasticity of this witness amidst religious diversity is seen as integral to the education of the whole person. In a seemingly information-hungry age, the conviction of *who* teaches in a Catholic school is primary and fundamental. However up-to-date the knowledge and learning of the teacher and the curriculum may be, teachers will fail to unify the student's learning or assist them in liberating themselves through knowledge and learning unless those teachers know and understand how and why their witness is vital, a witness that is primarily existential and lived. The witness of a teacher's life as expressed through the Catholic faith remains broadly educational, for while the split between Gospel and culture may sound narrowly Christian, it affects all believers in analogous ways. Similarly, the documents' emphasis on the teacher's role in the synthesis between faith and culture and between faith and life is equally educational for all students. The foundation of that synthesis lies in the personal unity and synthesis of the teacher's life. Furthermore, the synthesis emphasizes that religious faith and practice are to be realized in the transformation of the believer, individually and communally. Contemporary society has far too many atrocious and bloody examples where religious faith is confined in upon itself and its rituals, often at the expense of those who do not share in those beliefs. The documents stress that faith amidst diversity entails social, intellectual, cultural, and moral duties and responsibilities. Maritain contributes through the teaching of the charter, and through his expression of how, even though it focuses on practicalities, it can be integral to education amidst religious diversity. But it depends upon the convictions of teachers, not merely their intellectual convictions, but their religious and moral convictions as well.

Lonergan's contribution to the vocation and responsibility of the teacher is undoubtedly demanding because he does not approach the teacher's responsibilities in the usual and expected way: either how the teacher's educational and professional qualifications are manifested through their teaching, or how teachers overwhelmed amidst religious diversity and cultural plurality must accommodate all perspectives under the seemingly accommodating umbrella of tolerance. Lonergan demands a great deal from the teacher in the form of personal development and authenticity, intellectually, morally, and religiously. It seems that in every age, the advance of science and technology and the amount of new information put practical and utilitarian demands on education that fail to recognize the comprehensiveness of human knowing and learning. His call for self-transcendence, authenticity, conversion, and reflecting on one's intending and intentionality are all part of an anthropology of adulthood. But that call is also in response to the narrowing of vision that emerges through relentless empirical demands, often in fields other than science, and often leading to the dismissive view that many of the certainties and claims involving communal living are nothing more than personal opinions. Lonergan's transcendental method is empirical in a wider sense, for he confronts the limitations of subjectivity and objectivity narrowly conceived, saying that they are a figment and a distraction in avoiding the personal demands of authentic subjectivity and objectivity. Teachers bear witness to the truth through the authentic subjectivity of their lives. And their objective living it out is all the more necessary in a world divided by religion, where knowing – apart from what is narrowly empirical – is reduced to mere opinion or, at best, time-limited agreement.

Maritain's contribution to the vocation of the teacher might seem to have come to a chilling halt when he says that teachers can hardly be expected to rise above the limitations and biases of their society and culture. That, however, is maintained paradoxically, and he says that it is more a problem of culture than of education. Nonetheless, everything he says about the teacher's role in freeing the mind of the pupil to be articulate, autonomous, and free indicates that the freedom and the convictions of the teacher are what give them the claim to carry out an artistic endeavour – which is what teaching is – as well as providing their moral authority to teach. The transcendence that teachers offer their students will depend on the *why* and the *how* of knowing and learning, always, of course, united by the *what*. All this is vital for what Maritain refers to as the enlightenment of the intellect. In this regard, his distinction between the enlightenment of the intellect and the indirect formation of the will offers a perspective on education amidst religious and cultural diversity. However, the dynamism of intellectual enlightenment, far from being closed in on itself, is shown to be vibrant and alive and is realized through the convictions and witness of the teacher.

All three sources have essential contributions to make towards the education and formation of teachers, and the education of Catholic teachers faces cultural, social, moral, and intellectual challenges similar to those of teachers in other school systems. However, all three sources come at these challenges from a basis of knowing, understanding, choosing, and deciding as fundamentally educational and as being the source of the student's internal freedom; but they all depend upon the witness, the vocation, and the life of the teacher. All three stress that the *how* and *why* of teaching will be integral to whether education is narrowly conceived as preparation for the future, focusing on skills and professions, or whether it is seen as human transformation, which includes a future occupation or skill. Lonergan's understanding of the good, particularly the human good as the developing subject, stands beside Maritain's emphasis on teaching that witnesses to the freedom of life and the spirit over the passions and the senses. The document *Lay Catholics in Schools*

lays the ground for such an understanding of the good and such freedom
by developing what the lay and secular vocation of the Catholic teacher
means and must look like. Such a conception has come a long way from
the world being looked on with suspicion, as the source of temptation
and sin. Teachers are called to transform the secular order through the
witness and authenticity of their lives, and such a transformation has
implications for all students. What all three sources show is that while
such inspiration is certainly Christian, it has broader humanistic and
anthropological educational implications for communal living.

6

Society, Culture, and the
Common Good

I Introduction

The social and cultural dimensions of Catholic education find their roots
in the Council's documents. *Gaudium et Spes* refers to *the common good*
over thirty times.[1] There are frequent references to *society*, which is
never a completed project, and requires intentional and sustained vigilance to ensure human dignity.[2] Society is included as one of the three
orders – the others being the religious and moral orders – and the challenges to society undermine its foundations.[3] Finally, *Gaudium et Spes*
makes numerous references to *culture*, with chapter 2 of part 1 devoted
to "The Proper Development of Culture."

The first document from the CCE, *The Catholic School* (1977), refers to
Catholic education in a pluralist context. Subsequent documents refer
to education in the context of religious and cultural diversity: the growth
of society interacting with various forms of pluralism and contributing
to the diversity of human living. However, forces have arisen in the name
of pluralism and freedom that harm and diminish the student, such as
relativism, nihilism, and individualism. While the integral formation
of the student is the focus of the documents, it is carried out within a
particular society and particular cultures, and in the context of globalization. Later documents make culture, particularly the multi-religious
dimension of culture, their special focus, seeing diversity as a means
to enhance an integral education. There are frequent references to the
contribution that Catholic education offers to society in ensuring inter-
relational communion and fellowship. Catholic schools contribute to the

fabric of society, given their large number of non-Christian students, and to society, culture, and the common good, by preparing students as future active citizens committed to the communal renewal of society.

Society, culture, and the common good can appear, at first glace, to be removed, theoretical, and disengaged concepts. In fact, all three sources show why and how they are the living embodiment of who the human person is and grows into being. The documents show a steady progression from the changes that were brought in by the Council and the other social and moral concerns since then. The teachers must understand how and why the social nature of the student must be served through its intellectual mandate. Social and civic responsibility have moral and intellectual dimensions, which shape culture. Only the integral person, the moral and responsible person, enables the diversity and plurality of culture to be truly intelligible and life-giving. Maritain's social and political philosophy grounds his educational philosophy. While the social dimension of education is secondary, it has enormous implications, as society and the social dimension are essential elements in the realization of an integral personality. The common good protects against individualism and materialism. As well, human unity cannot be observed externally, but requires the transformation of minds and hearts, driven by the social nature of the person. Finally, for Lonergan, society, culture, and the common good are dependent on and shaped by who the subject is and is becoming through acts of self-transcendence and authenticity. The good is concrete, and realized through the authentic subject. The subject must move from the immediacy of the senses to thinking, reflecting, judging, and deciding. Thus culture is a way of living and choosing to live.

II The Documents of the CCE

II.1 CCE: CATHOLIC SCHOOLS IN A PLURALIST SOCIETY

Amidst diversity and plurality, the first document from the CCE recognizes the grave challenges that beset society in general and Catholic education in particular, such as the "relativism, materialism, pragmatism, and technocracy of contemporary society." However, in spite of these problems, Catholic education has a special role in "building up a secular society."[4] This strengthening of the mission of secular society gains increasing attention in later documents. The divisiveness of cultural pluralism necessitates assisting the young, through a Christian worldview, in growing in the virtues and the moral life, particularly given the societal emphasis on individual freedom. The documents are attentive to religious formation in the school, which is an essential part of the mandate of the CCE, especially "when a pluralist mentality dominates and the Gospel is pushed to the side-lines."[5] Later documents, however, include the religious nature of all students, and how growth in one's religious tradition and identity contributes to the overall strength of society, a community of persons who, given their transcendent nature and call, rise above the particularities of culture and society. However, the document *The Catholic School*, in paying special attention to values, to formation in self-control, to the ability to choose freely, and to students' ability to subject what they see and hear to a critical and personal analysis, attests to the wider societal contribution made by the Catholic school. Also of note is the recognition of parental rights in choosing a school for their children, and the acceptance of a diversity of schools representing the diversity of society.[6] Recognition of a variety of schools, including a religious variety, is not merely a nod to religious diversity but is an affirmation of schools forming persons, including their formation of the student's religious identity.

While the personal development of the individual student is fundamental, it is not apart from the social nature of the person, a nature that has a direct bearing on the educational community in particular and society in general. This social nature is not developed in a neutral school – which does not exist – but through a Christian conception of the person and life.[7] However, political, cultural, and social changes often make attending Catholic schools difficult, and there are many obstacles, including widespread poverty, that can prevent such schools from carrying out their mission.[8] The Catholic school prepares students for a scientific and technical society by providing them with the means, especially the intellectual means, for entry and participation into that society.[9] Such knowledge is vital, as new technologies have given rise to "questions concerning the future of human development. The vastness and depth of technological innovations influence the processes of access to knowledge, socialization, relations with nature and they foreshadow radical, not always positive, changes in huge sectors of the life of mankind."[10] This requires attention to the fundamental characteristics of a Catholic school, including offering oneself for the betterment of society and care for one's neighbour. Such care pertains to the nature of society in general, as well as to its particular cultural, political, and economic characteristics. The diversity of this approach, and its care in bringing together all the component parts of society into its educational vision, enables the Catholic school to be truly an integral and comprehensive form of education for the person.[11]

The school must be attentive to the cultural identity of the student, and to building a communal identity that rises above culture. While students must understand the inherent limits of any particular culture, they must remain open and receptive to other cultures. In the midst of diversity, the school must emphasize the world's cultural and intellectual patrimony, particularly the patrimony of values, and through this emphasis it must ensure ways of unifying persons, enabling them to grow as instruments of peace and harmony.[12] The school is an educational community and communion, and while this sense of communion is based on Christ, it has wider implications as a privileged context for educating the young in the "construction of a world based on dialogue and the search for communion, rather than on contrast; on the mutual acceptance of differences rather than on their opposition. In this way, with its educational project taking inspiration from *ecclesial communion and the civilization of love*, the Catholic school can contribute considerably to illuminating the minds of many, so that there will arise a generation of new persons, the moulders of a new humanity."[13] Such a civilization depends upon mutual understanding and respect. Education must include a respect not only for cultures but for religious identities as well, and so assist in dispelling fear and prejudice. Recognition of religious distinctiveness amidst religious diversity can assist in averting two negative outcomes of pluralism: "relativism and assimilation." Distinct religious identities, as well as all that binds human beings together, make for a healthy pluralism.[14] The theological foundation of the school includes a relational understanding of human beings: a vertical communion with God, and a horizontal communion with others. The anthropological foundation enables the human encounter wherein persons go beyond themselves to understand the other, an encounter that enhances personal identity. Human beings

cannot grow to the full stature of their integral humanity without as-
serting and manifesting themselves through their relational and social
nature.[15] The third foundation is pedagogical: persons encounter each
other, not cultures. Thus intercultural dialogue is neither disengaged
nor theoretical, but marked by a sense of care for the other. The other is
not isolated by virtue of a distinct culture, nor does the relative nature of
culture reduce the other's beliefs to an uncritical subjectivism. Rather,
the paradigm proposed "seeks, by every means, to foster a culture of dialogue, of understanding and mutual transformation, so as to reach the
common good."[16] A social dimension, which includes care for others,
for the cosmos, and for one's relationship with God, distinguishes the
anthropology of the Catholic school. The documents emphasize the role
that religious diversity plays in unifying the human family by drawing
attention to the social and communal dimensions of religious belief,
whereby religions can strengthen the fabric of a diverse society and the
social and relational unity of human beings. Education focuses on knowledge and learning, but on action as well, and in this it serves to secure
and build up society.[17] Thus the endorsement of the interreligious contribution of the Catholic school:

> Today, these establishments are found worldwide and the major-
> ity of their students come from different religious backgrounds,
> nations and cultures. However, students' confessional allegiances
> should not be seen as a barrier, but as a condition for intercultural
> dialogue, helping each pupil grow in their humanness, civic
> responsibility and learning.[18]

Education and schooling must be carried out amidst new social and
cultural challenges, exacerbated by the inherent divisiveness and dis-
unity that can mark pluralist societies, particularly in one's moral and
personal life. In addition, there are the challenges of globalization, mass
migration, rapid societal changes, the unparalleled growth of science
and technology, the disparity between the rich and the poor, and a crisis
of personal and communal values. The sheer breadth of these forces
contributes to undermining "any idea of community identity."[19] The
Catholic school serves society and the common good by not envisaging
students as passive recipients.[20] In order to assist students to understand

what they see, hear, and encounter in various forms of culture, teachers must accompany students, enabling them to make judgments that are truly life-giving and worthy of their dignity.[21] Students must "pass from simple and passive consumers to critical interlocutors, capable of positively influencing public opinion and even the quality of information."[22] Amidst the various forces that pull at the individual unity of the student, education must pay special attention to strengthening the personality of students, enabling them to make moral decisions and choices that are personal and free.[23]

II.2 CCE: EDUCATION, THE COMMON GOOD, AND SOCIETY

The documents do not define the common good, but refer to it in the context of the social and relational dimensions of human nature. The *Catechism of the Catholic Church* defines the common good as "the sum total of social conditions which allow people, either as a group or individuals, to reach their fulfillment more fully or more easily. The common good concerns the life for all. [And] it consists of *three essential elements*: first, *respect for the person*; second, the *social well-being* and *development* of the group itself; finally, *peace*, that is the stability and security of a just order."[24] Noteworthy is that the common good needs the political order for its realization, and it is always "oriented towards the progress of persons. The order of things must be subordinate to the order of persons, and not the other way around. This order is founded on truth, built up in justice, and animated by love."[25]

Education is an essential contributor to the common good.[26] And in order for education to contribute to the common good, it depends upon the establishment of schools and institutions of learning.[27] Given the challenges that are posed by individualism, the common good must contribute to shaping the evolution of society. In a pluralist world, Catholic education, secured upon the Gospel, collaborates with those who are seeking to build a new world "freed from a hedonistic mentality and from the efficiency syndrome of modern consumer society."[28] In the face of forces that impede human participation and coexistence, the school has a privileged task in preparing future adult citizens to build a society "in which structures of power give way to structures of cooperation, with a view to the common good."[29] While the common good is best realized in political society, educating for the common good is never apart from the citizen's transcendent nature as a person, and religious and moral education are integral parts of such preparation. These dimensions of education ensure the harmony between faith and culture. In attending to the personal and social dimensions of life, moral and religious education makes important contributions to the common good.[30] Through their truths, systems, and practices, religions draw attention to the social dimensions of life, and how the believer, personally and collectively, contributes to the common good. Religions proclaim that human beings are created by God, and thus inherently motivate believers towards dialogue and the recognition of all that binds the human family together. The educational value of dialogue stretches further as it seeks to discover the common and unifying ethical and moral truths found in different religions. This further strengthens working for the common good and seeking justice and peace. Such a unifying culture of dialogue enables the believer to grow in self-awareness, which is another contribution to the common good.[31] The mandate of the Catholic school includes the religious moral formation of students, as well as their personal and social growth, and the duties and responsibilities of citizenship, all essential in building up the common good.[32] So the documents call on civil authorities to work for the common good by protecting public morality, particularly that of the young.[33] Given the importance placed on dialogue and mutual understanding between students as religious believers, it would seem the documents recognize, however implicitly, the centrality of religious instruction for all students, each according to their tradition, though this is never stated explicitly. Such a provision would surely further strengthen the communal, pedagogical bonds that are formed by working and collaborating for the common good of a society composed of transcendent human persons. For, in ultimate terms, the citizen is never just a citizen.

The Church affirms a diversity of school systems where the young are "formed by value judgments based on a specific view of the world and to be trained to take an active part in the construction of a community through which the building of society itself is promoted."[34] The diversity of religions and various forms of human freedom characterizes a pluralist society. In the face of religious diversity, the pedagogical vision of the Catholic school promotes communal solidarity based on personal identity. The communal and personal dimensions constitute the school community, a united community where individual identities, far from being submerged, are recognized.[35] Thus the vision arises of moving beyond a united community to the human race as a single family:

> All of humanity is alienated when too much trust is placed in merely human projects, ideologies and false utopias. Today humanity appears much more interactive than in the past: this shared sense of being close to one another must be transformed into true communion. The development of peoples depends, above all, on a recognition that the human race is a single family working together in true communion, not simply a group of subjects who happen to live side by side.[36]

By recognizing the dignity of each individual student, the Catholic school plays its part in moving beyond religious and cultural differences to all that binds a diverse student body as human persons marked by personal dignity and united by their common humanity, who contribute to society and are bound upon a common human journey.[37] Dialogue is therefore intrinsic to human nature. Not only are human beings relational, they cannot live without love, which, "freed from egoism, is the way *par excellence* to fraternity and reciprocal help towards perfection among people ... Love is the strongest, most authentic and most desired bond, which unites people ... and makes them listen to one another ... love is the method and goal of life itself ... and [through self-sacrifice] the sublime and necessary path to spiritual and social change and renewal."[38]

Inspired by the Gospel, Catholic educators shoulder a social and civic responsibility in preparing students to become active citizens, engaged in and working for the betterment of the social and civic orders. So the renewal of the temporal order remains a special vocation of lay Catholic teachers.[39] A healthy school milieu is one essential way of enhancing the common good. The documents are aware of the various forces that beset society; they strike at the very integrity and dignity of the student, as well as at the welfare of society and the common good.[40] Christians must, therefore, engage in the transformation of the social order. The perennial slavery of sin does not just bear down on the person as a religious believer, but because of the social and communal nature of the person, it also weighs heavily upon the cultural, social, and political dimensions of life.[41] The world is the stage upon which to respond to Christ's call to follow him: "to live and work in history, without however allowing oneself to be imprisoned in it. Hope demands insertion in the world, but also separation [and] withdrawing in order to educate the children of God to freedom in a context of influences that lead to new forms of slavery."[42] Responsible citizenship requires going beyond the law to the "spirit of the law ... precisely in the measure that the law is at the service of the common good and puts everyone in a condition of reciprocity. Therefore, a community's identity is mature to the extent that it takes on and continually and faithfully seeks to renew the values of co-operation and solidarity."[43] In the context of plurality and diversity, the documents are concerned with those foundational issues that shape human existence; thus the added emphasis on the educational value of teaching students the importance of good and virtuous judgments, and the choices that flow from such judgments.[44]

II.3 CCE: EDUCATION AND CULTURE

The comprehensive definition of culture in article 53 of *Gaudium et Spes* is summarized in another document as the "particular way in which persons and peoples cultivate their relationship with nature and their brothers and sisters, with themselves and with God, so as to attain fully human existence. Culture only exists through man, by man, and for man. It is the whole of human activity, human intelligence and emotions, the human quest for meaning, human customs and ethics. Culture is so natural to human beings that they can only be revealed through culture."[45] In such a context, multiculturalism is critiqued as being unable to offer a real model of what communal human unity means in the face of diversity and plurality. Multiculturalism offers no measurement or evaluation of culture, of distinguishing between what is life-giving and what is not. It leads to relativism, which stands at the opposite side of the relational and dialogical aspects of social life.[46] There is the formative and emphatic assertion that diverse cultures reveal human nature more clearly.[47] However, the human condition is "located between universality and particularity."[48] Culture, too, exists between these poles of universality and particularity as it concerns individual persons and their integral development as whole persons, but it also serves the wider communal dimension in promoting a new humanism, marked by care and responsibility for the other. Thus culture is at the service of the integrity and dignity of the person as well as of society.[49]

Gaudium et Spes states that "the Church, sent to all peoples of every time and place, is not bound exclusively and indissolubly to any race or nation, any particular way of life or any customary way of life recent or ancient."[50] However, the difference between *culture as relative* and *relativism* is crucial. The historical and changeable nature of reality does not, in and of itself, advocate relativism.[51] So the complexity of the cultural situation, particularly cultural pluralism, provides opportunities and challenges to the relationship between faith and culture. This relationship includes a personal and communal appropriation, reminding us that "a faith that does not become a culture is a faith not fully accepted, not entirely thought out, not faithfully lived."[52] This understanding is the very opposite of religion or faith closed in upon itself and ghettoizing its followers. It is a relationship that recalls and serves the divine plan for the human race and the action of God in history: "this task requires the courage of testimony and the patience of dialogue; it is a duty before the cultural tendencies that threaten the dignity of human life, especially in the crucial moments of its beginning and its ending, the harmony of creation, and the existence of peoples and peace."[53] This requires clarity on the part of those responsible for education:

> A time emerges in which to process answers to the fundamental questions of the young generations and to present a clear cultural proposal that clarifies the type of person and society ... which it is desired to educate, and the reference to the anthropological vision inspired by the values of the gospel, in a respectful and constructive dialogue with the other concepts of life.[54]

As culture is ever-changing, either positively or negatively, the human relationship with culture is dynamic and heuristic, and it is communal. Consecrated persons have a special counter-cultural role in society in general and in the school in particular. Such men and women work in local situations and understand their immediate culture and context, but they also witness and apply the broader evangelical and humanistic principles of the Gospels and the Church's social and moral teachings locally and according to the particularities of their ministry. Through such dialogue, relationship, and interaction with culture, consecrated persons can offer students the example of being immersed in history and in one's context, strengthened by all that constitutes the Christian life, including the primacy of conscience and the strength of prayer. These dispositions enable the person to view the created order and the realities of the world from a Christian perspective. It is a contemplative stance, one distinguished from the frantic pace and the instrumentalist ideology that marks and disfigures modern living.[55] Such dispositions also stand in relation to more particular educational dispositions:

> Through study and research a person contributes to perfecting himself and his humanity. [Apart from the other benefits] knowledge can help to motivate existence, begin the search for God, it can be a great experience of freedom for truth, placing itself in the service of the maturation and promotion of humanity.[56]

The mission of consecrated persons in Catholic schools also serves to promote intercultural dialogue. Such persons belong to religious orders spread across the world, whose members are well versed in local contexts and histories and other social and cultural particularities. In this they play a special role in understanding the lived reality of human dignity and all that challenges and compromises it. The issue of global migration, so pertinent today, requires more than the model of multiculturalism; it requires dialogue and mutual understanding, as well as acknowledging the limits of any one culture.[57] In the context of such pronounced diversity, an education marked by openness, dialogical relationship, and a focus on life as a community of persons will not be easy. Cultural differences and conflicts are exacerbated by perceptions of cultural superiority, and new forms of individualism, atheism, and materialism further complicate this.[58] Cultures, like human beings, are marked by sin and are in need of being restored, redeemed, and thus serving the human person. The integrity and authenticity of culture are always judged in relation to its service to the human person.[59]

Among other things, the school prepares students to make good and life-giving judgments, and to do so in the context of cultural diversity. While culture must be critiqued and evaluated, it depends upon human dynamism for its growth and perfection. Culture is communicated and appropriated through the personal contact of teachers and students.[60] The Christian worldview includes an understanding of *communion*, and thus of the relational nature of persons and their ensuing reality. The notion of communion is twofold: vertically with God and horizontally with others.[61] Thus the Council calls for a new humanism where persons are responsible for history and to each other. The challenges of cultural diversity makes the education of the whole person all the more urgent, and yet the Church calls for a healthy appropriation of diversity as an essential means of realizing this new humanism, and it looks to education for leadership.[62] One of the prime responsibilities of culture is for an integral education, and in this respect, education goes beyond intellectual knowledge.[63]

A chronological reading of the educational documents reveals an increasing emphasis on the social and communal dimensions of education. While the seeds of this development are sown in the Council's documents, the progressive expansion of this theme attests to the urgency of the matter. However, what the documents offer is not a wholesale acceptance of diversity for diversity's sake, a smorgasbord of choices, but instead they see cultural and religious diversity as various forms of human expression in the perennial search for meaning and values. The documents, of course, keep their primarily Catholic focus and attention, but through this focus they show how the Catholic school, through its intellectual mandate, serves to draw out the greater meaning and values that religious diversity offers. The tone of the documents changes as the world has changed, and this new emphasis offers the world the educational and social patrimony of the Church, all in the service of meaning, value, and human dignity.

The educational documents are strengthened by the rich patrimony of the Church's teachings on society, culture, and the common good. This enables the Catholic school to give pedagogical reasons why education is more than instruction or preparing students for the narrow confines of future employment. The *common good* is a term associated with Catholics.

The documents offer a rich commentary on how the common good is to be conceived, and how it must be contributed to and built up, a perennial task. The claim that the common good needs the political and civic orders for its realization shows that it is not just a conceptual, theoretical category. It involves dialogue, mutual respect, the giving of the self, and the recognition that human beings are relational in nature. The documents' critique of an unreflective and undifferentiated multiculturalism shows that human dignity and the search for meaning and values in life are not served by celebrating diversity without reflection. Much more is required before the value of diversity can be affirmed. That begins with how various forms of diversity serve human nature and human freedom, as well how those gifts can also be compromised by diversity.

The intrinsic relationship between culture and education is another noteworthy theme. Today, the relationship can be polarized: either it is the ubiquitous culture of the Internet and other forms of electronic communication, or culture is limited to particular forms of social, geographical, and religious expression. The documents see culture as the sum total of human expression in living life at its deepest and most meaningful levels. Culture exists in the traditions that are handed down, but culture is also constantly being newly constituted and created. And while the particularities of cultures are essential (as human expressions depend upon such particularities), they are nourished and made whole by attending to the more universal themes of human living that enable culture to be at the service of the liberation and freedom of the person. The Catholic school emphasizes the relationship between culture and education though its intellectual mandate – that is, by enabling students to think, understand, judge, and decide how meaning and values shape their lives, and how they must become active agents in deciding what shape those lives take. In calling for a new humanism, the documents call for new ways of thinking about one's self. Knowledge and learning are in relation to action, but knowledge and learning also serve the relational and communal natures of the student as a person.

This leads smoothly to Maritain's position on society, culture, and the common good. While he insists on the primacy of the intellectual mandate of the school, it is this mandate that serves the secondary, though vital, social and communal nature of education. But in spite of this qualification, he shows how an education that did not know how to serve society, culture, and the common good would fail in its claim to educate.

III   The Contribution of Jacques Maritain

III.1   EDUCATION, SOCIETY, AND THE PERSON

Maritain's social and political philosophy pervades his works; he was instrumental in the realization of *The Universal Declaration of Human Rights*. His educational philosophy is a delicate balance between the intellectual mandate of the school and the social nature of the person. While education is not primarily concerned with "adapting a potential citizen to the conditions and interactions of social life, but first in *making a man*," however, "one does not make a man except in the bosom of social ties where there is an awakening of civic understanding and civic virtues."[64] The person's relationship to society is natural as it provides for a variety of needs, including those of "material, intellectual and moral life,"[65] but also for human nature and the realization of reason and freedom.[66] One way that persons realize their social nature is through intelligence and love. So while the ultimate end of education concerns "personal life and spiritual progress," the secondary aim of education is social in nature.[67] Thus the balance of the social dimension of education:

As a result, it is obvious, that man's education must be concerned with the social group and prepare him to play his part in it. Shaping man to lead a normal useful and cooperative life in the community, or guiding the development of the human person in the social sphere, awakening and strengthening both his sense of freedom and his sense of obligation and responsibility, is an essential aim. But it is not the primary, it is the secondary essential aim.[68]

In the seeming divisions between the social and individual dimensions of education, education has a decided social and communal role; it must emphasize "freedom and ... responsibility, human rights and human obligations, the courage to take risks and exert authority for the general welfare and the respect for the humanity of each individual person."[69] The curriculum is not an exclusively literary education – given Maritain's emphasis on the dignity of manual work – nor is everything learned in schools; there is much to learn that lies outside books or lectures, essential though they are. Education is not activism, but involves being and becoming somebody by virtue of one's ontological and rational nature.[70] Included in this learning *to be* is the place of leisure, which is related not only to the personal dimensions of life and growth as a spiritual being, but also to the person's life in the social and political spheres.[71] Accordingly, the school is not only where teaching occurs; it also has decided communitarian and social dimensions.[72] A more challenging assertion is that "teachers have neither to make the school into a stronghold of the established order nor to make it into a weapon to change society." Maritain reminds us that education is primarily intellectual and not social in nature. The prime purpose of the school is teaching students how to think, and hence to allow them "to become articulate, free, and autonomous."[73] And it is the democratic charter that is an essential part of such preparation. There is a balance between the status quo and change in society, which Maritain proposed in the context of the Second World War, where peace had to be established in society itself. For Maritain, peace would ultimately be realized when citizens were actively engaged in the transformation and the healing of their war-torn world. It would require an effort that had moral, social, and political dimensions, building society through greater human unity.[74]

The social dimension of education is grounded in human nature, and while part of freedom is won in the social and political orders, persons transcend the world, and being created in the image and likeness of God, they seek their satisfaction beyond the limits of society. And yet, human beings need and depend upon the society that provides for their needs.[75] Here again is a balance: persons constitute society and transcend it, while individuals needs society which is greater than them.[76] As earthly society is composed of persons who are not purely spiritual in nature, but rather a combination of spiritual and material individuality, so human beings need society, and upon entering into society, become members of a whole, which is superior and more perfect than its individual parts. However, it is by virtue of being a person, one whose personality is increasingly perfected in society, that one seeks to be a member of society. Nevertheless, it is because of the person's relationship with God and divine destiny that the person transcends and is higher than all forms of earthly societies.[77] Maritain's balance between the individual and the person results in the realization that both the individual and the person need society. The individual needs society for their more material and earthly needs, while the person's social and relational perfections can only be realized in society, and such perfection is ultimately spiritual in nature. Accordingly, a liberal and humanistic education can never be restricted to a few, the privileged, but must be made available to all because of the role that such an education plays in building and contributing to the ongoing civilization of society and the health of a vibrant and thriving democracy.[78] As the Church's documents emphasize the importance of the secular order for human perfection and realization, so too does Maritain, where persons, through their knowledge and love, come to greater internal and spiritual freedom, and are thus able to offer themselves to others and so build up society.[79] Society is a source of human freedom, not simply freedom of choice, but of expansion or autonomy, freedom that is ultimately realized in the moral and rational life of the person.[80] While the structures of society depend upon justice, "the internal creative force of society depends upon civic friendship."[81] In sum, society is more than the work of human reason; it also depends upon the intellectual and spiritual characteristics of the persons who form it.[82] Education is thus placed within this wider understanding of the nature and purpose of society and its relationship to human flourishing.

III.2 EDUCATION, CULTURE, AND THE COMMON GOOD

Maritain opens a work on the common good by asking: "does society exist for each one of us, or does each one of us exist for society?"[83] The answer is found in the distinction between the person and the individual. Social life is meant to free human beings from the constraints of matter and to place the individual in the service of the common good. The individual is subordinated to the common good "in order that the common good flow back upon the individuals, and that they enjoy that freedom of expansion or independence which is ensured by the economic guarantees of labour and ownership, political rights, civil virtues, and the cultivation of the mind."[84] The end of a materialistic and narrow individualism calls for a living connection between human beings and society, where the common good is truly a communal enterprise. Such individualism is not replaced by the extremes of a collectivist political ideology, such as totalitarianism or communism, but is enabled by recognizing the nature of the citizen as a person, a social and relational being.[85] Thus, among the principal and secondary aims of education is preparing students for participatory citizenship and working for the common good.[86] While an authentic common good recognizes the primacy of the person, it is more than a collection of individual goods gathered together.[87] The end of society is "neither the individual good nor the collection of individual goods of the persons who constitute it." The end of society, then, is a good that is social in nature and based upon the dignity of the person. So the common good is neither the totality of individual goods nor the good of the whole. Rather, "it is the good *human* life of the multitude, of a multitude of persons; it is the communion in good living. It is … common to *the whole and the parts* into which it flows back and which, in turn, must benefit from it."[88] An important inclusion in this definition is that "the common good is at once material, intellectual, and moral, and principally moral, as man himself is; it is a common good of persons."[89] While the temporal order is an end in itself, it is subordinated to the absolute ultimate end of the human person, union with God, and beyond time.[90]

This synopsis of the common good leads to its relationship with culture and civilization in the context of the diversity of modern living, where people who live in proximity to each other are no longer unified by a single creed or culture. Maritain uses the terms "civilization" and "culture" interchangeably, and says that a civilization is only worthy of its title if it is a truly human culture marked by the intellectual, moral, and spiritual dimensions – *spiritual* used in the widest sense. For Maritain, only a person is a cultured being, one in possession of a personality who has moved beyond the confines of nature, and who is marked by reason, and shaped by the intellectual and moral virtues.[91] He sees culture as the labour of "reason and virtue," and in answering to the "fundamental aspirations of human nature … it is the work of spirit and liberty."[92] And given its moral aspect, it includes a religious dimension. While historically religions have unified cultures and societies, in the new secular order Christians must now work for the transformation of the world as the stage for a fully human and authentic life, marked by justice, love, and the protection of human dignity. The temporal city is now distinguished by a secular creed, and while no longer united religiously, it is bound by the common desire to shape the temporal order so as to uphold human dignity and the continued flourishing of the person *qua* person, and thus, indirectly, to serve the transcendental nature of persons.[93] However, Maritain's pluralist principle is distinct from nineteenth-century liberalism, as it includes ethical and religious dimensions. Applying the principle of proportionality, Maritain says that the liberties of the pluralist city are not identical or equal. However, the unity of such a city is bound by friendship.[94] Nevertheless, on its own, friendship will not unify or shape a pluralist society, and particularly will not ensure the ethical dimensions of society, nor render religious plurality intelligible; without them there is no common good.[95] So civil society is not characterized by the freedom of choice of each citizen, but by their choosing the temporal common good.[96] In this temporal order, the end of society, the state, and politics is the common good.[97] Maritain decries how the economic and political orders have been diminished by a material and physical mindset. For "politics and economics are not as physical sciences, but as branches of ethics, the science of human actions."[98] This way of conceiving the temporal order has been inspired by Christianity and will depend upon the convictions of Christians for its realization, not in a creedal sense, but in safeguarding the secular order for the flourishing of human persons amidst religious diversity.[99] Thus a broad definition of culture:

> But culture itself consists in knowing *how* and *why* to use these things for the good of the human being and the securing of his liberty. Culture is essentially the inner forming of man. This forming is achieved by the development [of the] virtues, virtues of the mind, and virtues of the heart ... Culture implies the pursuit of human happiness, but it requires also that we know in what this happiness consists ... Culture implies the possessing of the means of liberty, but first it implies being inwardly free.[100]

III.3 HUMAN UNITY AMIDST DIVERSITY

Maritain's emphasis on the unity of the human race is not based on a post-war sentimentality or the desire for a utopia, but upon a philosophical humanism. He cautions that citizenship education and social behaviour are overemphasized at the expense of "justice, love, and integrated knowledge."[101] Natural morality is at home in the political, social, and civic spheres; persons must win their freedom in these orders, and thus transcend the confines of the natural and material orders.[102] In such a society, freedom of choice is not directed at "dominion over the external order of nature and history, but towards the realization and progress of the spiritual freedom of individual persons [making] justice and friendship foundations of social life."[103]

Communal and personal dimensions mark such a political philosophy, given that the good of civil society is more than a collection of particular or individual goods. Human beings are material and spiritual, possessed of individuality and personality, a unity of spirit, but a unity that is delicate and uncertain, and requires the inner spiritual dynamism of the person to move forward.[104] The individual needs society, however, and while the cumulative perfection of personality is realized in social and political society, "each person is a part or member of political society but not to the whole extent of his being and his existence."[105] So personal and communal unity also require a balance and a relationship of virtues, reason, and freedom.

The unity of the human race, and its equality and inequality, can be viewed through three lenses: nominalist (empiricist), idealist, and realist – realizing that equality can never be "visibly perceived because it is something perceivable only to the intellect."[106] Nominalism and empiricism deny the equality of nature, as opposed to the idealist's "deification of this equality."[107] Then there is a Christian realist position: "the equality in nature among men consists of their concrete communion in the mystery of the human species; it does not lie in an idea, it is hidden in the heart of the individual and of the concrete, in the roots of the substance of each man."[108] With every act of service and help to others, in reaching out to our neighbours, human beings understand our common human nature and the propensity towards goodness; Maritain asks poignantly: "How could we all be called upon thus to love one another in God if we were not all equal in our condition and specific dignity as rational creatures?"[109] Christian realism recognizes inequalities in human nature, but equality, by virtue of rational nature, is greater than the inequalities that are secondary.[110] What is lacking through social inequalities is made up through distributive justice, realizing that while "social inequalities proceed from society more than from nature … social equality proceeds from nature more than from society."[111] Equality must be realized through reason and freedom, and though inspired by Christianity, a new secular and integral humanism depends upon reason and freedom.[112]

So Maritain calls for *fellowship* rather than *tolerance*, and the place of friendship in the civic and social spheres. Maritain laments a world divided by racial and social prejudices that hinder personal human cooperation.[113] Religious believers are called to serve each other through social cooperation, seeking justice, the appropriation of goodness, and the defense of truth.[114] Based on analogical similarities and practicalities, Maritain calls for unity amidst religious diversity, not a philosophical or a theological, theoretical unity, but the unity of friendship and fellowship realized in the common pursuits of daily life, recognizing that there will be some disagreement. And how will such unity come about without some doctrinal agreement? A force more primordial than religious or philosophical concordance unifies human beings. It is the rational nature that is held in common, one that is more ancient than doctrinal unity; it is a common rational nature that is intellectually attracted to the same objects: the practical details and necessities of life, given flesh in a community of persons, and based upon an "analogical likeness of practical thought."[115] The good, of course, can always be manipulated and employed for something other than what is truly good. The human search for meaning has various and different expressions, and thus the search for a unity of doctrinal or philosophical thought will always prove to be fruitless. Yet in spite of this, human beings can be united around practical decisions and actions. Thus human cooperation can be secured upon an "analogical likeness between the practical principles ... in the acceptance of the law of love, and corresponding to the primary inclinations of human nature."[116] Maritain closes his essay "Who Is My Neighbour?" very movingly:

[God permits] religious divisions ... for the education of mankind, and in order to prepare them for final religious unity ... the Kingdom of God is that of a spiritual, supernatural, supra-racial, supra-national, supra-earthly community, open to all humanity ... Much suffering and many purifications throughout human history are necessary to extricate us from any restrictions and adulterations of spiritual unity brought about by fleshly unities.[117]

Unity in the practical order also serves the theoretical order and eases the divisions of theoretical and doctrinal differences.[118] The fact that God permits human diversity is placed in relation to the realization that all human beings are children of God.[119] However, a community of persons is truly respectful when one can follow one's conscience and religious convictions but also recognize the other's right to disagree, not because they are exempt from truth, but because they live by other truths.[120] Maritain's convictions of the unity of fellowship and friendship, amidst sharp doctrinal disagreements, are instructive for our day: "There is real and genuine tolerance only if we fully respect the right to exist, and speak his mind, of him who we are fully convinced is in error. Intolerance is created not by the essence of the absolute, but by the instinct of domination and the loss of the sense of transcendence."[121]

Maritain's contribution to education in the context of society, culture, and the common good is significant, given that the strength of its emphasis is displayed against the backdrop of the fact that the social dimension of education is a secondary aim of education, but a necessary secondary aim. It is particularly beneficial to read the later educational documents through a Maritainian lens. The documents emphasize how the context of religious and cultural diversity can serve human unity, and draw attention to all that binds the human race, offering humanity a more profound and personal way of imagining the social and temporal orders. Maritain's social and political analysis makes a formidable contribution not only for a renewed emphasis on friendship and cooperation, but for how coming to an integral understanding of human equality is not something that can be externally or empirically observed, but is the work of reason, virtue, and freedom. In the midst of world conflicts and divisions, especially those in the name of religion or culture, Maritain offers a way of looking at the world, and the perennial development of society, culture, and the common good, as a developmental path that would require the active, intentional, and moral agency of each citizen. The secular state cannot take the place of such agency, and the school must show students why.

Another significant contribution that Maritain makes, especially when culture, society, and the common good are diminished by envisaging them as being only tangible, externally verified, and material – though, of course, the practical dimensions of cooperation include these external and material dimensions – is how he understands the role of free will (freedom of choice) and how it must grow and be liberated into a more integral dimension of human freedom: that is, freedom as personal autonomy and independence. Further, such a development of personal freedom is then related back to society, culture, and the common good. Again, this requires the intentional agency and judgment of the student as a person, which in turn shapes how that person comes to see the religiously and culturally other. The secular nature of modern society could be left at the level of secularity as the confused collection of irreconcilable diversity and differences kept in check only by laws and regulations. Or, the secular nature of society could be envisaged as the arena where persons not only grow in their understanding of religious diversity and cultural difference, but, through their practical cooperation, liberate themselves through friendship, justice, protecting human dignity, and the quest for peace, which are all in service of the transcendent and spiritual nature of the citizen as a person.

Finally, there is a matter that weighs heavily on the world today: religious differences and their association with violence. Here again, like the other issues in Maritain's social and political offerings for an integral education, the emphasis will be on the intentionality and agency of the citizen – that is, the student as a future citizen. It is a way of seeing oneself anew, and Maritain frames this as transforming one's own metaphysical and ontological *being* into the *becoming* of active agency and intentional choices, judgments, and living. This movement from one's *being* to one's *becoming* is never achieved in any one act or one stage of life. It is a perennial movement of growth and personal development. And in this growth and movement, culture, society, and the common good are both shaped and liberated.[122] All this leads to Lonergan's understanding of being and becoming, and their relation to education.

IV The Contribution of Bernard Lonergan

IV.1 EDUCATION, COMMUNITY, AND HUMAN BECOMING

For Lonergan, society, culture, and the common good are concrete and realized through acts of self-transcendence leading to authenticity and enhancing human freedom. As they are realized in concrete, living, and manifested choices and judgments, education must attend to the "development of the individual up to the level of the times," which, as previously stated, is supported by a philosophy of education serving the concrete development of the individual and society, rather than by philosophy as timeless truths.[123] The human good is concrete and changes through the ages, so *society*, *school*, and the *good* are interrelated.[124] From the Christian perspective there are "three differentials: intellectual development on the level of civilization and culture; sin, contradicting, deforming both these types of development; and finally redemption. That analysis of the good, of course, makes it obvious why we want Catholic education ... [and why] the good cannot prescind from the tension between good and evil."[125] This is another reason why philosophy must be concrete, as the good is concrete; and another indication of how such a philosophy shapes the transformation of society and human living in its historical context. Such concrete living makes possible a series of other applied philosophies such as the philosophies of economics, politics, science, sociology, and, of course, education.[126]

Learning moves beyond the immediacy of the senses; it includes perceiving, and it is essential for the education of the whole person.[127] Such an education must be focused on human living, which "is a struggle for meaning, an effort, because meaning is constituent of human living. The effort to live is fundamentally the struggle for meaning."[128] Education must be responsible for transmitting common meaning, but it is meaning that grows, increases, and transforms the subject, or else it diminishes and distorts the subject.[129] However, Lonergan says that while there has been a growth and increase in meaning, and in understanding meaning, there has not been similar attention to judging meaning. And while understanding is generally communal, it is the individual who must be able to judge and decide. New knowledge and information pour forth relentlessly, leaving much for the individual to learn before judging, "yet judge he must and decide he must, if he is to exist, if he is to be a man."[130] Individuals and societies develop but also decline; individual and group egoism, biases, and alienation contribute to this decline.[131]

One's understanding of education is related to one's understanding of community, and community has to do with common meaning, and common meaning is realized through common agreement in judgments, either what is affirmed or what is denied. Commonality is rejected when one withdraws from common judgments, rejecting what is held as true or false. It is within common meaning, however, that individuals are born and grow, and where individuals decide what to make of them-selves. One of the common tasks in the search for meaning is education, but for human beings it is the existential dimension of growing as an au-thentic subject.[132] Lonergan's understanding of community has parallels with Maritain's understanding of the common good.

> Community is not an aggregate of individuals within a frontier, for that overlooks its formal constituent, which is common meaning. Such common meaning calls for a common field of experience and, when that is lacking, people get out of touch ... It calls for common judgments and, when they are lacking, people reside in different worlds. It calls for common values, goals and policies and, when they are lacking, people operate at cross-purposes. The genesis of meaning is an ongoing process of communication, of people coming to share the same cognitive, constitutive, and effective meanings.[133]

Common meaning shapes society, a systematic and methodical pur-suit of subjects seeking a common goal. A fear that this may lead to a ma-terialistic notion of society is countered by the structure of the human good.[134] Like Maritain, Lonergan sees human cooperation as essential in society, giving form to the social dimension. However, while society is a wide association, "the ideal basis of society is community, and the com-munity may take its stand on a moral, a religious, or a Christian prin-ciple. The moral principle is that men individually are responsible for what they make of themselves, but collectively they are responsible for the world in which they live. Such is the basis of universal dialogue."[135] Thus: "the annual crop of infants is a potential invasion of barbarians, and education must be conceived as the first line of defense."[136]

The world is more than a collection of objects; it is the stage of the subject's judging, acting, and deciding, all of which are historically con-ditioned by past and present.[137] Subjects are led by "their own inter-subjectivity both to satisfy their own appetites and to help others in the attainment of their satisfaction; but neither type of activity is necessarily egoistic or altruistic."[138] The roots of egoism lie not in intersubjectivity or a detached intelligence on their own, but emerge through the resulting tension and the realization that an authentic self-love is only possible when it is governed by virtue and wisdom.[139] And thus the primacy of the principle that the "subject communicates not by saying what he knows but by showing what he is."[140] Such self-constitution is concerned less with universal truths and more with the free choices and judgments of the subject that shape and form who they are and who they are becoming.[141] Recall Lonergan's emphasis that authentic human becoming depends upon the self-transcending subject and conversion, as well as on the relationship between subjectivity and objectivity. Human becoming is never complete, it is always precarious, and it happens within community, for human becoming is social in nature, and it depends upon understanding of oneself and of one's world.[142] The shaping and the transformation of the subject's environment are "effected through intentional acts that envisage ends, select means, secure collaborators, direct operations."[143]

IV.2 THE SUBJECT, CULTURE, AND PLURALISM

The good is realized through "human apprehension and choice ... [it] is not ... a legal system or a moral system. It is a history, a concrete, cumulative process resulting from developing human apprehension and human choices that may be good or evil. And that concrete, developing process is what the human good in this life is, the human good on which depends man's eternal destiny."[144] When religious belief passes out of the social frame, then history, which is either the manifestation or the diminishment of the human good realized through concrete judgments and choices, is no longer cooperation between human beings and God and the realization of God's will. The notion of "automatic progress" is an illusion of utopia, and springs from the unwillingness to admit that beyond the world there is "the good by its essence which is God, [and unwillingness to accept that truth] can lead to desperation and nihilism, the negation of the notion of value."[145] Human making can be changed and improved; subjects are responsible for their history and for their becoming.[146] And so the good is concrete, historical, and related to the philosophy of education:

> Are we to seek an integration of the human good on the level of historical consciousness, with the acknowledgment of man's responsibility for the human situation? If so, how are we to go

about it? These are the fundamental questions for a philosophy of education today. There is a need for a philosophy at the level of our time, a philosophy that is concrete, existential, genetic, historical, a "philosophy of...," and Catholic. There is required, too, an education that is at the level of our time.[147]

Such a concept of the good, concrete and informing a philosophy of education, must also be concerned with subjects in their becoming and in their increasing autonomy.[148] Human becoming can be compromised by bias, egoism, and sin, but it can also be incrementally and cumulatively liberated by acts of transcendence. Affirming something to be so is an act of judgment; it is to go beyond oneself; to judge something to be so, to culminate in a true judgment, confirms a truth beyond oneself, a truth that transcends the self.[149] So, while judgments of fact and value are different in content, they are similar in structure.[150] Acts of self-transcendence form the structure of the *good of order*. This order moves the identification of the good from the narrowness of desire in relation to the self to the good of order as systematic patterns of relationships where the desire of the self and the desire of others are related. The good of order does not exist independently of these subjects and their choices and actions.[151] It is because the good of order flows from subjects who make up that order that a series of subordinations follows in technology, economics, and values.[152] Ensuring the objectivity of a judgment of value "is the good conscience of the virtuous man."[153] Thus, the human good is individual and social; it is meeting the needs of others cooperatively, and is achieved intentionally, knowingly, and freely, and contributes to the subject's authenticity.[154]

Such a structure for human becoming is the foundation for culture defined as "a way of life."[155] No longer can a way of life be secured on the certainties of the classicist mindset, but neither need it be left to the ravages of relativism or individualism. So amidst pluralism, judgments of value become all the more important for an authentic way of life.[156] The unity of life is based on the conviction that "living is an art," and such living is not an individual enterprise, but grows and matures in the company and through the example of others. Such living is within a group, and groups are influenced by many factors. Yet this living is organized and united, and while it cannot be taught, as it has not been systematically and conceptually organized, one comes into such a culture and achieves understanding through birth and the assimilation that comes from community. However, "there is a culture that can be taught, and education is concerned with it."[157]

Lonergan understands culture as a "reflective level of development," while civilization is "connected with technology, economy, and the polity or state."[158] Culture is a prominent theme for Lonergan, and *Method in Theology* opens with the distinction between a classicist understanding of culture that was normative, and an empirical understanding of culture regarding the concrete living of life.[159] This distinction is an essential lens through which to understand not only the reasons for the shift from a normative to an empirical position, but also the intrinsic relationship between culture and history and the particularities of time and place.[160] Classicist culture meant the acquisition of an established religious, literary, and historical intellectual tradition, typified in the liberal arts and the humanities. It was an unchanging, established syllabus, and was concerned more with facts than with values; and in this it claimed universal sway. However, the "classicist is not a pluralist," for though classicists admit that circumstances change, they see change in material terms, and are convinced that beyond the accidents of such differences there lies "some substance ... that fits in the classicist assumptions of stability, immutability, fixity."[161] Pluralists disagree, as they understand culture empirically, where circumstance and the particularities of time and history shape concepts and understanding.[162]

Classicism is correct in its "assumption that there is something substantial and common to human nature and human activity. Its oversight is its failure to grasp that something substantial and common is something quite open. It must be expressed in the four transcendental precepts: be attentive, be intelligent, be reasonable, be responsible. But there is an almost endless manifold of situations to which men successively attend ... The standard both for human reasonableness and for the strength and delicacy of man's conscience is satisfied only by a complete and life-long devotion to human authenticity."[163] One notes the parallels between Lonergan and Aristotle's *Nicomachean Ethics*: the concrete manifold of human experience renders it impossible to produce a compendium of ethics for every concrete, particular situation. Yet, the relativist's objections cannot be ignored: that meaning is relative to context,

that contexts change, and that it is impossible to forecast a future context.[164] However, one does not counter relativism by the addition of further propositions; rather, what is beneficial is "found only by unveiling
the invariant structure of man's conscious and intentional acts."[165] This,
of course, is unveiled in Lonergan's transcendental principles and cognitional structure, and he responds to the relativist's objections by saying
that while meaning is dependent on context, it does not follow that the
context is an impenetrable mystery, and therefore unknown. Second,
while contexts change, hermeneutics and exegesis help in understanding the truth contained in any given context. Third, while one cannot
foretell future changes, "one can predict, for example, that the contexts
of descriptive statements are less subject to change than the contexts of
explanatory statements."[166] And so we return to Lonergan's questions:
What am I doing when I am knowing? Why is doing that knowing? And
what do I know when I do it?

Lonergan returns to the reality of historical consciousness.[167] As culture is ultimately concerned with meaning and value, people manifest
their selves through a particular culture. "The classicist was aware that
men individually are responsible for the lives they lead. Modern man is
aware that men collectively are responsible for the world in which they
lead them."[168] However, the modern view is hardly devoid of challenges,
and here it is the group that must be responsible for the transformation
of culture.[169] Rather than culture sheltering in abstract philosophical
theories of human nature, it concerns people as they live, concretely,
amidst their diversity, and understand what is universal through the
"common and invariant structures in human operations."[170] Those
structures are "experiencing, inquiring, and reflecting."[171] An empirical understanding of culture leads to an understanding of the person's
historicity, and thus the role of the concrete operations of the person.[172]
Finally, the modern notion of culture is faced by secularism that pushes
religions to the sidelines of society.[173] However, like religion, secularism
offers a way of life, and is no less a philosophy.[174] The future of humanity
will not be secured upon an uncritical traditionalism, but will depend
upon experience, intelligence, judgment, and decision, harmonious
with a religious disposition.[175] Recalling St Augustine's maxim that
the human heart remains restless until finding rest in God, Lonergan
notes: "what that restlessness is we see all about us in the mountainous

discontent, hatreds and terrors of the twentieth century. But what it is to rest in God is not easily known or readily understood." The clue is found in the Christian maxim of denying oneself daily, picking up one's cross, and following Christ. Lonergan, very movingly, applies this teaching to all human beings, realized through self-transcendence and authenticity: "For the fulfillment that is the love of God is not the fulfillment of any appetite or desire or wish or dream impulse, but the fulfillment of getting beyond one's appetites and desires and wishes and impulses, the fulfillment of self-transcendence, the fulfillment of human authenticity, the fulfillment that overflows into love of one's neighbour as oneself."[176]

Perhaps of all the three sources, Lonergan's contribution to society, culture, and the common good is the most demanding because of its emphasis on the personal transformation and transcendence of the subject. His method will please neither traditionalists – as there is far too much emphasis on personal responsibility and conversion – nor relativists – as the outcome of this personal emphasis is in relation to transformation, conversion, and an authenticity that stands in relation to something outside and is thus greater than the individual subject. That something outside and greater is, of course, God, but it is also the making and shaping of culture and history that demand personal accountability.

In ways that are parallel to Maritain's caution of the fruitlessness of searching for a theoretical and conceptual framework to unite a religiously and culturally pluralist society, Lonergan's method is not aimed at providing some wider conceptual framework. Perhaps in the context of society, culture, and the common good, the implications of Lonergan's transcendental method shine brightest as they anticipate many of the challenges and tensions that such society faces today. Amidst such diversity and difference, the societal conclusion often seems to veer in the direction of either a secular individualism or a communal sectarianism. Like the documents, Lonergan would agree that the uncritical celebration of multicultural diversity does not make any real and substantial contribution to the shaping and destiny of culture and history. Human growth and flourishing are realized in a continued conversion and authenticity, and his three levels of conversion – intellectual, moral, and religious – serve the broader integral understanding of the new secular order, upon which both the documents and Maritain also elaborate.

Another major contribution made by Lonergan is how he understands education in the context of society, culture, and the common good. His understanding of the good is also demanding, and, once again, places a great responsibility on the knowing, choosing, and judging subject – in this case, the student. The good is neither pre-existing in some empirical and external form, nor so personal as to excuse the individual from accountability, other than to the law. In many ways, Lonergan's method makes the task and mission of education and schools all the more demanding. Given this method, education and schools would be deemed to have failed if their only concern (and the concern of parents and students) were future careers and professions. Professionalism and early specialization are two prominent sources of challenge to an integral education. The *good* and *society* have also been reduced and diminished by a materialism that is found in early professionalism and specialization, which are often seen as the only legitimate and ultimate purpose of education.

Both the documents and Maritain make detailed reference to *being* and *becoming* in the context of the new understanding of the secular order; but this order is meant to promote an integral humanism, and not a materialist and atheistic secularism nor a religious intolerance and fundamentalism. Lonergan's transcendental method provides the foundation for this being and becoming, but his other contribution in the context of society, culture, and the common good is that without such a being and becoming, and without that back-and-forth relationship between them, society and history are diminished and imprisoned. Lonergan's thought offers the Catholic school both a humanism and an anthropology for adult living. To intentionally choose not to be attentive, intelligent, reasonable, and responsible is a contradiction. On the other hand, not to follow the conclusions of one's attentiveness, intelligence, reason, and responsibility leads to self-contradiction. Either contradiction shows how society, culture, and the common good are diminished, and in this how the student as a subject, a person, is diminished. While religious identity is a central part of Lonergan's humanism, his transcendental method is not defined only by religion and religious dictates. Lonergan's method, inspired by the Gospels and the Christian tradition, offers Catholic schools a way to unite religiously diverse students, first through the

accountability and responsibility of a common humanity, and second, by
applying the implications for this unity as to how the good, culture, and
history are envisaged as living and unfolding entities.

V Conclusion

This chapter has elaborated on the delicate and crucial balance between
the intellectual mandate of the school and teaching, on the one hand,
and the social implications of education, on the other. The breadth of
perspective that the documents, Maritain, and Lonergan provide is a re-
sounding testimony to the intellectual patrimony of the Catholic tradition. While at all times declaring the primacy of faith and the call of
Christ (given Lonergan's emphasis that falling in love with God leads to
self-transformation and a new sense of horizontal and vertical liberty),
this intellectual tradition unfurls the backdrop for an integral Catholic
philosophy of education, whose integrity and wholeness must necessarily include meeting society and culture where they are, and yet moving
them to a communal and collective higher plane. The documents, Maritain, and Lonergan offer a vision for society, culture, and the common
good that serves Catholic teachers and school administrators, parents,
and the many others who hold positions of social responsibility. The
contributions of all three sources can be synthesized into the classic and
fundamental Christian principles: love of God and love of neighbour
as oneself. The authenticity of all three loves is essential to individual
human unity, and to the transformation of communal and interpersonal life.

The progression of the documents on social matters is noteworthy,
and their ability to place the challenges of diversity and pluralism within
a Christian anthropology and a communion of persons expands the service that Catholic education provides in ways that would have been unthinkable prior to the Council. This is one important reason why Catholic
philosophy of education has necessarily remained open-ended since the
Council. The vision that the documents offer for Catholic education in a
religiously pluralist society is based upon an integral understanding of
the nature of society, and how culture either flowers through communal
living or withers. However, while it is clear that the freedom to make this
choice is not as simple as it may seem, neither is it any more complex

than trading in one's heart of stone for a heart of flesh. The documents offer their vision of society, culture, and the common good within a pedagogical framework, consistently pointing to how and why learning, knowledge, and the communal life of the school are essential means of human perfection, supported by built-in systems of accountability to oneself, to others, and for the common good of society.

Lonergan's writing provides a philosophy of education based upon his cognitional theory, epistemology, and metaphysics, and how they enlighten individual and communal accountability. The breadth of Lonergan's system – based upon the transcendental precepts, upon the three questions of philosophy, and upon the subject's transformation through self-transcendence, authenticity, and an authentic subjectivity – is staggeringly impressive and demanding. And while it is inspired by the Christian tradition and the call of the Gospel, it is really a humanism for communal living. What he provides society, culture, and the search for the common good is the ability to avoid the Scylla of the nostalgia for complete cultural systems, such as classicism, and the Charybdis of relativism and individualism, often synthesized by the dismissal: *that is your opinion*. Human living involves meaning, and meaning requires responses, communication, decisions, and judgments. Meaning cannot, without contradiction, be dismissed either by relativism or by a solipsistic individualism.

Maritain's contribution, like those of the documents and Lonergan, is equally impressive. While he remains convinced – as do the other two – of the contribution of the liberal arts and the humanities for human transformation, he sees this transformation in much wider terms than those envisaged by a particular culture (in this case Western culture, narrowly understood). He too provides a sophisticated humanism that is neither a hurried response to the terrors of the Second World War, nor a sentimental nostalgia for some golden past. He says repeatedly in *Integral Humanism* that the humanism he proposes is not harkening back to something similar to the medieval cultural, religious, and intellectual order. Rather, his humanism, like the documents' and Lonergan's, is not only historically based but is also offered for the very transformation and the liberation of history, which is called to be more than the collection of the inevitability of human decisions, choices, biases, and sin. For him, too, history is either liberated or imprisoned by what human beings make of themselves individually and communally. His social and political thought, encapsulated by his call to replace *tolerance* with *fellowship*, is a vast philosophical foundation that shows how human cooperation and fellowship, in the perennial shaping of society, culture, and the common good, have secure intellectual and moral moorings. Like the documents and Lonergan, Maritain shows how there is much more to be said and offered by the Catholic tradition, in the midst of religious plurality. There is more to this tradition than simply the regret that unity amidst diversity is not possible, and that secularism, the privacy of religion, individualism, and relativism are inevitable, and that the only satisfactory solution is some cobbled-together version of a secular humanism, distinguished by calls for *tolerance*, which hardly affirms human dignity or the spiritual and intellectual complexity of each human person.

The social and cultural implications of all three sources are vast, as they focus on the needs and challenges of education amidst religious diversity and cultural plurality. All three offer the Catholic school an intellectual tradition that is at the service of this plurality and diversity, one that is intrinsically pedagogical, revealing what is meant by the dignity of the human person. Such a dignity, which educators rightly affirm as vital to their task (though regrettably they do not often accompany this affirmation by clarifying how this is undertaken through the school's intellectual mandate), is personal and communal, and grows side by side with and is realized through personal accountability.

Finally, the documents, Maritain, and Lonergan offer more than just an inclusive vision for the education of the non-Christian student in the Catholic school. To *include* someone or something often sounds like a last-minute decision; it suggests that the whole would remain whole without such an inclusion. On the other hand, the vision that emerges from the documents, Maritain, and Lonergan is that society is only whole when, amidst its diversity and plurality, it is looked on as a whole from the start. All three sources see religious diversity as part of the providential plan of God. Responding to this diversity is more than just *including* the religiously other. Secular society, as distinct from a secularized society, has its own aims and its own ends, and so it should. The transformation of this society into one that is truly human is dependent upon individual and communal transformation. Catholic education can offer a vision of why this transformation is one major contribution to what is meant by the dignity of the student as a person, and how such a transformation is necessarily heuristic and open-ended, without the loss of individual and communal responsibility. Maritain's humanism and Lonergan's cognitional theory provide the philosophical basis for this conviction, and all three sources attest to how Catholic education contributes to society, culture, and the common good by celebrating intellectual, religious, and cultural diversity as part of a much wider cosmic plan. Human agency, choice, transformation, and good will are the means to participate in this plan; and however mysterious its purpose, it is yet unifying in its invitation.

7

Teach Me Goodness, Discipline, and Knowledge

Some Observations

The motto of my religious congregation – the Congregation of Saint Basil – is *Bonitatem, et disciplinam, et scientiam doce me: teach me goodness, discipline, and knowledge*, and is taken from Psalm 118.[1] It is a prayer addressed to God, and it has inspired my congregation dedicated to Catholic education. God is hidden behind a veil of mystery, incomprehensibility, and stillness – not silence, of course, for he has spoken through the Scriptures and prophets, but especially through his Son and Word Jesus Christ. God teaches the student goodness, discipline, and knowledge, and inspires and shapes the active agency of parents, teachers, and other educators in their pursuit of goodness, discipline, and knowledge. The Church calls on educators to purify and liberate their agency, a challenging and demanding task, particularly as the fruit of Christian transcendence does not always ripen during one's lifetime.

This has been an enlightening journey in keeping close company with the educational documents, Maritain, and Lonergan; bringing them into close proximity has been revelatory and an intellectual discovery for me. As suggested in the introduction, a study should be undertaken to consider the particular historical, social, and cultural influences that form the warp upon which each educational document is woven. However, as I am neither a historian nor sufficiently versed in social and cultural theories, I took a different, more familiar route, given my own discipline of the philosophy of education. I was interested to see whether the

Church's understanding of a Catholic philosophy of education could be culled from its documents. I am now confirmed in my conviction. While the authors and the times of the documents change, they are written against a background of the scriptural, pastoral, spiritual, moral, social, and intellectual tradition of the Church, where they find their foundations. The themes of the documents are varied, and the Church continues to add different colours and emphasis to the edifice of Catholic education, continually responding to the concerns and challenges of each age.

One historical note regarding Maritain and Lonergan's designations as Thomists. While Maritain was uneasy with the term "Neo-Thomism," as mentioned in chapter 2, in this book that designation is used in the context of the revival of Thomistic philosophy after Pope Leo XIII's encyclical *Aeterni Patris* in 1879. Maritain was not a Thomistic philosopher in the old Manualist Tradition. While Maritain scholars may well view the designation of "Neo-Thomist" as imprecise, as Lonergan scholars would view him as a Transcendental Thomist, both groups would likely agree that either designation is a helpful starting point, but requires further and nuanced clarification outlining areas of distinctiveness, divergence, and disagreement. In this book, Lonergan is not referred to as a Transcendental Thomist, because while he used the transcendental method, historically Transcendental Thomists represent a different interpretation of Thomism than that developed and subscribed to by Lonergan. On the other hand, here Maritain is referred to as a Neo-Thomist in the context of the Thomistic revival subsequent to *Aeterni Patris*.

Maritain's and Lonergan's writings complement the Church's educational stance. Their assistance is also beneficial given the Church's reliance upon and relationship with philosophy and philosophical methods, as the documents themselves see the need for an *educational philosophy*. Since the Council, the Church has not singled out, nor does it depend upon, any one philosophical system. I chose these two philosophers for a number of reasons as they have helped shape my own thought, most notably my growing appreciation that education, like life, is ultimately a mystery. First, they are both Catholics, and so Catholicism is the overall context for their philosophical systems and sensibilities. Second, both wrote on the philosophy of education. In this regard, Lonergan's development of a Catholic philosophy of education in light of the seismic

shift from a classicist model to historical-mindedness is exceedingly instructive. And while neither of their philosophies of education is recent,
they are not dated; they retain a freshness, rooted in a wider philosophical, theological, and anthropological tradition, and they continue to
inspire and challenge educators. Third, while education is an art, and
in making and doing art is a practical discipline, both philosophers
elaborate on how this art can quickly become imprisoned within itself
if the practical making and doing dominates and is not informed by the
theoretical and the speculative; and they warn of the dangers of education being overwhelmed by the empirically measurable and sensorially
perceptible. Education is an art, but given the nature of the student as
a person, it is necessarily subordinated within a wider anthropological,
intellectual, moral, and social hierarchy.[2] Fourth, both philosophers
raise meta-educational questions and issues, and so move the discussion of a Catholic philosophy of education to a higher, more universal
level, beyond the borders of nations and states, situating it amidst the
diversity of cultures and creeds, and so assist in revealing the audience
of a Catholic philosophy of education: the universal Church historically
constituted in every age. Fifth, teachers should be rightly concerned with
their professional qualifications, their curricular responsibilities, and
their knowledge of the latest methodologies, systems, and developments
concerning the practicalities of educating and teaching. However, the
practical *activity* of teaching as an art seems increasingly to be confused
with *activism*.[3] The demands of individual academic subjects and course
outcomes, standardized testing, a narrowing and specialized curriculum, education envisaged as a commodity and students reduced to cli-
ents, and the perception that schools are meant only to prepare students
for the future, with the present viewed simply as a stepping-stone to that
future – all contribute to a frenzied activism. This over-emphasis on preparing students for an economic and financial future disfigures and distorts education, but it also fails to acknowledge how and why the present
is utterly formative of how students will look upon themselves, others,
and the world in the future. Maritain and Lonergan are keenly aware of
the dangers when the necessary practicalities of education (including
preparing the student for adulthood, for a career, and for citizenship)
are eclipsed by an *educational activism* that is driven by reducing the

school year from one period to the next, and when at the end of schooling students are expected to emerge as completed products, only to be finally polished off by a specialized university education or professional and skill training in preparation for a future whose hallmarks are material prosperity, financial security, accumulated wealth, and individual success. In such a flattened and arid landscape, education for freedom and liberation are nowhere to be seen because they cannot survive. Rather, both philosophers emphasize that education is never completed at any one stage, and that the school must prepare students to understand why such completion is never possible; *educational completion* – as opposed to the completion of professional qualifications, skills, and abilities – is likened to *educational stagnation*. Both philosophers emphasize the need for education to cultivate a contemplative stillness, more challenging when information overload and instant accessibility lack a centre and unity. Finally, it seems to me that contemporary Catholic education is in need of philosophical muscle. While there are other philosophers and philosophical systems, to be sure – existentialism, phenomenology, analytical philosophy, schools of personalism – that could also be put into conversation with the Church's educational documents, I find Maritain's and Lonergan's thought to be enlightening because of the breadth of their philosophical interests. Their educational theory is one chamber in their houses of philosophy, secured upon lasting foundations; the diversity and unity of their thought gives education a much wider context beyond schools and the school day. In short, there are many ways to examine a more universal philosophy of education from the perspective of the Universal Church; my approach is one among them.

Placing these three sources side by side, under the four headings of chapters 3 to 6, has revealed that while each offers a different emphasis and perspective on each of these themes, there is a remarkable unity and congruity amongst them. What those chapters also reveal is that the three sources do not offer lockstep symmetry of intellectual correspondence on the topic in question, but they do offer a unity of a more enduring order: the unity of the human person. Over the years I have grown increasingly convinced that human unity, the personal unity of the student, is one of the fundamental themes and concerns of the Church's educational documents, and this is true for Maritain and Lonergan as well. What the three sources have revealed is that this unity is enhanced by a tradition that highlights the perennial relationship between being and becoming, vital for human unity.

Human unity is also essential for Christian service. I am reminded of Gilson's essay, *The Intelligence in the Service of Christ the King*, where the unity of intelligence is presupposed.[4] Christian service must respond to each age, and such service is in response to Christ's invitation to follow him, and amidst increasing diversity and plurality this service is necessarily heuristic. The Christian service of Catholic education must respond to its age and the challenges therein. However, in order for it to be dynamic, liberating, and transformative, Catholic education must be enduring and recognizable in each age. That enduring feature, it seems to me, is the unity of the student, and is manifested in a variety of dimensions, including the religious, moral, social, intellectual, and cultural dimensions. Christ's call is an invitation to salvation, and responding to that invitation leads to growth in personal unity, manifested in freedom and liberation. However, persons are much more than *intellectual beings*, and history records too many instances of harm and terror when the intellectual and the rational dominate the other dimensions that constitute human living and being. Intellectualism and rationalism can easily imprison, and they stand at the opposite end from the freedom and liberation in following Christ.[5] Human unity is sophisticated and complex, and much care is required to protect its integrity and ensure its perennial growth; growth in unity is also simple, and is surely encapsulated in the command to love God and one's neighbour as oneself. Human intelligence is at the service of human unity, and intelligence plays a prominent role in the progressive, cumulative, and heuristic growth of personal unity. Over the years I have noted that Catholic educators tend to bristle when reminded of the *intellectual mandate* of the Catholic school, and this bristling is well founded if *intellectual* is narrowed in its scope and meaning to suggest heady, disengaged, ivory-tower ruminations and a snobbery of shuffling ideas, a bourgeois concept of education. I hope what has emerged in this work is that the intellectual mandate of the Catholic school must always be at the service of human unity, and more fundamentally, at the service of Christ and his call to pick up one's cross and follow him.[6] This call is personal and communal, and invariably involves interacting with and responding to the levels and dimensions of the created order, human knowledge, and learning. The Catholic school contributes to this interaction and response, but all towards enhancing human unity and freedom, and enabling a unified human response to the unity of the Gospel, which outlines what living and being in the world as pilgrims in time entail and should look like.

There are many ways to reflect on a Catholic philosophy of education. Since the Council, there is a greater appreciation for more local and regional Catholic philosophies of education,[7] a need to attend to the varied issues of the Catholic school,[8] and the guiding role of a universal oversight.[9] There are calls for a more detailed Catholic *philosophy* of education in light of the Council's changes and the diversity of philosophical methods. Catholic philosophers of education have also enriched the field through their scholarship.[10] For their part, religious educators have made a significant contribution in clarifying and expanding the understanding of a Catholic education, informed by Scripture scholarship, systematic and practical theology, pedagogical and hermeneutical theories, social sciences, cultural theories, pastoral practice, the arts, etc. These influences have added richly to why Catholic education now needs *methods* rather than *a method*. There is as much need for a Catholic theology of education and a Catholic theology of religious education as there is for a Catholic philosophy of education.

My approach to a Catholic philosophy of education is coloured by my own experience of attending a Catholic school, but it is also shaped by my continued appreciation of why there are now many approaches to and formulations of Catholic philosophy of education. The Congregation for Catholic Education exercises a universal oversight over that education, and it must necessarily speak in broad terms that are, in spite of regional and continental differences and applications, clearly identifiable as Catholic anywhere in the world. What I have been proposing is that these foundational categories – anthropological, pedagogical, philosophical, theological, moral, social, and communal – as they appear in the Church's documents and teaching tradition form the structure of a Catholic philosophy of education, but a structure that is living and growing. Ongoing work will be required on more particular issues as knowledge increases and specializes; as moral and social challenges confront educators; as the curriculum expands in some ways and contracts in others; as the ways change in which the school is envisaged in relation to society and to higher and professional education; as the state's influence and even interference in shaping what education and schools should look like increases; as various ideologies and cultural perspectives mould educa- tion; as an increasingly scientific and technical world makes demands of schools and universities; as educators discover how new forms of testing can actually limit knowledge and learning; etc. Attention is also required for Catholic education globally, and the challenges, threats, and oppor- tunities faced through countries and across continents.

I, however, have taken one approach to see how Catholic education can be at the service of a diverse and pluralistic society, and why the Church, Maritain, and Lonergan confirm this to be urgent in the cause of human unity. Some would rightly be critical of this approach, saying that it weakens the Catholic identity of the school, particularly in our age when that identity is already threatened by a host of pressing issues, not least of which are the increasing criticisms that Catholic schools have outgrown their usefulness; that apart from religious education, Catholic schools are often indistinguishable from their secular counterparts; that the Catholicity of Catholic teachers and their education has not received the attention of the Church that they rightly deserve, and that the identity of the Catholic teacher is increasingly compromised and questionable; that Catholic students are often woefully ignorant of the basic elements of the Catholic faith at the conclusion of their schooling in ways that would not be tolerated in their study of other scholastic subjects; that Catholic education as envisaged by the Church is out of step with the de- mands of modern living, particularly in sexual and social morality; that a broad humanistic education such as the Church envisages is no longer possible given social changes and what skills and knowledge students are expected to possess at the end of schooling; that education, of neces- sity, must now be utilitarian, pragmatic, and practical, and any humanis- tic, spiritual, and religious education should be taken care of elsewhere by parents and religious institutions; that Catholic education privileges one group over all others, not just when it receives public monies, but also by privileging one faith tradition over all others; and that faith- based schools are a source of division in an already religiously divided and culturally fragmented world. There are other objections, of course, and of those listed here, some are undoubtedly urgent: the identity of the Catholic teacher and the faith formation of Catholic students. As a priest and as one who has spent his career in the education of Catholic teachers, these two issues could not be closer to my heart. However, I do not believe that an inward-looking Catholic education for Catholics benefits anybody, least of all students, teachers, and parents living amidst diversity and plurality. Local churches and dioceses must play a far more active and collaborative role than they seem to be playing (particularly in the West) in the education of Catholic teachers and in supplementing the faith formation of Catholic students. Collaboration must also come from Catholic colleges and universities. The faith education of adult Catholics is also a pressing need. If parents are the first and most formative educators, as the Church rightly teaches, then the formation of Catholic parents needs urgent attention.[11] Church attendance once a week may have been sufficient in a world that could identify a broad Catholic culture. Such a world has long passed.

In spite of the urgency of these concerns, I have taken the approach that I have because of the change in the way the Church now understands herself since the Council, as well as through my reading of the educational documents, Maritain, and Lonergan.[12] The age prior to the Council, which gave a place of prominence to Thomistic and Neo-Thomistic studies, was one where a unified and detailed Catholic philosophy of education was possible; but even then, it was hardly universally accepted, particularly given the changes that accompanied the shift to historically minded worldviews. Biblical studies, hermeneutics, existentialism, social and moral scholarship, philosophical personalism, and the transcendental method that Lonergan developed, all show why a single method would be neither possible nor desirable. This, I believe, is a moment of liberation for the Catholic philosophy of education, and indeed a collaborative moment. After the Council, Catholics flocked to secular universities and began to take their place in those academies. The advances in knowledge and learning emanating from those universities, while not always attentive to the requirements and demands of human unity, freedom, and liberation, have contributed to human advancement and social and communal change and progress. Studies in psychology, sociology, cultural hermeneutics, and pedagogical theories are obvious examples. Catholic educators have learned from the social sciences; today it is unthinkable for education to be uninformed by those disciplines. All these advances must continue to shape the discipline of Catholic philosophy of education, as is clearly evidenced in the progression of the educational documents. Catholic educators need to learn from and be informed by the academy, and to collaborate with diverse specialists, from social workers to clinical psychologists, and from pedagogical theorists to religious leaders. They all help shape particular Catholic philosophies of education sensitive to local, national, and continental particularities.

My interest has been to explore the universal themes and challenges of a Catholic philosophy of education: human flourishing and the subject as developing in relation to the good, as Lonergan sees it; the role of Catholic education in the heuristic discovery of the common good, as Maritain envisioned; and how the tremendous advances in working for human unity, liberation, and freedom are also beset with dangers leading to the diminishment of the student as a person, as laid out in the Church's educational documents. All this must be part of a Catholic philosophy of education amidst religious plurality and cultural diversity. The collaboration that Catholic educators build with scholars and other professionals will enable them to draw on knowledge and learning that truly is at the service of human unity and human flourishing, and that enhances the search for and the contribution to the common good. What education and the study of education seem to lack, however, are not necessarily the many practicalities, particularities, and methodologies concerned with the school day, such as imparting the curriculum, the professional qualifications of teachers, the obligations and duties of parents, etc. What education appears to lack, rather, is an appreciation of the whole for which students ought to be prepared and to take responsibility, beginning with the individual student, as a whole person, in the company and fellowship of other such whole persons. There are, undoubtedly, many competing visions of the whole and its constituent parts. However, Catholic education does have a vision of the whole, and it does have a vision of who the student is as a person with regard to that whole. Catholic education can map out what is required of education and the school to actualize this potential of personhood, and how this influences the common good, giving it a form and structure to enhance the unity, freedom, and liberation of the student. Knowledge and learning are essential sources for human unity, freedom, and liberation. However, knowledge and learning must be situated within a wider anthropological and humanistic context, a personalist context, and Catholic education has the ability to make these contexts available to all its students, regardless of caste or creed. These contexts are spelled out in the educational documents, and Maritain and Lonergan offer additional ways of understanding them, from the relationship and distinction between the person and the individual, freedom of choice culminating in freedom of autonomy, and the legitimate ends of secular society, to the transcendental method and the emphasis on interiority, authentic subjectivity, and transcendence.

However, one is cautioned against painting too a rosy a picture in the face of a growing *religious illiteracy*, and not just of students but of parents as well. Religious illiteracy is not new to Christianity, even in its present form of viewing reality, and especially religious reality, in material and tangible terms.[13] While what the student learns from the family, the Church, and the school must be understood and appropriated, and not just memorized, it would seem that responding to religious illiteracy is not simply a matter of increasing doctrinal and catechetical instruction, important though these are. For on their own, they run the risk of remaining external and not part of one's personal, appropriated experience. More than instruction, religious illiteracy is responding to the natural human yearning for knowledge and values. It is to know and understand why the deeper questions and answers that religions provide make for a meaningful, integrated, and happy life, and beyond religion narrowly conceived.

Lonergan's analysis reveals the resulting imprisonment when reality is viewed in exclusively material terms, as picture thinking; reality reduced to the experience and encounter with one's senses alone; reality as *out there*, external and material. Thus, immaterial realities such as God, salvation, and eternal happiness are, in the context of a Western materialist worldview, practically unimaginable, and even if imagined, are generally viewed in material terms. Salvation is equated with having one's needs met, with *needs* again understood in material terms: physical, sensible, and tangible. If *life* means one's present experience, and if *eternal* means unending, then *eternal life* is reduced to something continuing in its present form, bedecked with never-ending happiness and joy all around, understood in material terms. It is important to note that in spite of the challenges, religious illiteracy is not a moral failing, but a philosophical and intellectual one. It is the failing of the reduction of a materialist worldview. What Lonergan and Maritain show, as do the documents, is that a comprehensive and Christian understanding of reality has material and spiritual dimensions – hence our fundamental dependence on the senses for knowledge – but that reality is also revealed and unfolds as a consequence of human freedom and choices. What a Catholic philosophy of education offers is the broadening and widening of the horizon against which reality is perceived, understood, and responded to. I quickly note that this is not particular to Christianity; theistic religions such as Judaism and Islam face similar challenges. To propose a rejection of religion based on materialistic terms and categories is intellectually dishonest, because most religions do not formulate a worldview or an anthropology in materialistic terms, and hence to declare oneself as an atheist in materialist terms is to fail to understand the worldview and anthropology of a religion. A Catholic philosophy of education can help show why the intellectual and philosophical inadequacies that underlie religious illiteracy have a bearing on more than just religious matters; religious illiteracy seriously diminishes human living in its social, moral, intellectual, communal, and psychological dimensions. Through its worldview and anthropology, and its moral and social teaching, and the increasing stress on the interreligious context of modern societies, the Catholic school is well positioned to respond to religious illiteracy, a task that must be principally shouldered by teachers and educators. However, parents have their role to play, and the Church must play a far more intentional and engaged role in responding to the crises and challenges of religious illiteracy.

In all this, the other trap to be avoided is the facile distinction between conservative and liberal, traditional and progressive. Recall Lonergan's distinctions between the traditionalist and modernist approaches to education, referred to in chapter 2. The traditionalist and modernist responses lead to the either/or trap; the former calcifies religion and religious belief, while the latter leads to the progressive materialization of reality. While the five positions proposed by the modernist – rejection of authority; reality is not fixed but in process; the only viable method is that of empirical science; philosophy must submit to the scientific method; and experience is what matters ultimately – only contribute to the diminishment of one's understanding of reality. The traditionalist simply holds on to a golden and idealized past, with no regard for the historicity and cultural constitution of human living, while the modernist is mesmerized by progress and the seeming rigour and objectivity of a narrow conception of science, thus rejecting other forms and expressions of human knowing. Again, a Catholic philosophy of education must avoid the Scylla of the traditionalist, and the Charybdis of the modernist. Once again, the intellectual mandate of the Catholic school must serve in showing why its worldview and anthropology are essentially unifying; it offers a unity that is based on the student as one who seeks to know, understand, and choose, and in this transcends religious and cultural distinctions.

Teach Me Goodness, Discipline, and Knowledge

I propose that the three virtues of my congregation's motto can unite democratic societies marked by religious diversity and cultural plurality: striving for *goodness*; the need for personal and communal *discipline*; and the freedom and liberation that come from *knowledge*. Religions and cultures all express the yearning for goodness, discipline, and knowledge in different ways and with different emphases. The motto of my congregation is a prayer addressed to God in seeking Christian perfection, particularly in the evangelical councils of poverty, chastity, and obedience. I propose that another way to look at this motto is in the context of the Catholic school as a subconscious and unarticulated plea, a petition from the personhood of the student to the personhood of the educator. *Teach me goodness, discipline, and knowledge* is a supplication made from the depths of the student, a spiritual being, whose fulfillment and perfection includes knowledge and understanding. The school must pursue each of these virtues in a particularly educational way, distinguished – while acknowledging the obvious relationship – from the quest for goodness, discipline, and knowledge that parents and the Church also undertake.

Moreover, it is these distinctions that place these virtues at the service of a religiously diverse student body in a Catholic school, and in this respond to the philosophical and intellectual limitations of religious illiteracy.

GOODNESS

To be good requires a vision of goodness. Religions provide such a vision, and in the midst of religious diversity there are competing visions of the good. My contention has been that by offering religious instruction for all pupils, according to the religious diversity of the student population, the Catholic school sends a powerful educational message regarding the good. It is a message that engenders respect for the goodness of religions and religious beliefs. There is a certain hermeneutic that would suggest that the face of religious plurality and the expectations from religions that make up that plurality change, progress, and contribute to the whole through such an inclusion. This inclusion seems to ask for an accountability of the religious expression of the good. The second, unspoken message in placing religious instruction as a subject of the curriculum requires it to take its place besides other subjects, with the rigour and accountability expected of all the other subjects. While religion holds a place of primacy in human flourishing, its rightful place beside other subjects has the effect of levelling it, without belittling or disrespecting it. Placing religious instruction in the curriculum requires and demands that all the teachers show how and why more is expected of human flourishing than is shown by confining the good to religions and moral codes alone, as religion is *one* subject in the curriculum. Excluding religion suggests that it is a private pursuit, and extreme positions can flourish as religion then lacks a wider, accountable context. One requirement of such inclusion could be that all students in a Catholic school must be introduced to religions other than their own, and in each other's company.[14] One essential pedagogical outcome of placing religious instruction and religious education – according to the diversity of the school population – in the curriculum is that it has the implicit effect of showing that goodness is not limited to beliefs and morality born from religion alone, and that the existence and manifestation of goodness need to be explored in other areas of knowing and in the communal living of life as well. What Catholic education can show is that goodness is found in every subject in the curriculum, and it can do this secured on an anthropology that explores goodness in relation to knowing, and that emerges from right knowing. This is not to downplay one of the fundamental convictions of Catholic education: that faith, religious observance, and moral rectitude are intrinsic to knowing the good and living by it. However, widening one's understanding of goodness and what it means to be a good person is surely the mark of an educated person, and the obligation of an educated person amidst religious plurality. In a free, religiously diverse society, the relationships between believers must be expected to be of a higher communal order, more than that characterized by tolerance.

A Catholic philosophy of education has the intellectual wherewithal to ask the crucial question: what does goodness look like for modern living? What does it mean to be a good person beyond being informed by one's religion and its accompanying beliefs, values, and moral code, fundamental as they are? And, in spite of the complexity of modern life and living, another question in this genre could be: is it good to be alive?[15] Religions usually answer the last question with great clarity: life is a gift from God, and human beings will be called to give an account of that gift at the end of time. While this sense of final accountability could be seen as an opportunity to strengthen a multi-religious society, modern living seems to add a nuance to this question: is it good to be alive in the company of those of another religion, culture, or worldview than mine? It depends in what political form this company is being kept; a dictatorial or totalitarian government would suppress and persecute minorities. Here it is presupposed that the context is democratic, a free society where the freedom of religious diversity and cultural plurality is guaranteed. It seems that in order to answer yes to the question, one must have a wider understanding of the good, and what a Catholic philosophy of education can offer is how and why the good is a comprehensive and expansive term. And while the good is laid out by religious and cultural traditions, communal living demands that other aspects of the good need to be discovered through a heuristic openness, marked by good will and fellowship. A society marked by religious diversity can be handicapped by differing conceptions of the good. A Catholic education acknowledges this diversity of opinions, but what it offers is the understanding that the good has been reframed and broadened by diversity,

though not easily. Not only does Catholic education confront the relativist position that one can do what one wants as long as others are not
harmed and the law is respected, but it reminds all students that in being
created by God, the good is sought personally and communally, and that
while students have a right to follow and live by their religious beliefs,
they also have the obligation to allow others such freedom. This freedom
introduces a third obligation: the duty to work for the common good,
for this is surely the context from which one will have to give a final account of one's personal goodness before God's throne. While pursuing
goodness according to the demands of one's religion is certainly foundational, it can quickly become ghettoized where the good is narrowed to
religious beliefs alone.

Again, the critic is likely to say that many Catholic students are not
sufficiently knowledgeable of the teachings on the good as contained
in the Catholic faith and its moral teachings, without the additional requirements of knowledge of other religious traditions. That this only
leads to a watering down, resulting in religious and moral relativism.
The Church affirms the primacy of religious faith and morals, but it also
recognizes that in light of religious diversity, the notion of the good must
be expanded, and that expansion must lie primarily in how students see
themselves and others with regard to the good. The failure of such expansion will surely disintegrate into a competition and rivalry between
religious understandings of the good. In addition, the criticism does not
take away from the larger opportunity of the Catholic school to educate
for a vision of the good that is informed by religion, certainly, but also
through all the studies and the other aspects that make up the school day.
Failing this, the good becomes ghettoized and fails to be communally
accountable, an accountability that seems essential for life in pluralist
societies. What the documents, Maritain, and Lonergan offer is a much
wider understanding of the *secular* nature of society, as distinct from a
society marked by *secularism*. The former is based upon an anthropology marked by responsibility, accountability, mutuality, fellowship, and
morality in the midst of diversity. The latter identifies diversity as the
reason why unity is not possible, and takes for granted that individualism, materialism, moral relativism, and self-absorption are the inevitable and unaccountable outcomes. Here goodness withers and shrinks
through a selfish subjectivism, as opposed to responsible subjectivity.

The anthropology and worldview of Catholic education also offer a vision of the good that emerges communally, where students understand what is involved in freeing the self from external forces, societal and cultural, and internal forces culminating in prejudices and selfishness. This vision of goodness is related to freedom, and the anthropology of Catholic education is in the service of an integral freedom.

A great deal has been written on the secular public square and on what secular public living should look like.[16] The documents, Maritain, and Lonergan are all in agreement that the religious diversity of secular societies should not be seen as a corruption of society to be accepted only grudgingly, but as an opportunity to see how the nature of the citizen as a person can be perfected amidst the opportunities and demands of diversity, which exists through God's providence. Lonergan's understanding of the good as developing subject places the onus for pursuing and being good on the student – as a religious believer, certainly, but also as one who increasingly understands why the pursuit of the good cannot be formulated in its entirety, foreseeing every human situation, and placed in a self-sufficient textbook. Pursuing the good is neither absolutely determined by religion nor absolutely determined by the self. There is a third way where the good is explored and appropriated through communal commitment, and this in turn means that the person is gradually becoming good through that pursuit. Knowing and choosing the good are demanding, for they depend upon self-renunciation and self-transcendence.[17] Finally, goodness and happiness are also inextricably linked. Religions offer their understanding, but there are other competing understandings of this relationship, ranging from the renunciation of self to the self as the only and ultimate measure of goodness and happiness. Catholic education teaches that human beings are created for beatitude, and explains why the wealth of the nations is unable to fulfill that yearning. Goodness is indispensable for happiness, and goodness and happiness must undoubtedly be striven for in the company of others. What such an education can offer is the knowledge that one's historical context makes demands of the good: one can only be a good religious person within a culture and history. To reject this either calcifies religious beliefs as purely conceptual in the way that Lonergan warns against, or rejects the modern secular state and the necessary pursuit of the common good in the way that Maritain cautions against. And finally, it rejects what the documents emphasize: becoming a good person happens in the company of others, also created by God.

DISCIPLINE

School discipline justifiably remains enveloped in suspicion and mistrust; it can quickly deteriorate into ruthless and inhumane behaviour, all in the name of education and the betterment of the student. Indeed, and Catholic schools are hardly exempt from this, there are too many instances where teachers and educators have been nothing short of barbaric and criminal in the name of discipline. Even such a brief preface must frame any discussion of school discipline.

All religions teach what it means to be disciplined in the pursuit of holiness, goodness, and following the commandments and precepts. The Bible often speaks of the discipline that God instills in order to make one a true disciple. The disciplined life as a result of external discipline may or may not be a hindrance to the necessary internal discipline that one places upon oneself. It is obvious that the discipline that religions expect, and that families instill, is of a related but different order from the discipline that a school and a teacher must implement. The image of the student as soft, supple clay needing moulding and shaping is one way of envisioning school discipline. Educational discipline comes with great responsibility and trust; it is precarious and delicate, and never apart from supervision.

Today, and all three sources confirm this in their own way, a Catholic education sees discipline as ultimately being perfected in self-appropriation. Rules and regulations establish an initial structure, but it culminates when students become aware of why they must consciously choose a disciplined and accountable life. I am reminded here of a response that would surely have unsettled Pontius Pilate's question, what is truth? George Eliot says in *Daniel Deronda*, "The truth is something different from the habitual lazy combinations begotten by our wishes."[18] Eliot's succinct observation is apt for our age where wishing one's truth *into* and *as* reality is not uncommon. Relativism, individualism, and subjectivism confuse the distinctions between right and wrong. Who one is becoming through choices, decisions, and actions is easily neutralized by the assurance of not harming others and obeying the law. Account-ability now has an exclusive and limited audience: the self and the law.

Often non-Christian parents cite discipline as one main reason that they enrol their children in a Catholic school. Even with the best def-initions of that discipline as good behaviour, politeness, and respect, Catholic education must advocate discipline at a higher level: the student as a person who gradually and incrementally appropriates discipline and lives by a disciplined life in the company of others. And while school discipline should change according to the different stages of mental and moral growth, a higher-order discipline is required if students are to take their places as future citizens in the context of diversity and plural-ism. Making moral and ethical choices for oneself with implications for others and the common good has never been more demanding. One way to frame this higher-level sense of discipline is the expectation, increas-ing as students advance in age and maturity, that they are able to say who they are and who they would like to become as a result of their choices and decisions; why their becoming is never a finished process; why it must grow in the company of others and in society; and why there must be an inbuilt sense of personal responsibility and accountability. There are many influences on whom one becomes and chooses to become, both internal and external. Using the time that one has been granted wisely, justly, and prudently is a quest that has occupied human beings through the ages. Time can either be conceived as one day collapsing into the next, and increasing in speed the older one gets, or seen as mysterious and filled with possibility; and a Catholic philosophy of education em-ploys this latter sense of time by introducing an implicit philosophy of history within the curriculum and the school day. Students study in time, their time, and the evolution and shaping of their time through their choices and judgments must be an integral part of that study. What is the relationship of the student to time? And who is the student becoming in time through study and learning in the company of other students? Such a philosophy of history is exemplified in the first instance in the understanding of Christian service, to one's neighbour and to society as a whole. Today's cultural and religious conflicts appear to be between those who have conflicting philosophies of history and those who have no philosophy of history. If interacting with matter and the materiality of life is an end in itself and the sure source of happiness, then the *discipline* of acquiring such happiness is of a different order from the *discipline* of a life lived by the conviction that human beings have a spiritual nature, that they are accountable to God and destined for eternal life, and that selflessness, generosity, love, transcendence, and service give meaning and shape to history, rendering it *human* history, as opposed to history as *chronological inevitability* recorded in the annals of the past. The myth of eternal progress shapes the discipline of human becoming in a different way from the idea of becoming in the context of religious tradition, communal and personal morality, and service to others and the common good, all marked by personal accountability.

To appropriate and live by the conviction that education, knowledge, and learning are not ultimately about material prosperity, financial success, and a self-referential sense of fulfillment requires a personal discipline of a higher order. It is insufficient to say that such a vision does not need defending precisely because that vision no longer has the accompanying support of religious or cultural unity, nor wider support from society. Society expects schools to produce students who will quickly take their places in the work force and contribute to the prosperity and progress of the economic machine, leading to rapid personal, material, and financial success. The only communal language that pluralist societies seem to use is connected to the realization of such goals. Such a language does not reveal a linguistically ordered world that offers human persons the ability to reveal themselves and their nature by communicating with each other beyond the call for material and economic betterment and success, where the resulting inevitable emptiness of the practicalities of life is placed in the service of such success. The only discipline required for such a limited vision of the purpose of life and living is the frantic pace to acquire such prosperity, and to keep acquiring more.

Evidence would suggest that in the West, cultural and religious pluralism is ghettoizing society, and that attempts to free oneself from such a mentality are associated with liberalism and the rejection of religion and tradition. On the other side, Enlightenment humanism evolves into ever-changing shapes of anthropocentricism and secularism.[19] The danger is that in proposing personal accountability and responsibility, authenticity, and conscious choice of who one is becoming might seem to have the erroneous ring of contributing to anthropocentricism and individualism. On the contrary, even with the support of one's religious tradition and community it would seem that the human way to unite a diverse and plural society is through the efforts and good will of a consciously choosing, disciplined person in the company of other such persons. The philosophy of history of Catholic education can offer a vision of such disciplined company, of human community and societies moving toward an end – not necessarily an ultimate eternal end, as all citizens are not religious believers, but an end that is given meaning and purpose through conscious choices, decisions, and actions, and grounded in personal accountability and generosity. It is a secular end of human persons, both believers and non-believers, who see that without disciplined intentionality, society collapses into either an organized animalism driven by impulses, desires, and materialism, or a chaos riven by the conflicting dictates of religions that can miniaturize the identity of the citizen as *only* a religious believer, and often an extreme one at that. Continually discovering and working for the common good requires an act of personal discipline, not simply the discipline of a work ethic, but more importantly, the discipline of convictions, commitments, and the shared belief that all human beings are on a journey. The diversity of those on this journey declares that the worldviews of *only* secularism or *only* religions are insufficient and further divide society. A human world will require the disciplined understanding of why the common good is necessarily a heuristic concept, and such discovery only adds to the humanity of the world.[20]

In making religious instruction available to all students, a Catholic school stands tall in the face of a secularism that sees religions as the archaic residue of an unpurified and undifferentiated consciousness. In spite of various predictions, it would appear that religions are not about to disappear through an inescapable historical dialectic. Religions, of course, enforce personal and communal discipline. What pluralist societies seem to need is for religious citizens to grow in the discipline of their faith and to be accountable to others, supporting the freedom of others to practice their faith and to work for the common good. As it stands, pluralist societies encourage diversity and pluralism, but they have nothing to say about the *end* of diversity and pluralism, and the ensuing differences regarding life in common are papered over by inviting all to feast at the common table of material and financial progress.

The state assures this through laws and through guaranteeing rights and freedoms in the public square of secularism. Living amidst diversity and pluralism requires personal discipline if the public square is to be truly human and free beyond the manipulation of only the freedom of choice and material success. Diversity for diversity's sake is ultimately meaningless. Students brush against diversity every day. What they need is a way to see how they are united as persons and how such a unity demands a personal responsibility and accountability for communal living. A disciplined life, Catholic education teaches, is not only a responsible life but a truly human, free, and social life; human diversity is part of divine providence, and human wholeness, personal wholeness, can never be acquired on one's own.

KNOWLEDGE

The psalmist places knowledge third, and the descending order from goodness to discipline to knowledge suggests a governance of knowledge by goodness and discipline, and implies that the purpose and end of knowledge changes in this relationship. While the intellectual mission of the Catholic school, like any school, enjoys a place of primacy, this requires a great deal of qualification, as the previous chapters have demonstrated, particularly given the social and communal nature of education. There is a similar deceptive simplicity, also in need of perennial qualification, to St Augustine's maxim, "love God and do what you will."

To educate students from diverse religious and cultural groups together is pedagogically symbolic. The diverse ways of acquiring knowledge – here I am using "knowledge" and "understanding" synonymously – are integral to personal and communal unity. And doing this together signals that the accidental differences of culture and religion – accidental in that one is born into a culture and religion, but they do not change the essence and nature of one's humanity in seeking to know – are unified in the desire to know all of reality and to know it in common. Students are united in their common, human entreaty: teach me goodness, discipline, and knowledge, and introduce me to the diversity of knowledge. To fail to provide this diversity is to ignore this plea, and furthermore, students are not unified in their common humanity, that seeks knowledge in all its diversity. In this case, the Catholic school fails to be catholic – defined as "universal; of interest or use to everyone; having sympathies with all; all-embracing; broad minded, tolerant."[21] As a person, the student has the innate capacity to understand the diversity of knowledge, and that diversity is in service of the student's unity, which in turn is the basis of personal freedom and liberation. To deprive students of diversity, as in premature specialization at the expense of other subjects – not just the diversity of the curriculum but the diversity of the entire school day as well – is to compromise their personal unity. It also compromises their communal unity in rendering them unable to communicate with one another on a wide array of issues regarding life in common, a communication that is urgently needed today. Secular schools also educate a diverse group of students. The difference is that a Catholic school unifies diversity through an anthropology and worldview with implicit hierarchies and values, and though Christian, they are in service of the student as a person through the dignity and freedom that comes from the diversity of knowledge. Education is ultimately mysterious and spiritual. By mysterious I mean that education, as a search for truth, is not open to examination as biological dissection is.[22] Truth comes in many forms, as the curriculum and other school activities attest, and knowledge of the truth in all its diversity transforms the student. Knowledge of the truth serves the student's journey in time, but that journey also transcends time. Education is a spiritual activity whereby judgments, choices, and actions free one from the constraints of space and time and the constraints of matter. Human transcendence, and not just in matters religious, is another aspect of this spiritual dimension. Education is also spiritual through the personal appropriation of knowledge; rather than remaining external and conceptual, what is learned and known is internalized and spiritualized.[23]

Today the danger is in equating education with information. The Internet and other electronic forms of communication are never at a loss for information, and are constantly being freshly stocked. However, the medium suggests that what one sees on a screen is what one knows; the internal, spiritualizing movement of knowledge seems to be put aside, ignored, and truth is determined by what one sees. The danger is that this picture-based form of thinking and knowing results in naïve realism, upon which, as we have seen, Lonergan elaborates with great philosophical dexterity. There are many distinctions between knowledge and information, but an essential one is between information as data, as external and linear, and knowledge as appropriated through insights, understanding, and judgments; such a distinction highlights crucial differences. Knowledge is also related to wisdom and to the intellectual and moral virtues. Information and data are crucial for knowledge, but it is quite another matter to respond to, think about, and appropriate what one has learned as the foundation for judgments, decisions, and actions. How would a diverse group of students studying together respond to the question of the purpose of knowledge in their education? Are they likely to confuse the acquisition of information with knowledge and understanding? Are they likely to evaluate knowledge solely in the service of their future professions and employment, and what the business and financial world will expect them to know? Such likely confusion regarding the purpose of knowledge gives rise to a language with a very limited vocabulary, where human beings are in the service of employment, labour, and the endless demands of a material existence, and where the continued tide of information is equated with knowledge. Such a language hardly befits the dignity of human persons as an essential means of self- and communal revelation. It would appear that such a language fails to reveal the self in all its depth and complexity because the object and goal of such a language has no need of, nor depends upon, such depth and complexity.

A great disservice to the student is when education and knowledge are shrunken to the demands of *relevance*. The state and educational bureaucracy will ensure that the school remains *relevant*, and that is not without its own challenges. That aside, the nature of the student as a person, and the requirements for the continued maturity of personhood, cannot be governed by relevance alone. Students must be assisted to understand that their growth through knowledge and understanding is dependent upon what they learn in school, both inside and outside the classroom, and that such learning is essential for their liberation and freedom. The curriculum, religious exercises, sports, social outreach, debates, and interpersonal relations are some of the varied ways through which students come to know, and the means of liberating their individual and communal experiences. It is true that the goal of education is not simply to communicate knowledge, but this too needs qualification before its clarity can be comprehended. The teacher teaches in order to strengthen the student's powers of thinking and reasoning, understanding and judging, and then deciding and choosing, all as a means toward their personal freedom and liberation. Education is not the sum total of what is imparted through intellectual knowledge alone. However, what is required is a governing agency that gathers the different ways of knowing and understanding into unity, and that is to be found in the student's active intellectual and spiritual agency in the knowing and understanding process, realized through insights, making connections, seeing implications, making judgments, carrying out decisions. It is the student who must understand that there are many different ways of knowing, apart from the empirical, the observable, and the measurable.

St Justin Martyr said, "As the good of the body is health, so the good of the soul is knowledge, which is indeed a kind of health of soul, by which a likeness to God is attained."[24] How does knowledge promote the health of the common good and thus of society? If knowledge is equated with information and data, then it is likely that the good will be equated with all that can be controlled, manipulated, and redirected to serve a vision of society and persons based on a scientific, technological, and mechanistic rationality. Knowledge and understanding are transformative and liberating. In democratic societies where education is often freely provided for all, knowledge can easily be taken for granted, and this can easily lead to confusion as to its purpose, what it entails, and how it is related to the freedom and liberation of the student, particularly in relation to understanding. The title of a recent book sums up the matter rather well: *Where Is Knowing Going?*[25] One of the themes of the book is how personal knowing is one essential means of self-revelation. Where indeed knowing is going is a question that should be of perennial concern to a Catholic philosophy of education. All our wealth of systems, methods, technologies, and other educational innovations will be of no use if the fundamental purposes of knowing and understanding are not clearly placed at the centre of the intellectual mandate of the school.

The universality of Catholic education is not primarily its international reputation and recognition, but rather its ability to educate the student as an integral person, to educate all students through a particular worldview and anthropology, and to be able to do so without compromising the particular religious and cultural identity of the student. Catholic education is universal because the person's desire to know and understand is universal. Such an education seeks to help the student not only to know reality in all its diversity, but to be able to distinguish the kinds of realities, the different kinds and levels of truth, and the different kinds of knowledge required to respond to these realities. How reality is understood and constituted is ultimately dependent upon how one grows in goodness through choices, decisions, and actions, and thus the Catholic school is equally interested in the becoming of students for their world and society.

Jesus did not come to establish Catholic schools. He came to save men and women from the never-ending, imprisoning, and destructive cycle of sin and death. However, once people are so saved, everything changes, for human beings are, in the words of St Paul, " a new creation," and how they live their lives by seeking, yearning, and striving for the good and all that ennobles one's humanity is in response to being so saved. Catholic education is the indispensable secondary reflection of the implications of being saved by Christ: the decisions made and the choices carried out. In this world, men and women must learn to love and yearn for the right things, for which knowledge, learning, and understanding are essential. It would appear that at the final judgment we will each be asked to given an account not of how much we know, but of how much we have loved. For this, Catholic education can offer a vision of ordering and unifying one's life, personally and communally, by loving wisely and well.

NOTES

INTRODUCTION

1 In his book *Educating for Life: A Spiritual Vision for Every Teacher and Parent*, Thomas Groome says, "The first Catholic schools in Pakistan were founded in 1856 at Sialkot by the Sisters of Jesus and Mary, a French order, and the system burgeoned thereafter. It now numbers about 550 schools of various kinds, many of which are huge institutions, providing schooling from kindergarten to college. St. Joseph's Karachi [St Joseph's Convent School is an institution which Groome visited during his time in Pakistan] is more than one hundred years old and has over three thousand students. Clearly a jewel in the crown, yet it is only one example of what is widely considered the best educational system in Pakistan." Groome, *Educating for Life*, 9–10.

2 Ibid., 11, 40.

3 Taylor, "Multiculturalism and the Politics of Recognition," 34.

4 Maritain, *Ransoming the Time*, 125.

5 Sen, *Identity and Violence*, 14–15, 13. The following passage, from the same work, is also worthy of note: "Perhaps the worst impairment comes from the neglect – and denial – of the role of reasoning and choice, which follows from the recognition of our plural identities: The illusion of unique identity is much more divisive than the universe of plural and diverse classifications that characterize the world in which we actually live. The descriptive weakness of choice less singularity has the effect of momentously improvising the power and reach of our social and political reasoning. The illusion of destiny exacts a remarkably heavy price" (17).

6 See D'Souza, "The Distinctiveness of Catholic Education," 45–72.

7 Paul VI, *Nostra Aetate / Declaration on the Relation of the Church to Non-Christian Religions*, para. 1.
8 See *Code of Canon Law, Latin-English Edition*, canons 802–6 on the Catholic school, and canons 807–14 on the Catholic university.
9 See D'Souza, "Religious Particularism and Cultural Pluralism."
10 See, for example, Morris, ed., *Catholic Education: Universal Principles, Locally Applied*.
11 The University of Toronto Press is publishing the *Collected Works of Bernard Lonergan*.
12 The two most historic encyclicals issued well before the Second Vatican Council are Pope Leo XIII's *Rerum Novarum / Of New Things* (1892), on the principles for a just society, including protecting the right of workers and the defense and limits of private property; and Pope Pius XI's *Quadragesimo Anno / On the Fortieth Year* (1931), condemning dictatorship and fascism and the oppression of child and female labour.

CHAPTER ONE

1 In later documents, the Sacred Congregation for Catholic Education refers to itself as "The Congregation for Catholic Education" and "Congregation for Catholic Education." References in the bibliography will appear as the document is designated.
2 See *Papal Teachings: Education*. See also Franchi, ed., *An Anthology of Catholic Education*.
3 See McCool, *From Unity to Pluralism*, 224–30.
4 See Brezik, ed., *One Hundred Years of Thomism*; Reilly, *The Leonine Enterprise*; Ventresca, "A Plague of Perverse Opinions: Leo XIII's Aeterni Patris and the Catholic Encounter with Modernity"; and Watzlawik, *Leo XIII and The New Scholasticism*.
5 See McCool, *Nineteenth Century Scholasticism*, 32.
6 Jedin, *Crisis and the Closure of the Council of Trent*, 5. Also see ch. 19, "The General Council of Trent, 1545–63," in Hughes, *The Church in Crisis*, 265–93.
7 Gallicanism was a French movement that sought to limit papal authority to the spiritual realm, thus drawing a sharp line between spiritual and temporal powers; its origins stretch from the Middle Ages to the French Revolution. It stood in opposition to Ultramontanism, which looked to Rome for universal leadership and authority. The Catholic Church was caught between two extreme positions, and it could agree to neither in order to retain its Catholicity: a Church organized solely on a national model, or a Church totally autonomous from the state and relying exclusively on papal

supremacy. See McEvoy, *Leaving Christendom for God*, 67–8, and Warner, *Confessions of an Interest Group*, 56–9.

8 See Hayward, *The Vatican Council*. See also ch. 20, "The First General Council of The Vatican, 1869–70," in Hughes, *The Church in Crisis*, 294–324.

9 Watzlawik, *Leo XIII and the New Scholasticism*, 78.

10 Ibid, 83.

11 Leo XIII, *Aeterni Patris: On the Restoration of Christian Philosophy*, para. 31.

12 Edwards, ed., *The Encyclopedia of Philosophy, vol. 8*, 121.

13 McCool, *From Unity to Pluralism*, 161.

14 It is maintained that the very "timelessness" of the thought of St Thomas, its relevance for each age, means that there "can be no such thing as Thomism." See Pieper, *The Silence of St. Thomas*, 85. For a brief exposé on the rise of scholasticism after the First Vatican Council and its relation to Catholic education, see the chapter "Vatican I and the Revival of Scholasticism," in Bryk, Lee, and Holland, *Catholic Schools and the Common Good*, 35–41.

15 A Thomist philosopher or theologian, then, is one "who believes that his seminal, or core, ideas agree with those of the thirteenth-century Dominican theologian, St. Thomas Aquinas, as that philosopher or theologian reads the Thomistic texts ... Obviously this understanding of 'Thomist' does not baptize or anoint any particular brand of Thomism. Rather, it establishes a definite-enough context to distinguish a Thomist from a Kantian, Hegelian, or Heideggerian, yet possesses the logical space to permit the various Thomists to argue and settle the issue of which Thomism is authentic or inauthentic, philosophically correct or incorrect, etc." Knasas, "Whither the Neo-Thomist Revival," 121–2.

16 See Pieper, *The Silence of St. Thomas*, 83.

17 Maurer, "Gilson and *Aeterni Patris*," 101.

18 Gilson, *The Christian Philosophy of St. Thomas Aquinas*, 8. Also, "It has become customary to label 'theological' any conclusion whose premises presuppose faith in a divinely revealed truth, and to label 'philosophical' any conclusions whose premises are purely rational, that is, known by the light of reason alone. This is not the point of view stated by St. Thomas himself at the beginning of his Prologue to the Second Book of his commentary on the *Sentences* of Peter Lombard" (9).

19 Wallace, *The Elements of Philosophy*, 291.

20 Maurer, "Gilson and *Aeterni Patris*," 94, 97.

21 Egan, *Philosophy and Theology: A Primer*, 52.

22 See McCool, *The Neo-Thomists*, 1.

23 See Wallace, *The Elements of Philosophy*, 327.

24 "It is part of the paradox of Thomism that it claims to be an exception to the generally valid principle that the proper name of no philosopher should be

used to circumscribe perennial philosophy because it is not a system but a wisdom, a synthesis and a spiritual organism capable of assimilating truth wherever it may be." Gallagher, "Contemporary Thomism," 455.

25 Knasas, *Being and Some Twentieth-Century Thomists*, 3.

26 See McCool, *From Unity to Pluralism*, 8–10.

27 In replying to the objection that God is not one, St Thomas replies, "Thirdly, this is shown from the unity of the world. For all things that exist are seen to be ordered to each other since some serve others. But things that are diverse do not harmonize in the same order, unless they are ordered thereto by one. For many are reduced into one order by the one better than by many: because one is *per se* cause of one, and many are only the accidental cause of one, inasmuch as they are in some way one. Since, therefore what is first is most perfect, and is so *per se* and not accidentally, it must be that the first which reduces all into one order should be only one. And this one is God." *The Summa of St. Thomas Aquinas*, vol. I, 47–8.

28 Pius X, *Pascendi Dominici Gregis / On the Doctrines of the Modernists*, 39.

29 Daly, *Transcendence and Immanence*, 5.

30 Reardon, "Introduction," in *Roman Catholic Modernism*, 9.

31 McCarthy, *The Catholic Tradition*, 51, 129.

32 O'Connell, *Critics on Trial*, 33.

33 Ginther, "Notre attitude en face du Pragmatisme: George Tyrell's Relation to Pragmatism," 196–7.

34 Schultenover, *A View from Rome*, 2. See also Daly, *Transcendence and Immanence*, 2. See also Thompson, ch. 1, "The Legacy of the Modernist Crisis," in *Between Science and Religion*, 1–30.

35 Mayer, *The Philosophy of Teaching of St. Thomas Aquinas*, 10, 89–90, 161.

36 Marique, *The Philosophy of Christian Education*, vii, 27, 45, 71, 84, 335, 27–9; Pius XI, *Divini Illius Magistri / On Christian Education*.

37 Slavin, "The Thomistic Concept of Education," 313, the four causes, 313–14, and 331.

38 Leen, *What Is Education?*, 7, 53–4, 253, 237, 225.

39 Redden and Ryan, *A Catholic Philosophy of Education*, 31, 353, 371–2, 86, 91, 15.

40 Pegis, *Christian Philosophy and Intellectual Freedom*, 30, 33, 48, 65, 68, 73.

41 Cunningham, *The Pivotal Problems of Education*, 4, 9, 267, 272, 551, 552, 467–70.

42 See for example Maritain, *An Essay on Christian Philosophy*, on the *nature and state* and *the order of specification and the order of exercise of Christian philosophy*, 11–13.

43 Ward, *New Life in Catholic Schools*, 34, 14, 53, 66, 71, 72.

44 Smith, *The School Examined: Its Aim and Content*, 29, 33, 12, 235, 248, 231, 201, 199, 35, 41.

45 See Brennan, *Thomistic Psychology*.

46 McLean, ed., *Philosophy and the Integration of Contemporary Catholic Education*, 6, 7, 16, 18, 24, 33, 35, 36, 231, 232.

47 Copleston, *Aquinas*.

48 Goodrich, "Neo-Thomism and Education," 167, 168, 170, 172, 173.

49 Gleason, *Contending with Modernity*, 301, and see also 300–4.

50 See Faggioli, *Vatican II*.

51 Gaillardetz and Clifford, *Keys to the Council*, 40.

52 O'Malley, "Introduction," in *After Vatican II*, xiv.

53 Knightley, "Vatican II: The Church's Self Understanding," 1, 4.

54 Sullivan, *The Road to Vatican II*, 4, 5–8, 12.

55 Byron, "Communio as the Context for Memory: On the Universal-Local Church Relationship," 77–8.

56 See Congar, *Traditions and Tradition: An Historical and a Theological Essay*, 252, 253, 348, 264–5.

57 Dulles, *Models of Revelation*, 15.

58 Paul VI, *Dogmatic Constitution on Divine Revelation / Dei Verbum*, para. 10.

59 See D'Souza, "Tradition in the Context of Religious Education," 9–15.

60 Paul VI, *Pastoral Constitution on the Church in the Modern World / Gaudium et Spes*, para. 25.

61 Paul VI, *Dogmatic Constitution on the Church / Lumen Gentium*, para. 41 and 31. See also para. 46–7.

62 Ashley, "Contemporary Understanding of Personhood," in *The Twenty-Fifth Anniversary of Vatican II*, 38, 39, 41.

63 Hess and Allen, *Catholicism and Science*, 97.

64 Egan, *Philosophy and Catholic Theology*, 49.

65 Faggioli, *Vatican II and the Battle for Meaning*, 75–6.

66 Kelty, "Catholic Education: The Historical Context," in *The Catholic School: Paradoxes and Challenges*, 28.

67 See Knasas, *Being and Some Twentieth-Century Thomists* and "Whither the Neo-Thomist Revival?"

68 Bryk et al., *Catholic Schools and the Common Good*, 54.

69 For a helpful article on the distinctions between the Council's terminology of "constitutions," "declarations," "decrees," etc., see Grote, "Rome's Official Statements: How and What? Towards a Typology of Documents."

70 Pius X, *Acerbo Nimis / On Teaching Christian Doctrine*, para. 12, 5.

71 Pius XI, *Divini Illius Magistri*, para. 3, 5, 11, 21, 92, 68, 7.

72 Briel, "The Declaration on Christian Education, *Gravissimum Educationis*," 389.

73 Carter, "Education," 634–5.

74 While *Gravissimum Educationis* is a very broad document under the title of *Christian Education*, since the close of the Council, the Congregation for Catholic Education (one of the Roman Congregations, and part of the government of the Holy See) has assumed the work of Catholic education. The establishment of this Congregation can be traced back to Pope Sixtus V in 1588, when it was intended to oversee Roman universities, including universities in Bologna, Paris, and Salamanca. Gradually it came to oversee Catholic universities, and more recently under Pope Benedict XVI it assumed responsibility for seminaries as well.

75 Paul VI, *Declaration on Christian Education / Gravissimum Educationis*, para. 1, 2, 6, 7, 3, 5, 10.

76 Burke, "Vatican II on Schools," 106.

77 O'Malley, *What Happened at Vatican II*, 270.

78 Leckey, *The Laity and Christian Education*, 22, 23.

79 O'Malley, *What Happened at Vatican II*, 270.

80 Donohue, *Catholicism and Education*, 7, 13, 28, 31, 32.

81 Boys, *Educating in Faith*, 80, 81, 89, 91, 90.

82 Moran, "Religious Education after Vatican II," 151, 151–2, 153, 156, 159, 162.

83 Kelty, "Toward a Theology of Catholic Education," 7, 10, 13–14, 12, 22.

84 Elias, "Whatever Happened to Catholic Philosophy of Education," 92, 96, 101, 102, 103, 105–9.

85 John Paul II, *Fides et Ratio / Faith and Reason*, para. 63.

86 See, for example, The Sacred Congregation for Catholic Education, *Lay Catholics in Schools: Witnesses to Faith*, para. 38, 39, 47, 80; and Congregation for Catholic Education, *The Religious Dimension of Education in a Catholic School: Guidelines for Reflection and Renewal*, para. 22, 23, 34, 63.

CHAPTER TWO

1 Phelan, "First Award of the Cardinal Spellman Aquinas Medal," 3.

2 Jacques Maritain, "Angelic Doctor," 7. *"There is a Thomist philosophy; there is no neo-Thomist philosophy"* (Maritain, *St. Thomas Aquinas*, 18).

3 On the breadth of Maritain's understanding of philosophy as the search for wisdom, see Thompson, *Between Science and Religion*, ch. 2, "Jacques Maritain's Search for Wisdom (1882–1973)," 31–56.

4 Raïssa Maritain, *We Have Been Friends Together: Memoirs*, 72–9.

5 McInerny, *The Very Rich Hours of Jacques Maritain*, 23.

6 See de Lubac, "Retrieving the Tradition: On Christian Philosophy," and Jordan, "The Terms of the Debate over Christian Philosophy." For a wider historical context see Nédoncelle, *Is There a Christian Philosophy?*

7 See, for example, Rice, "Jacques Maritain and the Problem of Christian Philosophy."

8 Maritain, *An Essay on Christian Philosophy*, 17, 29.

9 See Maritain, *The Education of Man: The Educational Philosophy of Jacques Maritain*, 39–41.

10 Ibid., 40.

11 See ibid., 40–1.

12 See ibid., 42–3.

13 See ibid., 44–5.

14 Ibid., 45–6.

15 Ibid., 46–7.

16 Ibid., 41–2.

17 Maritain, *Integral Humanism: Temporal and Spiritual Problems of a New Christendom*, 22.

18 Maritain, *Education of Man*, 42, 43.

19 Ibid., 130.

20 See ibid., 129–30.

21 Saracino, *On Being Human*, 15.

22 Ibid.

23 Mathews, *Lonergan's Quest*, 8.

24 Crowe, *Appropriating the Lonergan Idea*, 70.

25 For example, "Moreover, there is the problem of Christian philosophy, in that philosophy involves a man's unrestricted reflection upon himself, where 'man' is not considered in the abstract but as human[s] actually exist and therefore as affected by original sin, by grace, and by the acceptance or rejection of supernatural gifts, all of which lie within the domain of theology. What then remains of philosophy?" Lonergan, *Early Works on Theological Method 2*, 153. See also Lonergan, *Topics in Education*, 18–24.

26 Kerr, *After Aquinas*, 208.

27 Lonergan, *Collection*, 223.

28 Lonergan, *Method in Theology*, 14–15.

29 Ibid., 17, 16.

30 See, for example, "Insight: A Preface to a Discussion," in Lonergan, *Collection*, 142–52; see also "Insight Revisited," in Lonergan, *Second Collection: Papers by Bernard J.F. Lonergan SJ*, 263–78.

31 Crowe, *Lonergan*.

32 Lonergan, *Topics*, 4–5.

33 See ibid., 6–7.

34 Ibid., 7–8.

35 See ibid., 6–8, 9.

36 See ibid., 15–16, 17–18.

37 See ibid., 18–19.

38 Ibid., 20.
39 Lonergan, *Verbum: Word and Idea in Aquinas*, 41.
40 Lonergan, *Topics*, 20–1.
41 Ibid., 21.
42 Ibid., 23–4.
43 Ibid., 24.
44 Allard, *Education for Freedom*, 114.
45 See O'Malley, "The Education of Man," 7.
46 See Tierny, "M. Maritain on Education," 22.
47 See O'Donnell, "Jacques Maritain – Political Philosopher," 178.
48 Beales, "Jacques Maritain," 76.
49 Egan, "Review of *Education at the Crossroads*," 418.
50 Buford, *Toward a Philosophy of Education*, 419.
51 See Sullivan, "Catholic Education as Ongoing Translation," 206–7.
52 See also Carr, Haldane, McLaughlin, and Pring, "Return to the Cross-roads," 163. This article emphasizes particular aspects of Maritain's Thomistic educational theory.
53 Lonergan, *Second Collection*, 37. Topley's article, "Meeting Lonergan's Challenge to Educators," offers helpful suggestions on how these three questions can be addressed in a classroom.
54 See Lonergan, *Collection*, 208.
55 Topley, "Meeting Lonergan's Challenge to Educators," 371.
56 See Walker, "Lonergan, Science, and Religious Education," 147.
57 Shea, "From Classicism to Method: John Dewey and Bernard Lonergan," 304.
58 See Fitzpatrick, "Subjectivity and Objectivity: Polanyi and Lonergan."
59 O'Shea, "The 'Critical Realism' of Jacques Maritain and Bernard Lonergan," 1–2, 22. For similarities between Maritain and Lonergan see 117–18, 120, 122–8, 136–7.
60 Lonergan, *Insight: A Study of Human Understanding*, 717.
61 Lonergan, *Second Collection*, 74.
62 See Lonergan, *Philosophical and Theological Papers 1958–1964*, 46.
63 See Lonergan, *Understanding and Being*, 238.
64 See Lonergan, *Second Collection*, 241.
65 See Lonergan, *Method in Theology*, 6.
66 See Lonergan, *Second Collection*, 241.
67 Lonergan, *Verbum*, 192.
68 See Lonergan, *Collection*, 193, 194.
69 See O'Shea, "The Critical Realism of Jacques Maritain and Bernard Lonergan," 117–18.
70 Maritain, *Education at the Crossroads*, 50–1.

71 Maritain, *Education of Man*, 135, 136.
72 Maritain, *Theonas: Conversations of a Sage*, 58.

CHAPTER THREE

1 "A Catholic school is a 'civic institution:' its aim, methods and characteristics are the same as those of every other school. On the other hand, it is
a 'Christian community,' whose educational goals are rooted in Christ and
his Gospel." CCE, *Religious Dimension of Education*, para. 67.
2 See Sacred Congregation for Catholic Education, *Educational Guidance in
Human Love: Outlines for Sex Education*, para. 41, 42.
3 See Leo XIII, *Spectata Fides / On Christian Education*, para. 4.
4 See Pius X, *Acerbo Nimis*, para. 5, 7, 2.
5 See ibid., para. 26; see also para. 12, 24.
6 Pius XI, *Divini Illius Magistri*, para. 7.
7 See ibid., para. 11.
8 See ibid., para. 11, 6, 7, 28, 56.
9 Paul VI, *Gravissimum Educationis*, para. 1.
10 Ibid.
11 Ibid., para. 8.
12 The Sacred Congregation for Catholic Education. *The Catholic School*, para.
36.
13 See ibid., para. 43, and also para. 53, 39.
14 Congregation for Catholic Education, *Consecrated Persons and Their Mission
in Schools: Reflections and Guidelines*, para. 52.
15 CCE, *Lay Catholics*, para. 17.
16 "Every type of education is inspired by a specific concept of man and
woman. Christian education aims to promote the realization of man and
woman through the development of their being, incarnate spirits, and of
the gifts of nature and of grace by which they are enriched by God. Christian education is rooted in the faith which throws a new light on all things
and makes known the full ideal which God has set for man." CCE, *Educational Guidance*, para. 21. See also para. 19.
17 "The Catholic school should be able to offer young people the means to acquire the knowledge they need in order to find a place in a society which is
strongly characterized by technical and scientific skill." CCE, *The Catholic
School on the Threshold of the Millennium*, para. 8.
18 CCE, "Introduction," in *Presentation of Consecrated Persons*. See also *Catholic School on the Threshold*, para. 100.
19 CCE, *Catholic School*, para. 67.
20 Ibid., para. 56.

21 See CCE, *Religious Dimension of Education*, para. 69.

22 See CCE, *Catholic School*, para. 30.

23 See ibid., para. 29.

24 "It should be no surprise that young people bring into the classroom what they see and hear in the world around them, along with the impressions gained from the 'world' of mass media. Perhaps some have become indifferent or insensitive." CCE, *Religious Dimension of Education*, para. 71. See also CCE, *Educational Guidance*, para. 67.

25 See CCE, *Religious Dimension of Education*, para. 82.

26 See CCE, *Consecrated Persons and Schools*, para. 50, 53.

27 "Real education is not possible without the light of truth." CCE, *Educating Together in Catholic Schools: A Shared Mission Between Consecrated Persons and the Lay Faithful*, para. 7.

28 See ibid., para. 67.

29 See CCE, *Catholic School*, para. 39, and *Religious Dimension of Education*, para. 53.

30 See CCE, *Religious Dimension of Education*, para. 55, 58.

31 See ibid., para. 60, 51.

32 See CCE, *Consecrated Persons and Schools*, para. 39.

33 CCE, *Educating Today and Tomorrow: A Renewing Passion: Instrumentum Laboris*, Section III.

34 See CCE, *Educating to Intercultural Dialogue in Catholic Schools: Living in Harmony for a Civilization of Love*, para. 67.

35 See CCE, *Circular Letter to the Presidents of Bishops' Conferences on Religious Education in Schools*, para. 12, 10, 18.

36 See CCE, *Lay Catholics*, para. 38, 17, 18, 69.

37 "Contemporary pedagogy of Christian inspiration sees in the person being educated, considered in all of his or her totality and complexity, the principle subject of education." CCE, *Educational Guidance*, para. 37.

38 See CCE, *Educating Today and Tomorrow*, Section III, e.

39 "The criterion of Catholic identity"; "building up a common vision"; "reasoned openness to globalization"; forming "strong personal identities"; development of "self-awareness"; respect for "the values of other cultures and religions"; and enhancing a sense of "sharing and responsibility." CCE, *Intercultural Dialogue in Schools*, para. 63.

40 CCE, *Religious Dimension of Education*, para. 98.

41 See, CCE, *Catholic School*, para. 40.

42 The curriculum's diversity ensures a balance of knowledge, without an exaggerated emphasis upon sciences and the scientific method, which "cannot grasp the essence of experience and the inner reality of things." Pontifical Council for Culture, *Towards a Pastoral Approach to Culture*, para. 13, 11.

43 See CCE, *Catholic School*, para. 50.

44 See CCE, *Religious Dimension of Education*, para. 6.

45 CCE, *Intercultural Dialogue in Schools*, para. 69.

46 "Education contains a central challenge for the future: to allow various cultural expressions to co-exist and to promote dialogue so as to foster a peaceful society. These aims are achieved in various stages: (1) discovering the multicultural nature of one's own situation; (2) overcoming prejudices by living and working in harmony; and (3) educating oneself 'by means of the other' to a global vision and a sense of citizenship. Fostering encounters between different people helps to create mutual understanding, although it ought not to mean a loss of one's own." Ibid, "Introduction."

47 CCE, *Catholic School on the Threshold*, 11.

48 See CCE, *Educating Today and Tomorrow*, Section III, and *Intercultural Dialogue in Schools*, para. 57.

49 See Maritain, *Crossroads*, 1–28.

50 See ibid., 4–10.

51 "If we are concerned with the future of civilization we must be concerned primarily with a genuine understanding of what knowledge is, its value, its degrees, and how it can foster the inner unity of the human being." Maritain, *Range of Reason*, 3.

52 See Maritain, *Crossroads*, 10.

53 Ibid., 4, and Maritain, *Education of Man*, 43.

54 Maritain, *Crossroads*, 22.

55 Ibid., 23.

56 See Maritain, *Creative Intuition in Art and Poetry*, 124, 130.

57 See Maritain, *Crossroads*, 44.

58 Ibid., 19.

59 The person who is also a "material individual, a fragment of a species, a part of the physical universe, a single dot in the immense network of forces and influences, cosmic, ethnic, historic, whose laws we must obey." Ibid., 9.

60 Ibid:, 7–8.

61 See ibid., 5.

62 See Maritain, *Education of Man*, 180.

63 "[H]uman life [is] ordered simultaneously to two different absolute ultimate ends, a purely natural ultimate end, which is perfect prosperity here on earth, and a supernatural ultimate end, which is perfect beatitude in heaven." Maritain, *Integral Humanism*, 22. Also, "the good life on earth is not the [human] absolute ultimate end ... which is eternal life." Maritain, *Range of Reason*, 143.

64 Maritain, *Crossroads*, 11.

65 Ibid., 3.

66 Education without clear aims and simply focused on growth "is no more an art than … architecture which would not have any idea of what is to be built, and would only tend to the growth of the construction in whatever direction a new addition of materials is feasible." Ibid., 17.

67 See Maritain, *Education of Man*, 112.

68 See ibid., 50–1, 58.

69 See ibid., 59, and Maritain, *Crossroads*, 4–15.

70 See Maritain, *Crossroads*, 18. "[E]ducation in the broad sense of the word continues during the entire lifetime of everyone of us. The school system is only a partial and inchoate agency with respect to this task." Maritain, *Education of Man*, 83.

71 See Maritain, *Crossroads*, 20.

72 Ibid., 11–12.

73 See ibid., ch. 3, "The Humanities and Liberal Education," 58–87.

74 See, ibid., 2.

75 Ibid., 10–11.

76 See ibid., 30–1.

77 See ibid., 59–60; see also 55–6.

78 Ibid., 59, 50, 52–3.

79 Ibid., 55. The examples include handicrafts, games, sports, gardening, beekeeping, rustic lore, cooking, and home economics.

80 Ibid., 53.

81 Ibid., 45, 64.

82 See Maritain, *Education of Man*, 135–6, on the *Christian-inspirited enlargement* of the curriculum.

83 See Maritain, *Crossroads*, 24; see also *Education of Man*, 74.

84 See Maritain, *Education of Man*, 72, 48.

85 See ibid., 89–90, 97–8.

86 See Maritain, *Crossroads*, 36.

87 This is a theme in Jacques and Raïssa Maritain's work *Prayer and Intelligence*.

88 "[I]t is not the aim of Catholic education to produce colonial administrators." Lonergan, *Topics*, 103.

89 Lonergan, *Insight*, 12.

90 Lonergan is concerned with the two positions of knowledge: "I ask … about the nature rather than about the existence of knowledge because in each of us there exist two different kinds of knowledge. They are juxtaposed in Cartesian dualism with its rational *Cogito ergo sum* and with its unquestioning extroversion to substantial extension" (ibid., 11). Lonergan is seeking a third way between rationalism on the one side and empiricism on the other.

91 (1) It "comes as a release to the tension of inquiry"; (2) it happens "suddenly and unexpectedly"; (3) it is a "function not of outer circumstances but of inner conditions"; (4) it "pivots between the concrete and the abstract"; and (5) once grasped, it becomes part of the "texture of one's mind." Ibid., 28; see also 27–31.

92 See Lonergan, *Method in Theology*, 13.

93 Lonergan, *Philosophical and Theological Papers 1965–1980*, 338.

94 See Lonergan, *Insight*, 304, 348.

95 See Lonergan, *Collection*, 209.

96 Lonergan, *Method in Theology*, 8–9.

97 See Lonergan, *Second Collection*, 241, 76–7.

98 Ibid., 241–3, 239.

99 "seeing, hearing, touching, smelling, tasting, inquiring, imagining, understanding, conceiving, formulating, reflecting, marshalling and weighing the evidence, judging deliberating, evaluating, deciding, speaking, writing ... To say that the operations intend an object is to refer to such facts as that by seeing there becomes present what is seen, by hearing there becomes present what is heard, by imagining there becomes present what is imagined." Lonergan, *Method in Theology*, 6–7.

100 See Lonergan, *Papers 1965–1980*, 136.

101 Intending moves one from "ignorance to knowledge ... intelligence takes us beyond experiencing to ask what and why and how and what for. Reasonableness takes us beyond the answers of intelligence to ask whether the answers are true and whether what they really mean is so. Responsibility goes beyond fact and desire and possibility to discern between what truly is good and what only apparently is good." Lonergan, *Method in Theology*, 11.

102 See Lonergan, *Insight*, 273, 296–9, 367–8.

103 Recall from ch. 2 that Lonergan prefers *subject* to *person*.

104 See Lonergan, *Insight*, 407.

105 All three questions appear across Lonergan's works; see for example *Second Collection*, 37, and *Method in Theology*, 83.

106 Lonergan, *Insight*, 437.

107 Lonergan is referring to the Augustinian "vision of eternal truths." Lonergan, *Verbum*, 85.

108 For Plato, "the ultimate answer is not something that we are but something that we see; it supposes that knowledge essentially is not identity with the known but some spiritual contact or confrontation with the known" (ibid.).

109 The validation of knowledge "cannot be something we know, for the knowing and the known must themselves be validated in an ultimate validation.

The ultimate validation lies in what we are, namely something attuned to the absolute." Ibid., 231.

110 See ibid., 232.

111 See Lonergan, *Topics*, 215–16.

112 Lonergan, *Collection*, 149. See also 148, "being and the concrete are identical terms."

113 See ibid., 217.

114 See Lonergan, *Papers 1958–1964*, 216.

115 "[I]ntellectual operations have their objectivity, not because they resemble ocular vision, but because they are what ocular vision never is, namely intelligent and rational." Lonergan, *Collection*, 218.

116 Lonergan, *Early Works on Theological Method 1*, 14.

117 Lonergan, *Topics*, 188.

118 See ibid., 85: "But what is one's world? It is a horizon of horizons. It is the totality of objects ... the organized whole of intelligibility varying objects in which I happen to have an interest, for which I have any concern. And that totality is a totality that we construct out of our experience, where the construction is governed by our concern."

119 Ibid.

120 Ibid., 90.

121 See ibid., 210.

122 "Consciousness is undifferentiated where the whole person is involved, operating simultaneously and equally with all of his powers. Differentiated consciousness, on the other hand, is capable of operating exclusively, or at least principally, on a single level, while the other levels are entirely subordinated to the attainment of the goal at that level ... the whole person, with all his powers, tends towards a goal that is proportionate to man. In contrast the scientist or speculative thinker, tends towards a goal that is not that of the whole man, but only of his intellect." Lonergan, *The Way to Nicea: The Dialectical Development of Trinitarian Theology*, 2–3.

123 Lonergan, *Method in Theology*, 303.

124 See Lonergan, *Second Collection*, 240–1.

125 Ibid., 241.

126 See Lonergan, *Papers 1965–1980*, 117. Lonergan's example of how a smile communicates meaning is particularly thought-provoking. See 110–11.

127 Ibid., 145.

128 See ibid., 142.

129 See ibid., 136.

130 Compare Aristotle (1979), *Metaphysics*, "All men by nature desire understanding" (12), with Aristotle (1941), *Metaphysics*, "All men by nature desire to know" (689).

CHAPTER FOUR

1 See CCE, "Introduction," in *Presentation of Consecrated Persons*. See also Paul VI, *Evangelii Nuntiandi / On Evangelization in the Modern World*, para. 78, on the difficulties facing parents and teachers.
2 CCE, *Catholic School*, para. 55.
3 See CCE, *Religious Dimension of Education*, para. 55.
4 CCE, *Consecrated Persons and Schools*, para. 52.
5 See CCE, *Catholic School*, para. 9, 12, 25.
6 See CCE, *Religious Dimension of Education*, para. 24.
7 See CCE, *Lay Catholics*, para. 17.
8 See ibid., 33, and CCE, *Educational Guidance*, para. 97.
9 See CCE, *Consecrated Persons and Schools*, para. 5.
10 CCE, *Educating Today and Tomorrow*, Section III.
11 See CCE, *Intercultural Dialogue in Schools*, para. 34, 63.
12 Compare CCE, *Catholic School*, para. 47 with CCE, *Intercultural Dialogue in Schools*, which has at least twenty-one references to unity amidst diversity.
13 CCE, *Religious Dimension of Education*, para. 107.
14 "Catholic schools, being Catholic, are not limited to a vague Christian inspiration or one based on human values. They have the responsibility of offering Catholic students, over and above a sound knowledge of religion, the possibility to grow in personal closeness to Christ in the Church." CCE, *Intercultural Dialogue in Schools*, para. 56.
15 See CCE, *Circular Letter*, para., 12, 10, 13, 18.
16 See ibid., para. 10.
17 "[A]ll children and young people must have the same possibilities for arriving at the *knowledge of their own religion* as well as of elements that characterize other religions" (CCE, *Intercultural Dialogue in Schools*, para. 18). See also CCE, *Religious Dimension of Education*, para. 108.
18 See Congregation for the Clergy, *General Directory for Catechesis*, para. 75, and CCE, *Circular Letter*, para. 17.
19 CCE, *Educating Today and Tomorrow*, Section III.
20 CCE, *Consecrated Persons and Schools*. The earliest declares, "The school must begin from the principle that its educational programme is intentionally directed to the growth of the whole person" (CCE, *Catholic School*, para. 29).
21 See CCE, *Lay Catholics*, para. 70, 62.
22 See CCE, *Educational Guidance*, para. 16, 38.
23 See CCE, *Religious Dimension of Education*, para. 101b, and CCE, *Educating Together*, para. 30.
24 See CCE, *Intercultural Dialogue in Schools*, para. 63 and "Introduction."

25 See CCE, *Religious Dimension of Education*, para. 69.

26 See ibid., para. 11, 12, 13, 19.

27 "The Internet places in the grasp of young people at an unusually early age an immense capacity for doing good and doing harm, to themselves and to others. It can enrich their lives beyond the dreams of earlier generations and empower them to enrich others' lives in turn. It also can plunge them into consumerism, pornographic and violent fantasy, and pathological isolation." Pontifical Council for Social Communications, *The Church and Internet*, para. 11. "The situation in which the Catholic school must educate today is still fraught with serious difficulties. The climate of moral disorientation to which the same document refers [CCE, *Educational Guidance in Human Love* (1983)] is made worse by the reduction of sexuality to something commonplace in the environment surrounding young people. Through the mass-media, above all, sexual realities and the most intimate aspects of genital experience are displayed without reserve, while information on the use and abuse of sexuality is offered to young people before they are capable of understanding and assimilating it." Pio Cardinal Laghi, "Letter from the Congregation of Catholic Education on the Document, *Educational Guidance in Human Love*" (Rome, 2 May 1997).

28 CCE, *Religious Dimension of Education*, para. 9.

29 See CCE, *Educational Guidance*, para. 35.

30 CCE, *Religious Dimension of Education*, para. 105.

31 See ibid., para. 49, 106.

32 See ibid., para. 103.

33 Education could be defined as the "acquisition, growth and possession of freedom" (CCE, *Consecrated Persons and Schools*, para. 39; see also para. 52).

34 Ibid., para. 60.

35 See CCE, *Educating Together*, para. 13.

36 CCE, *Educational Guidance*, para. 19.

37 CCE, *Educating Together*, para. 24. One document elaborates on the dangers of "instrumental reason and competitiveness" and a "functional view of education," serving only a "market economy and the labour market." While recognizing that students will need to develop skills for later life, they cannot be acquired to "the exclusion of a multiplicity of skills that enrich the human person, such as creativity, imagination, the ability to take on responsibilities, to love the world, to cherish justice and compassion." See CCE, *Educating Today and Tomorrow*, Section III, 1, e.

38 CCE, *Lay Catholics*, para. 18.

39 See CCE, *Catholic School*, para. 27, and *Lay Catholics*, para. 22. The term *people of God* finds its more recent origin in the Documents of the Second

Vatican Council. See, for example, chapter II, "On the People of God," in Paul VI, *Lumen Gentium*.

40 CCE, *Lay Catholics*, para. 33, 32.

41 "The fundamental aim of teaching is the assimilation of objective values, and, when this is undertaken for an apostolic purpose, it does not stop at an integration of faith and culture but leads the pupil on to a personal integration of faith and life" (CCE, *The Catholic School*, para. 44).

42 See CCE, *Consecrated Persons and Schools*, para. 34, 35.

43 See ibid., para. 35, 36.

44 Phrases such as *spirituality of communion*, *to participate in the humanity of the other*, and *a reciprocity* that enables one to offer oneself as a *gift* to the other, leading to *closeness and a sense of solidarity* characterize this document (ibid., para. 35).

45 Ibid., para. 60.

46 CCE, *Educating Together*, para. 42.

47 See CCE, *Intercultural Dialogue in Schools*, para. 57.

48 See Paul VI, *Gravissimum Educationis*, para. 8, 11, 10.

49 See Maritain, *Crossroads*, ch. III, "The Humanities and Liberal Education," 58–87.

50 "[I]n the educational process the vital principle which exists in the student is the 'principal agent,' while the causality exercised by the teacher is, like medicine, only cooperating and assisting activity" (Maritain, *Education of Man*, 131).

51 See Maritain, *Crossroads*, 30–1.

52 Ibid., 45.

53 "[P]ersonality, metaphysically considered … bears witness in us to the generosity and expansivity of being which, is an incarnate spirit, proceeds from the spirit and which constitutes, in the secret springs of our ontological structure, a source of dynamic unity and unification from within" (Maritain, *Existence and the Existent*, 81–2).

54 See Maritain, *Crossroads*, 47.

55 See ibid., 62, 136.

56 See Maritain, *The Peasant of the Garonne*, 178–9n14, and *The Person and the Common Good*, 41–2.

57 See Maritain, *The Person and the Common Good*, 44–5. See also Maritain, *Education of Man*, 164.

58 It is maintained that Maritain's essay "The Conquest of Freedom," in *Education of Man*, is the "most comprehensive treatment on this theme and one of the most original statements of the Thomistic philosophy of freedom" (Donald and Idella Gallagher, "Introduction," in *Education of Man*, 10).

59 Maritain, *Crossroads*, 10–11. "The freedom that I shall treat of subsequently [in his essay "The Conquest of Freedom," in *Education of Man*, 159–79] is the freedom of independence and of exultation, which can be called also – in a Pauline but not Kantian sense – freedom of autonomy, or also freedom of expansion of the human person. It takes for granted freedom of choice in us, but it is substantially distinct from it." Maritain, *Education of Man*, 159.

60 Maritain, *Freedom in the Modern World*, 34.

61 See Maritain, *Education of Man*, 165.

62 See ibid., 109, 166.

63 See Maritain, *Existence and the Existent*, 81–2.

64 Maritain, *Education of Man*, 149–50.

65 Ibid., 168.

66 See Maritain, *Distinguish to Unite; or, The Degrees of Knowledge*, 439.

67 See Maritain, *Freedom in the Modern World*, 30.

68 Ibid.

69 Maritain, *Scholasticism and Politics*, 112.

70 Maritain, *Crossroads*, 13.

71 Ibid., 45.

72 "It is a pity that so many young people [are] bewildered by highly developed and specialized, but chaotic, instruction about anything whatever in the field of particular sciences and miserably ignorant of everything that concerns God and the deepest realities" (Maritain, *Education of Man*, 55; see also 69).

73 Maritain, *Crossroads*, 19.

74 See Maritain, *Education of Man*, 70.

75 "[T]he task of the school in preparing the young person for adult life must involve a twofold function: on the one hand it must provide the equipment in knowledge required by the vocations and activities which consist mainly of manual work; on the other hand it must provide the equipment in knowledge required by those vocations and activities which consist mainly in intellectual work" (ibid., 150).

76 Ibid., 130.

77 Ibid., 150.

78 Ibid., 137.

79 See Maritain, *Crossroads*, 18–19. For Maritain's seven misconceptions of education, see 2–25.

80 Ibid., 22.

81 On the abstractive, immaterial, and universal nature of the intellect, see Maritain, *Untrammelled Approaches*, 120.

82 See Maritain, *Crossroads*, 16. See also Maritain, *Education of Man*, 83.

83 Maritain, *Crossroads*, 16.
84 Ibid., 63.
85 Maritain, *Education of Man*, 105. Maritain elaborates on wisdom, saying it is a "superior kind of knowledge ... because it deals not only with mastering natural phenomena but with penetrating the primary and most universal raisons d'être and with enjoying, as a final fruition, the spiritual delight of truth and the sapidity of being, fulfills the supreme aspiration of the intellectual nature and its thirst for liberation" (47).
86 See ibid., 118, 119, 144, 112.
87 Maritain, *Crossroads*, 46.
88 As the Second World War rages, Maritain condemns the "*irrationalist* tide wave"; "the tragic opposition between life and intellect"; "anthropocentric humanism," as opposed to a theocentric humanism; various forms of totalitarianism; and Nazi racism. See Maritain, *The Twilight of Civilization*, 7, 8, 17, 19.
89 Ibid., 49, 50–1.
90 See ibid., 28.
91 Maritain, *A Preface to Metaphysics: Seven Lectures on Being*, 20.
92 See Maritain, *Education of Man*, 105, 114–17.
93 See Maritain, *Crossroads*, 14. Maritain lists five "fundamental dispositions to be fostered" in education: "with regard to truth and justice"; "with regard to existence"; "with regard to work"; and "with regard to others" (36–8).
94 Maritain, *Education of Man*, 158.
95 Ibid., 134.
96 Ibid., 172.
97 See Maritain, *The Degrees of Knowledge*, 6–7.
98 See Lonergan, *Method in Theology*, 239.
99 See ibid., 110. Lonergan says, "today's resolutions do not predetermine the free choice of tomorrow, of next week or next year ... What has been achieved is always precarious: it can slip, fall, shatter" (Lonergan, *Collection*, 224).
100 See Lonergan, *Method in Theology*, 286, 262.
101 Lonergan, *Insight*, 197, and see also 311.
102 Lonergan, *A Third Collection: Papers by Bernard J.F. Lonergan SJ*, 172–3.
103 See Lonergan, *Topics*, 147.
104 Lonergan, *Method in Theology*, 101, and see 102.
105 Lonergan, *Verbum*, 71.
106 Teachers possess a "view of the whole" (Lonergan, *Topics*, 149).
107 See Lonergan, *Method in Theology*, 240.
108 Lonergan, *Topics*, 150.

109 See Lonergan, *Insight*, 311.
110 See ibid., 197.
111 Ibid., 29.
112 Ibid., 315.
113 Lonergan notes that a blackboard is there to help students acquire a correct phantasm. See Lonergan, *Topics*, 114.
114 See Lonergan, *Verbum*, 41. Also, "Insight into a phantasm ... is the process that moves from sense to understanding to essential definition" (38).
115 Lonergan, *Topics*, 110. Lonergan speaks of "an act of understanding with respect to a phantasm" and follows with a definition, an "inner word," proceeding to understanding. Also, "The definition is the inner word, an ·expression, an unfolding of what one had got hold of in an insight" (218). See also Lonergan, *Verbum*, 40–1.
116 Lonergan, *Verbum*, 41.
117 See ibid., 42.
118 On intelligibility, see ibid., 46–7. See also 179 on the intelligible as the object of intellect. Also, "when one abstracts, one grasps the intelligible in the sensible" (Lonergan, *Topics*, 124).
119 See Lonergan, *Topics*, 47–8.
120 See ibid., 100, 101, 106.
121 See Lonergan, *Papers 1965–1980*, 12–13, 213, 217. See also Lonergan, *Method in Theology*, 292, on genuine subjectivity and objectivity.
122 See Lonergan, *Topics*, 206–7, 221.
123 Ibid., 174. Also "the idea of being is an act of understanding." Thus, while "knowledge may be abstract and universal ... all realities are particular and concrete" (Lonergan, *Verbum*, 16).
124 Lonergan, *Third Collection*, 180–1.
125 See Crowe, *Old Things and New: A Strategy for Education*.
126 Ibid., 2.
127 Lonergan, *Papers 1965–1980*, 362.
128 Lonergan, *Third Collection*, 197.
129 See Lonergan, *Insight*, 17, and Crowe, *Old Things and New*, 65n2.
130 "Generally speaking, human development from above downwards depends on gift, love, affectivity and tradition. More specifically, human development from above downwards revolves around love in its threefold manifestation, namely family love, civic love and divine love." Rusembuka, *The Two Ways of Human Development According to B. Lonergan*, 64.
131 Crowe, *Old Things and New*, 39.
132 See ibid., 51, where Crowe warns against the *banking concept of education*. See also 48.
133 Lonergan, *Method in Theology*, 38.

134 See Crowe, *Old Things and New*, 57, 58.

135 See ibid., 15, 64.

136 Ibid., 75.

137 See Lonergan, *Third Collection*, 106.

138 See Crowe, *Old Things and New*, 79.

139 See Lonergan, *Topics*, 209, 210.

140 Lonergan says that human subjects "are the products of artistic living" (ibid., 217).

141 Lonergan, *Insight*, 208.

142 See Crowe, *Old Things and New*, 81–2.

143 See ibid., 82. Crowe says, "both tradition and belief are values embodied in experience, and … teachers can assist the pupil to understand this experience, just as they can assist in the understanding of geometry" (83).

144 Ibid., 26. See Crowe's diagram regarding this integration of development across the three stages of human growth: childhood, adolescence, and adulthood.

145 See ibid., 22–4.

CHAPTER FIVE

1 CCE, *Lay Catholics*, para. 16.

2 See CCE, *Educating Today and Tomorrow*, "Conclusion."

3 See CCE, *Catholic School*, para. 40, 43, 29.

4 See Paul VI, *Gravissimum Educationis*, para. 7.

5 CCE, *Catholic School*, para. 53.

6 See CCE, *Religious Dimension of Education*, para. 96.

7 See CCE, *Educating Together*, para. 38. There are references (for example, para. 21, and see also para. 26) to the teacher's witness in CCE, *Religious Dimension of Education*.

8 Paul VI, *Gravissimum Educationis*, para. 3, 8.

9 See CCE, *Religious Dimension of Education*, para. 97.

10 CCE, *Lay Catholics*, para. 18.

11 Ibid., para. 16.

12 "[T]he educator who does not educate can no longer be called an educator. And if there is no trace of Catholic identity, the educator can hardly be called a Catholic educator." Ibid., para. 25.

13 See ibid., para. 24.

14 Paul VI, *Lumen Gentium*, para. 31.

15 See CCE, *Educating Today and Tomorrow*, para. 1, g.

16 See CCE, *Consecrated Persons and Schools*, para. 18.

17 See CCE, *Lay Catholics*, para. 74.

18 John Paul II, *Apostolic Exhortation Catechesi Tradendae / On Catechesis in Our Time*, para. 61.
19 See CCE, *Catholic School*, para. 78, 60.
20 Paul VI, *Gravissimum Educationis*, para. 5, 8.
21 See CCE, *Lay Catholics*, para. 27, 60.
22 CCE, *Catholic School on the Threshold*, para. 6.
23 See CCE, *Lay Catholics*, para. 71.
24 See CCE, *Educating Today and Tomorrow*, III, 1, b.
25 See CCE, *Intercultural Dialogue in Schools*, 81, 83.
26 CCE, *Lay Catholics*, para. 72.
27 The teacher's worldview "is unavoidable in education because it comes into every decision that is made. It is, therefore, essential, if for no other reason than for a unity in teaching, that each member of the school community, albeit with a differing degree of awareness, adopts a common vision, a common outlook on life, based on an adherence to a scale of values. This is what gives teachers and adults authority to educate." CCE, *Catholic School*, para. 29.
28 See ibid.
29 See ibid., para. 40.
30 See ibid., para. 43, 44.
31 See CCE, *Lay Catholics*, para. 33.
32 See ibid., para. 28, 30.
33 CCE, *Educating Today and Tomorrow*, III, 1, g.
34 See, ibid., II, 3.
35 It is because "education is arduous, and very important, for that reason, its realization is delicate and complex," and thus it "requires calm, interior peace, freedom from an excessive amount of work, [and] continuous cultural and religious enrichment" (CCE, *Lay Catholics*, para. 73).
36 See ibid., para. 78.
37 See, for example, CCE, "An Urgent Need," in *The Presence of the Church in the University and in University Culture*, and Pontifical Council for Culture, *Where Is Your God? Responding to the Challenge of Unbelief and Religious Indifference Today*, para. 2.2.3.
38 Pontifical Council for Culture / Pontifical Council for Interreligious Dialogue, "Foreword," in *Jesus Christ the Bearer of the Water of Life: A Christian Reflection on the New Age*.
39 See CCE, *Lay Catholics*, para. 20.
40 See ibid., para. 29.
41 Ibid., para. 64.
42 See CCE, *Religious Dimension of Education*, para. 52, 62.
43 See CCE, *Catholic School on the Threshold*, para. 14.

44 Ibid.

45 CCE, "The Contribution of the Catholic School to the Educational Project," in *Presentation of Consecrated Persons*.

46 See CCE, *Educating Together*, para. 2.

47 In the formation and education of the teacher it is vital "to attain a special sensitivity with regard to the person to be educated in order to grasp not only the request for growth in knowledge and skills, but also the need for growth in humanity" (ibid., para. 24).

48 See CCE, *Educational Guidance*, para. 35, 86, 91, 87.

49 CCE, *Religious Dimension of Education*, para. 84.

50 See CCE, *Lay Catholics*, para. 19, 38, 55.

51 See CCE, *Educational Guidance*, para. 92.

52 See CCE, *Religious Dimension of Education*, para. 15, 88, 89, 90.

53 Teachers must direct their "greatest energy and skills [in encouraging students] towards a positive construction of themselves and their lives, and to be serious and credible witnesses of the responsibility and hope which the school owes to society" (CCE, *Educating Together*, para. 22).

54 See CCE, *Intercultural Dialogue in Schools*, para. 83, 84.

55 See CCE, *Educating Today and Tomorrow*, III, 1, 1, and "Conclusion." See also *Catholic School on the Threshold*, para. 15.

56 "Certainly in schools, education is essentially accomplished through teaching, which is the vehicle through which ideas and beliefs are communicated. In this sense, words are the main roads in educating the mind." CCE, *Educating Together*, para. 38.

57 See Maritain, *Crossroads*, 30.

58 See ibid., 26.

59 See ibid., 30–1.

60 See ibid., 31.

61 See Maritain, *Education of Man*, 59.

62 See ibid., 61.

63 See Maritain, *Crossroads*, 47.

64 Maritain, *Education of Man*, 109.

65 See Maritain, *Crossroads*, 42–3. Maritain also refers to "the subconscious and the irrational" forces that influence behaviour and education.

66 Ibid., 43.

67 See Maritain, *Education of Man*, 137.

68 See Maritain, *Crossroads*, 33.

69 Maritain, *Education of Man*, 138.

70 See Maritain, *Crossroads*, 26.

71 Ibid., 33.

72 Maritain, *St. Thomas Aquinas*, 110–11.

73 Maritain, *Crossroads*, 45.

74 "Nothing is more necessary to man than to discern, and nothing does he find more difficult. Ordinarily we work with intellectual instruments that we have not taken the trouble to sharpen, we use steam hammers to crush a fly, and telegraph posts to mount a butterfly; and we bring the paws of bears to the task of following out and drawing apart the threads of a spider's web." Maritain, *Theonas*, 173–4.

75 Maritain, *Education of Man*, 60.

76 "[I]t would be nonsense to demand from teachers that they should be wiser than the general culture of their time and its great representatives, and that they should make up for the failure of the latter in doing the constructive work than mankind expected of them. This means the most crucial problem with which our educational system is confronted is not a problem of education, but of civilization." Ibid., 82.

77 Maritain, *Art and Scholasticism and the Frontiers of Poetry*, 49.

78 See Maritain, *Education of Man*, 136–7.

79 "[Teaching mathematics] is not by trying to make mathematics say something Christian, but in praying for one's students and loving them, and the very manner in which one treats them, and the very manner in which one teaches, for teaching is something concrete that betrays, without our noticing it, many things that we have within us, and through which we are in a human relationship with others, while speaking to their minds." Maritain, *Peasant of the Garonne*, 211.

80 See Maritain, *Crossroads*, 27.

81 Ibid., 34.

82 See ibid., 35.

83 Ibid.

84 See ibid., 36.

85 See Maritain, *Education of Man*, 124.

86 See ibid., 183.

87 Ibid, 127.

88 See Maritain, *Crossroads*, 47–8.

89 See Maritain, *The Degrees of Knowledge*. The book, his major work on epistemology, elaborates on unity behind diversity. The various degrees of knowledge are explored (the physical, mathematical, and metaphysical), as well the degrees of wisdom (metaphysical, theological, and mystical). There are different degrees as there are different objects to be known – not limited physically – and these are known by degrees of abstraction and the intelligible nature of the intellect. Further, the degrees are distinct and united, and are ordered hierarchically.

90 Wisdom is defined as "that knowledge ... which penetrates and embraces things with the deepest, most universal, and most united insights" (Maritain, *Crossroads*, 48).

91 Ibid.

92 Ibid.

93 "The contents of the charter include ... political and social rights and responsibilities ... rights and duties of persons who are part of a family society ... and toward the body politic and the state ... functions of authority in a political and social democracy ... civil friendship and an ideal of fraternity, religious freedom, mutual tolerance and mutual respect between various spiritual communities and schools of thought ... obligations of each person toward the common good ... and the necessity of becoming aware of the unity of the world and of the existence of a community of peoples." Maritain, *Man and the State*, 112–13.

94 This is a freedom of "minds and consciences." See ibid., 111–12.

95 Ibid., 108, 110.

96 See ibid., 119.

97 See Maritain, *Education of Man*, 62.

98 See ibid., 64. See also Maritain, *Man and the State*, 121–2.

99 See Maritain, *Education of Man*, 65.

100 See ibid., 65–6.

101 See ibid., 66–7.

102 Ibid., 68.

103 See Lonergan, *Second Collection*, 69.

104 See ibid., 85.

105 Lonergan, *Collection*, 210.

106 See ibid.

107 See Lonergan, *Insight*, 498.

108 See ibid., 423.

109 Lonergan, *Method 1*, 133.

110 Lonergan, *Papers 1958–1964*, 125–6.

111 See Lonergan, *Understanding and Being*, 226, 227.

112 See ibid., 227.

113 See ibid., 228.

114 See Lonergan, *Insight*, 636.

115 Bias is defined as " a block or distortion of intellectual development." Bias is of four kinds, "unconscious motivation; individual egoism; group egoism; and 'common sense'" (Lonergan, *Method in Theology*, 231). For Lonergan, common sense, though essential for human living, is the "mode of concrete understanding and judgment," and in this it is always "egocen-

tric" (Lonergan, *Topics*, 72, 73). "The business of common sense is daily life" (Lonergan, *Insight*, 255).

116 See Lonergan, *Method 1*, 507.
117 Lonergan, *Verbum*, 86.
118 See ibid., 86, 87.
119 See ibid., 101.
120 See Lonergan, *Papers 1958–1964*, 41.
121 See Lonergan, *Phenomenology and Logic*, 282.
122 See Lonergan, *Papers 1965–1980*, 12.
123 See Lonergan, *Papers 1958–1964*, 238.
124 See ibid., 171.
125 Ibid., 240.
126 See Lonergan, *Topics*, 79–106.
127 Ibid., 28.
128 See ibid., 69–70.
129 See Lonergan, *Phenomenology and Logic*, 221, 237.
130 See ibid., 238.
131 See Lonergan, *Topics*, 80.
132 See ibid., 81.
133 Ibid.
134 See ibid., 82.
135 See Lonergan, *Phenomenology and Logic*, 304.
136 "[I]mpartiality, intellectual detachment, intellectual curiosity, intellectual interest" enable the subject to know in an authentic and truly objective way (Lonergan, *Topics*, 86).
137 See ibid., 90.
138 See ibid., 92.
139 Lonergan, *Collection*, 225, 226.
140 See ibid., 235.
141 Lonergan, *Method in Theology*, 78.
142 Lonergan, *Topics*, 106.
143 Lonergan, *Collection*, 148; see also 225.
144 See Lonergan, *Topics*, 62.
145 See Lonergan, *Verbum*, 193–4.
146 See Lonergan, *Shorter Papers*, 259.
147 Lonergan, *Papers 1965–1980*, 141.
148 See Lonergan, *Second Collection*, 153.
149 See Lonergan, *Method in Theology*, 130.
150 See Lonergan, *Second Collection*, 29.
151 Ibid., 71–2.

CHAPTER SIX

1 "[T]he common good finds its ultimate fulfillment in the eternal law ... the concrete demands of the common good are constantly changing as time goes on, peace is never attained once for all, but must be built up ceaselessly" (Paul VI, *Gaudium et Spes*, para. 78).

2 "[F]or the human person to be preserved; human society deserves to be renewed" (ibid., para. 3).

3 See Paul VI, *Apostolicam Actuositatem / Decree on the Apostolate of the Laity*, para. 6.

4 CCE, *Catholic School*, para. 12.

5 Ibid., para. 66.

6 See ibid., para. 14, 81. The presence of the Catholic school "guarantees cultural and educational pluralism" (CCE, *Catholic School on the Threshold*, para. 16).

7 See CCE, *Lay Catholics*, para. 34, 47.

8 See CCE, *Catholic School on the Threshold*, para. 7.

9 See ibid., para. 8.

10 CCE, *Consecrated Persons and Schools*, para. 32.

11 See CCE, *Catholic School on the Threshold*, para. 4, 16.

12 See CCE, *Consecrated Persons and Schools*, para. 79.

13 CCE, *Educating Together*, para. 53.

14 CCE, *Intercultural Dialogue in Schools*, para. 18, and see para. 21.

15 See ibid., para. 39, 37. See also para. 34–41.

16 Ibid., para. 42.

17 See CCE, *Educating Today and Tomorrow*, III.

18 Ibid., II, 6.

19 CCE, *Catholic School on the Threshold*, para. 1.

20 See CCE, *Educational Guidance*, para. 66: Pope John Paul II on the readiness of children to accept whatever is offered to them, whether good or bad.

21 See ibid., para. 67.

22 CCE, *Consecrated Persons and Schools*, para. 49.

23 CCE, *Presentation of Consecrated Persons*, in the section "Problems with education, the school today, loss of a sense of mission."

24 *Catechism of the Catholic Church*, para. 1906–9.

25 Ibid., para. 1912. See also Pontifical Council for Social Communications, *Ethics in the Internet*, para. 3, on the characteristics of the common good.

26 See CCE, "Introduction," in *Educating Today and Tomorrow*, para. 1, a.

27 See Paul VI, *Gravissimum Educationis*, para. 3.

28 CCE, *Catholic School*, para. 91. See also para. 62.

29 CCE, *Consecrated Persons and Schools*, para. 80.

30 CCE, *Circular Letter*, para. 10.

31 See CCE, *Intercultural Dialogue in Schools*, para. 10, 13, 42.

32 See ibid., para. 73.

33 See CCE, *Educational Guidance*, para. 68.

34 CCE, *Catholic School*, para. 13.

35 See CCE, *Intercultural Dialogue in Schools*, para. 36.

36 Benedict XVI, *Caritas in Veritae*, para. 53.

37 See CCE, *Intercultural Dialogue in Schools*, para. 21.

38 Ibid., para. 41.

39 See CCE, *Lay Catholics*, para. 19, 8.

40 The state must "safeguard its citizens against injustices and moral disorders, such as the abuse of minors and every form of sexual violence, degrading dress, permissiveness and pornography, and the improper use of demographic information." Permissive societies harm the common good through "alienating escapism," and when "drugs, mistaken autonomy, and sexual disorders are often found together." CCE, *Educational Guidance*, para. 64, 65, 104.

41 CCE, *Religious Dimension of Education*, para. 94.

42 CCE, *Consecrated Persons and Schools*, para. 22.

43 CCE, *Intercultural Dialogue in Schools*, para. 49.

44 CCE, *Religious Dimension of Education*, para. 57.

45 Pontifical Council for Culture, *Pastoral Approach to Culture*, para. 2.

46 See CCE, *Intercultural Dialogue in Schools*, para. 23.

47 See Paul VI, *Gaudium et Spes*, para. 44.

48 Pontifical Council for Culture, *Pastoral Approach to Culture*, para. 10.

49 See Paul VI, *Gaudium et Spes*, para. 55, 59.

50 Ibid., para. 58.

51 CCE, *Intercultural Dialogue in Schools*, para. 22.

52 Pontifical Council for Culture, *Pastoral Approach to Culture*, para. 1.

53 CCE, *Consecrated Persons and Schools*, para. 2.

54 Ibid., para. 5.

55 See ibid., para. 14, 23.

56 Ibid., para. 39.

57 See ibid., para. 65.

58 See ibid., para. 66, 67.

59 "The authenticity of each human culture, the soundness of its underlying *ethos*, and hence the validity of its moral bearings, can be measured to an extent by its commitment to the human cause and by its capacity to promote human dignity at every level and in every circumstance" (ibid., para. 68).

60 See CCE, *Lay Catholics*, para. 12, 20, 21.

61 See CCE, *Intercultural Dialogue in Schools*, para. 34.

62 See Pontifical Council for Culture, *Pastoral Approach to Culture*, para. 10.

63 The "*primary and essential task of culture* is education ... For this purpose man must be able to 'be more' not only 'with others,' but also 'for others.' Education is of fundamental importance for the formation of inter-human and social relations." John Paul II, *Address to* UNESCO (2 June 1980), para. 11. Given this breadth of reposnibilbiity, "education cannot be seen merely as the transmission of knowledge. It forms people and prepares them for their participation in social life by fostering their psychological, intellectual, cultural, moral and spiritual." Pontifical Council for Culture, *Pastoral Approach to Culture*, para. 16.

64 Maritain, *Crossroads*, 15.

65 Maritain, *The Rights of Man and Natural Law*, 4.

66 See Maritain, *Crossroads*, 14.

67 "[P]ersonal freedom itself is at the core of social life, and that a human society is veritably a group of human freedoms which accept obedience and self sacrifice and a common law" (ibid., 14–15).

68 Ibid.

69 Ibid., 89.

70 Maritain emphasizes *being* over *doing*. See Maritain, *Education of Man*, 155.

71 See Maritain, *Crossroads*, 89, 90.

72 See Maritain, *Education of Man*, 110.

73 Ibid., 59.

74 See Maritain, *Crossroads*, 101, 102.

75 Maritain, *Education of Man*, 171.

76 See ibid.

77 "A single human soul is of more worth than the whole universe of bodies and material goods. There is nothing above the human soul except God. In light of the eternal value and absolute dignity of the soul, society exists for each person and is subordinate thereto." Maritain, *Rights of Man and Natural Law*, 13; see also 11, 12.

78 See Maritain, *Education of Man*, 89.

79 See Maritain, *Christianity and Democracy*, 94.

80 See Evans and Ward, eds., *The Social and Political Philosophy of Jacques Maritain*, 336.

81 Maritain, *Rights of Man and Natural Law*, 35.

82 See Maritain, *Man and the State*, 2.

83 Maritain, *Person and the Common Good*, 11.

84 Maritain, *Crossroads*, 14.

85 See ibid., 89.

86 See Maritain, *Education of Man*, 89.

87 See ibid., 171.

88 Maritain, *Person and the Common Good*, 49–51.
89 Maritain, *Range of Reason*, 142.
90 See Maritain, *Freedom in the Modern World*, 50–1.
91 See Maritain, "Religion and Culture," in *Essays in Order*, 4, 7.
92 Maritain, *Integral Humanism*, 96.
93 See ibid., 111, 119, 168.
94 See ibid., 173.
95 See ibid., 174.
96 See Maritain, *Freedom in the Modern World*, 42.
97 See Maritain, *Rights of Man and Natural Law*, 8; *Scholasticism and Politics*, 56; and *Person and the Common Good*, 21.
98 Maritain, "Religion and Culture," 26.
99 See Maritain, *Freedom in the Modern World*, 70–1.
100 Maritain, *Education of Man*, 154–5.
101 Ibid., 104.
102 See ibid., 127, 171.
103 Maritain, *Freedom in the Modern World*, 45.
104 Ibid., 46, 48.
105 Ibid., 50. For an elaboration on persons and individuals in political society, see 46–54.
106 Maritain, *Ransoming the Time*, 3.
107 Ibid., 10.
108 Ibid., 17.
109 Ibid., 19; see also 18.
110 "[B]ecause ... the community of essence is of greater importance than individual differences; the root is more important than the branches ... [equality is] primary ... as it relates to the fundamental rights and common dignity of human beings" (ibid., 21–2).
111 Ibid., 26.
112 See ibid., 31.
113 Ibid., 116, 127.
114 See ibid., 130.
115 Ibid., 132, 133.
116 Ibid., 138.
117 Ibid., 139.
118 "The more we fraternize on the level of practical principles and common action, the more we should strengthen the edges of the opposite convictions, which divide us in the speculative order and on the level of truth, the first to be served" (Maritain, *Peasant of the Garonne*, 70).
119 See Maritain, *On the Church of Christ*, 190; *Twilight of Civilization*, 39.
120 Maritain, *On the Use of Philosophy: Three Essays*, 24.
121 Maritain, *Moral Philosophy*, 319.

122 "The unity of such civilization no longer appears as a unity of an essential or constitutional character guaranteed from above by the profession of the same doctrine and the same faith. Though the unity is less perfect, and material rather than formal in character, it is nonetheless real; it is a unity of Becoming or of orientation which springs from a common aspiration and gathers elements of heterogeneous culture (of which some may indeed be very imperfect) into a form of civilization which is fully consonant with the eternal interests of human personality ad with man's freedom of autonomy." Maritain, *Freedom in the Modern World*, 70–1; see also 80–1.

123 Lonergan, *Topics*, 20–1. "[P]hilosophy has become existential; it is concerned with man in his concrete living; and there the issue is authenticity" (Lonergan, *Second Collection*, 155).

124 See Lonergan, *Topics*, 24.

125 Ibid., 69.

126 See ibid., 62. See also Lonergan, *Second Collection*, 233, 262.

127 "[T]o perceive is to complete that hypothetical entity, the raw datum, with memories, associations, a structure, and one's emotive and expressive reactions" (Lonergan, *Third Collection*, 17).

128 Lonergan, *Papers 1958–1964*, 106.

129 See Lonergan, *Method in Theology*, 78, 79.

130 Lonergan, *Collection*, 244.

131 See Lonergan, *Method in Theology*, 52–5.

132 See ibid., 79.

133 Ibid., 356, 357.

134 See ibid., 359.

135 Ibid., 360; see also 369.

136 Lonergan, *Topics*, 59.

137 See Lonergan, *Papers 1958–1964*, 73.

138 Lonergan, *Insight*, 244.

139 See ibid., 244–5.

140 Lonergan, *Collection*, 220.

141 See ibid.

142 Lonergan, *Third Collection*, 23.

143 Lonergan, *Collection*, 234.

144 Lonergan, *Topics*, 33.

145 Ibid., 47.

146 See ibid., 76–7.

147 Ibid., 78; see also 262.

148 See Lonergan, *Papers 1965–1980*, 315.

149 See ibid., 349.

150 "[I]nsofar as both proceed from self-transcending subjectivity, from attention, intelligence, reasonableness, and responsibility; insofar as

both claim to be objective; insofar as the judgment of value is an *assent* rather than a *consent*, and a judgment of fact is also an assent: That is so." Ibid., 350.

151 See Lonergan, *Insight*, 238.

152 "Thus judgment of value set the good of order above private advantages, subordinate technology to economics, refers economics to social welfare, generally, mete out to every finite good appreciation and criticism" (Lonergan, *Collection*, 109). See also Lonergan, *Topics*, 263.

153 Lonergan, *Second Collection*, 221.

154 See Lonergan, *Method in Theology*, 52.

155 Lonergan, *Topics*, 262.

156 "What is a way of life? Externally, it is a series of observable actions. Internally, it is a flow of consciousness, and the flow is organically united ... It is coming together in vital organic unity of precepts, images, and affects, of insights and judgments, decisions and choices. They all form part of a total flow." Ibid., 251–2.

157 Ibid., 253. See also 252.

158 Ibid, 55.

159 "The classicist notion of culture was normative ... there was but one culture that was both universal and empirical ... Besides the classicist there is also the empirical notion of culture. It is a set of meanings and values that informs a way of life. It may remain unchanged for ages. It may be in process of slow development or rapid dissolution." Lonergan, *Method in Theology*, xi.

160 See Lonergan's essay "The Transition from a Classicist World-View to Historical-Mindedness," in *Second Collection*, 1–9.

161 Lonergan, *Doctrinal Pluralism*, 5.

162 "[H]uman concepts are products and expressions of human understanding, that human understanding develops over time, and that it develops differently in different places and in different times ... that a human action, determined solely by abstract properties, abstract principles, abstract laws, would be not only abstract but also inhumanely inept on every concrete occasion" (ibid., 6).

163 Ibid., 8.

164 See ibid., 10.

165 Ibid.

166 Ibid., 11–12.

167 "[T]he relevance of human intelligence and wisdom to the whole of life ... [is that] the entire fabric of human existence appears as a historical product, as the result of man's apprehension, judgment, choice, action" (Lonergan, *Topics*, 76).

168 Lonergan, *Second Collection*, 93.
169 See ibid., 99. Here Lonergan says that "modernity lacks roots," and that modern culture "has to be known, assimilated, and transformed."
170 Ibid., 161.
171 Lonergan, *Insight*, 754.
172 See Lonergan, *Second Collection*, 233.
173 "By modernity I do not mean just anything that exists or functions today. I mean the basic developments out of which has come the modern world" (ibid., 183).
174 See Lonergan, *Third Collection*, 106–7.
175 See Lonergan, *Second Collection*, 115.
176 Ibid., 146, 147.

CHAPTER SEVEN

1 *Biblia Sacra Juxta Vulgatae*, 640.
2 I will use the term *person*, aware, of course, that Lonergan prefers the term *subject*. However, *person/subject* is more cumbersome in this context.
3 See D'Souza, "The Preparation of Teachers for Roman Catholic Schools."
4 Gilson, *A Gilson Reader: Selected Readings of Etienne Gilson*, 31–48.
5 "Again, reason seeks its goal of the good life not only in the purely rational pursuits of knowledge and virtue, the Aristotelian beatitude, but also in a greater excellence added to nature's pursuit of life; and so it is that by arts and crafts, by applied science and technology, by economics and medicine, by marriage and politics, reason transforms the natural *nisus* towards life into a rational attainment of a historically unfolding good life. In like manner grace takes over both nature and reason. The purely rational pursuit of philosophy is made into an instrument as the hand-maid of theology; reason itself as reasonable faith is elevated to the level of grace; virtuous living is transformed into merit unto eternal life; repetitive preaching becomes the space-time manipulation of a unique revelation; repetitive doing is elevated into sacraments and liturgy. Inversely, the distinctive eternity of the order of grace is submitted to human progress inasmuch as grace sets up a human society or a human science or human advance in virtue; and it is submitted to natural repetitiveness inasmuch as it embraces even the recurrent aspects of human existence." Lonergan, *Collection*, 40.
6 See D'Souza, "The Pascal Mystery and Catholic Education."
7 See Grace and O'Keefe, eds., *International Handbook of Catholic Education: Challenges for School Systems in the 21st Century*.
8 See McLaughlin, J. O'Keefe, and B. O'Keefe, eds., *The Contemporary Catholic School: Context, Identity and Diversity*.

9 See Miller, *The Holy See's Teachings on Catholic Schools*.

10 In this regard, the scholarship of Terrence McLaughlin and John Haldane deserves particular note. See, for example, *Liberalism, Education and Schooling: Essays by T.H. McLaughlin*, edited by Carr, Halstead, and Pring; and Haldane, *Faithful Reason: Essays Catholic and Philosophical*.

11 "In what might be regarded as the domestic church, the parents by word and example, are the first heralds of the faith with regard to their children ... As the domestic church, the family is *school of the richest humanity*" (Pontifical Council for the Family, *The Truth and Meaning of Human Sexuality*, para. 26, 48).

12 Particularly the Council's *Dogmatic Constitution on Divine Revelation / Dei Verbum*; the *Dogmatic Constitution on the Church / Lumen Gentium*; and the *Pastoral Constitution on the Church in the Modern World / Gaudium et Spes*.

13 This was one of St Augustine's great intellectual difficulties before he was introduced to the thought of those who enabled him to expand his understanding of reality. See Augustine, *The Confessions*, Book VII.

14 The work by Feinberg, *For Goodness Sake: Religious Schools and Education for Democratic Diversity*, explores this matter in detail.

15 This question is part of a wider discussion undertaken by Ratzinger in *A Turning Point for Europe? The Church in the Modern World – Assessment and Forecast*.

16 Taylor's essay is very instructive in this regard: "Why We Need a Radical Redefinition of the Secular."

17 In his book *Happiness and Contemplation*, Pieper says that human beings have been placed on earth to practice virtue.

18 Eliot, *Daniel Deronda*, 258.

19 In the collection of essays *Between Naturalism and Religion*, Habermas explores the theme of the Enlightenment vision of existence and the religious resistance to it.

20 On the heuristic understanding of the common good, see Patrick Riordan, *A Grammar of the Common Good: Speaking of Globalization*.

21 *Shorter Oxford English Dictionary vol. 1*, s.v. "catholic."

22 In *The Risk of Education: Discovering Our Ultimate Destiny*, Giussani develops the mysterious identity of education as related to the humanity of the student.

23 See D'Souza, "The Spiritual Dimension of Catholic Education."

24 Roberts and Donaldson, eds., *The Ante-Nicene Fathers*, 302.

25 Haughey, *Where Is Knowing Going? The Horizons of the Knowing Subject*.

BIBLIOGRAPHY

Allard, Jean-Louis. *Education for Freedom: The Philosophy of Education of Jacques Maritain*. Translated by Ralph Nelson. Notre Dame, IN: University of Notre Dame Press, and Ottawa: University of Ottawa Press, 1982.

Aquinas, Thomas. *The Summa of St. Thomas Aquinas*. 3 vols. New York: Benziger Brothers, Inc., 1947.

Aristotle. *Metaphysics*. In *The Basic Works of Aristotle*, translated by W.D. Ross and edited with an introduction by Richard McKeon, 681–926. New York: Random House, 1994.

— *Metaphysics*. Translated with commentaries and glossary by Hippocrates G. Apostle. Grinnell, IA: The Peripatetic Press, 1979.

Ashley, Benedict, OP. "Contemporary Understanding of Personhood." In *The Twenty-Fifth Anniversary of Vatican II: A Look Back and a Look Ahead. Proceedings of the Ninth Bishops' Workshop, Dallas Texas*, 35–48. Edited by Russell E. Smith. Braintree, MA: The Pope John Center, 1990.

Augustine. *The Confessions*. Translated by E.B. Pusey. London: J.M. Dent & Sons Ltd, 1953.

Beales, Arthur C.F. "Jacques Maritain." In *The Function of Teaching: Seven Approaches to Purpose, Tradition, and Environment*, edited by A.V. Judges, 67–88. London: Faber and Faber, 1959.

Benedict XVI. *Caritas in Veritae Encyclical Letter*. Rome: 29 June 2009. http://w2.vatican.va/content/benedict-xvi/en/encyclicals/documents/ hf_ben-xvi_enc_20090629_caritas-in-veritate.html (accessed 1 May 2015).

Biblia Sacra Juxta Vulgatae. Paris: Librairie Letouzey et Ané, 1887.

Boys, Mary C. *Educating in Faith: Maps & Visions*. Kansas City, MO: Sheed and Ward, 1989.

Brennan, Robert Edward. *Thomistic Psychology: A Philosophical Analysis of the Nature of Man*. New York: The Macmillan Company, 1941.

Brezik, Victor B., ed. *One Hundred Years of Thomism: Aeterni Patris and Afterwards: A Symposium*. Houston, TX: Center for Thomistic Studies, University of St Thomas, 1981.

Briel, Don J. "The Declaration on Christian Education, *Gravissimum Educationis*." In *Vatican II Renewal within Tradition*, edited by Matthew L. Lamb and Matthew Levering, 383–96. Oxford, UK: Oxford University Press, 2008.

Bryk, Anthony S., Valerie E. Lee, and Peter B. Holland. *Catholic Schools and the Common Good*. Cambridge, MA: Harvard University Press, 1993.

Buford, Thomas O. *Toward a Philosophy of Education*. New York: Holt, Rinehart and Winston Inc., 1969.

Burke, Colm. "Vatican II on Schools." *The Furrow* 26, no. 2 (1975): 104–12.

Byron, J. Michael. "Communio as the Context for Memory: On the Universal-Local Church Relationship." In *Revelation and the Church: Vatican II in the Twenty-First Century*, edited by Raymond A. Lucker and William C. McDonough, 67–85. Maryknoll, NY: Orbis Books, 2003.

Carr, David, John Haldane, Terrence McLaughlin, and Richard Pring. "Return to the Crossroads." *British Journal of Educational Studies* 43, no. 2 (1995): 162–78.

Carr, David, Mark Halstead, and Richard Pring, eds. *Liberalism, and Education and Schooling: Essays by T.H. McLaughlin*. Exeter, UK: Imprint Academic, 2008.

Carter, Gerald Emmett. "Education." In *The Documents of Vatican II: In a New and Definitive Translation with Commentaries and Notes by Catholic, Protestant, and Orthodox Authorities*, edited by Walter M. Abbott, SJ, with translations directed by Joseph Gallagher, 634–6. New York: Herder and Herder, 1966.

Catechism of the Catholic Church. Vatican City: Libreria Editrice Vaticana, 1994.

Code of Canon Law, Latin–English Edition. Translation prepared under the auspices of the Canon Law Society of America. Washington, DC: Canon Law Society of America, 1983.

Congar, Yves M.J., OP. *Traditions and Tradition: An Historical and a Theological Essay*. New York: The Macmillan Company, 1967.

Congregation for Catholic Education (CCE). *Educating Today and Tomorrow: A Renewing Passion / Instrumentum Laboris*. Rome: 7 April 2014. http://www.vatican.va/roman_curia/congregations/ccatheduc/documents/rc_con_ccatheduc_doc_20140407_educare-oggi-e-domani_en.html (accessed 12 January 2015).

– *Educating to Intercultural Dialogue in Catholic Schools: Living in Harmony for a Civilization of Love*. Rome: 28 October 2013. http://www.vatican.va/roman_curia/congregations/ccatheduc/documents/rc_con_ccatheduc_doc_20131028_dialogo-interculturale_en.html (accessed 12 January 2015).

– *Circular Letter to the Presidents of Bishops' Conferences on Religious Education in Schools.* Rome: 5 May 2009. http://www.vatican.va/roman_curia/congregations/ccatheduc/documents/rc_con_ccatheduc_doc_20090505_circ-insegn-relig_en.html (accessed 12 January 2015).

– *Educating Together in Catholic Schools: A Shared Mission Between Consecrated Persons and the Lay Faithful.* Rome: 8 September 2007. http://www.vatican.va/roman_curia/congregations/ccatheduc/documents/rc_con_ccatheduc_doc_20070908_educare-insieme_en.html (accessed 11 January 2015).

– *Consecrated Persons and Their Mission in Schools: Reflections and Guidelines.* Rome: 28 October 2002. http://www.vatican.va/roman_curia/congregations/ccatheduc/documents/rc_con_ccatheduc_doc_20021028_consecrated-persons_en.html (accessed 11 January 2015).

– *Presentation of Consecrated Persons and their Mission in Catholic Schools: Reflections and Orientations.* Rome: 19 November 2002. http://www.vatican.va/roman_curia/congregations/ccatheduc/documents/rc_con_ccatheduc_doc_20021119_press-release_en.html (accessed 12 January 2015).

– *The Catholic School on the Threshold of the Third Millennium.* Rome: 28 December 1997. http://www.vatican.va/roman_curia/congregations/ccatheduc/documents/rc_con_ccatheduc_doc_27041998_school2000_en.html (accessed 12 January 2015).

– *The Presence of the Church in the University and in University Culture.* Vatican City: 22 May 1994. http://www.vatican.va/roman_curia/pontifical_councils/cultr/documents/rc_pc_cultr_doc_22051994_presence_en.html (accessed 10 April 2015).

– *The Religious Dimension of Education in a Catholic School: Guidelines for Reflection and Renewal.* Rome: 7 April 1988. http://www.vatican.va/roman_curia/congregations/ccatheduc/documents/rc_con_ccatheduc_doc_19880407_catholic-school_en.html (accessed 7 December 2014).

Congregation for the Clergy. *General Directory for Catechesis.* Rome: 11 August 1997. http://www.vatican.va/roman_curia/congregations/cclergy/documents/rc_con_ccatheduc_doc_17041998_directory-for-catechesis_en.html (accessed 6 March 2015).

Copleston, Frederick C. *Aquinas.* Harmondsworth, UK: Penguin Books, 1955.

Crowe, Frederick E., SJ. *Lonergan.* Series edited by Brian Davies, OP. Collegeville, MN: The Liturgical Press, 1992.

– *Appropriating the Lonergan Idea.* Edited by Michael Vertin. Washington, DC: The Catholic University of America Press, 1989.

– *Old Things and New: A Strategy for Education.* Atlanta, GA: Scholars Press, 1985.

Cunningham, William F., CSC. *The Pivotal Problems of Education: An Introduction to the Christian Philosophy of Education.* New York: The Macmillan Company, 1953.

Daly, Gabriel, OSA. *Transcendence and Immanence: A Study in Catholic Modernism and Integralism*. Oxford, UK: Clarendon Press, 1980.

de Lubac, Henri. "Retrieving the Tradition: On Christian Philosophy." *Communio: International Catholic Review* (Fall 1982): 478–506.

Donohue, John, SJ. *Catholicism and Education*. New York: Harper & Row Publishers, 1973.

D'Souza, Mario O., CSB. "The Distinctiveness of Catholic Education." In *Discipline, Devotion, and Dissent*, edited by Graham P. McDonough, Nadeem A. Memon, and Avi I. Mintz, 45–72. Waterloo, ON: Wilfrid Laurier University Press, 2013.

– "The Pascal Mystery and Catholic Education." *The Heythrop Journal: A Bimonthly Review of Philosophy and Theology* 54, no. 5 (September 2013): 846–58.

– "Tradition in the Context of Religious Education." *Religious Education Journal of Australia* 29, no. 2 (2013): 9–15.

– "The Spiritual Dimension of Catholic Education." *International Studies in Catholic Education* 4, no. 1 (March 2012): 92–105.

– "Religious Particularism and Cultural Pluralism: The Possible Contribution of Religious Education to Canadian Political Identity." *Religious Education* 95, no. 3 (2000): 234–49.

– "The Preparation of Teachers for Roman Catholic Schools. Some Philosophical First Principles." *Paideusis: Journal of the Canadian Philosophy of Education Society* 9, no. 2 (1996): 5–19.

Dulles, Avery, SJ. *Models of Revelation*. Garden City, NY: Image Books, 1985.

Edwards, Paul, ed. *Encyclopedia of Philosophy, vol. 8*. New York: Macmillan Publishing Company, 1967.

Egan, James M. "Review of *Education at the Crossroads* by Jacques Maritain." *The Thomist* 7 (July 1944): 415–25.

Egan, Philip A. *Philosophy and Theology: A Primer*. Collegeville, MN: Liturgical Press, 2009.

Elias, John L. "Whatever Happened to Catholic Philosophy of Education?" *Religious Education* 91, no. 1 (1999): 92–110.

Eliot, George. *Daniel Deronda*. New York: Everyman's Library, 1999.

Evans, Joseph W., and Leo R. Ward, eds. *The Social and Political Philosophy of Jacques Maritain*. New York: Charles Scribner's Sons, 1955.

Faggioli, Massimo. *Vatican II: The Battle for Meaning*. New York and Mahwah, NJ: Paulist Press, 2012.

Feinberg, Walter. *For Goodness Sake: Religious Schools and Education for Democratic Diversity*. New York: Routledge, 2006.

Fitzpatrick, J. "Subjectivity and Objectivity: Polanyi and Lonergan." *Higher Education Quarterly* 36, no. 2 (1982): 183–95.

Franchi, Leonard, ed. *An Anthology of Catholic Education*. London: Scepter, 2007.

Gaillardetz, Richard R., and Catherine E. Clifford. *Keys to the Council: Unlocking the Teaching of Vatican II*. Collegeville, MN: Liturgical Press, 2012.

Gallagher, Donald A. "Contemporary Thomism." In *A History of Philosophical Systems*, edited by Vergilius Ferm, 454–70. New York: The Philosophical Library, 1950.

Gilson, Etienne. *The Christian Philosophy of St. Thomas Aquinas*. Translated by Lawrence K. Shook, CSB. New York: Random House, 1956.

Ginther, Clara. "Notre attitude en face du Pragmatisme. George Tyrell's Relation to Pragmatism." In *The Reception of Pragmatism in France and the Rise of Roman Catholic Modernism, 1890–1914*, edited by David G. Schultenover, SJ, 185–215. Washington, DC: Catholic University of America Press, 2009.

Giussani, Luigi. *The Risk of Education: Discovering Our Ultimate Destiny*. Translated by Rosanna M. Giammanco Frongia. New York: The Crossroad Publishing Company, 1996.

Gleason, Philip. *Contending with Modernity: Catholic Higher Education in the Twentieth Century*. New York: Oxford University Press, 1995.

Goodrich, Rachel M. "Neo-Thomism and Education." In *Philosophy of Education: Essays and Commentaries*, edited by Hobert W. Burns and Charles J. Brauner, 166–74. New York: The Ronald Press Company, 1962.

Grace, Gerald, and Joseph O'Keefe, eds. *International Handbook of Catholic Education: Challenges for School Systems in the 21st Century*. Dordrecht, Netherlands: Springer, 2007.

Groome, Thomas. *Educating for Life: A Spiritual Vision for Every Teacher and Parent*. Allen, TX: Thomas More, 1998.

Grote, Heiner. "Rome's Official Statements: How and What? Towards a Typology of Documents." *The Ecumenical Review* 46, no. 1 (1994): 109–17.

Habermas, Jürgen. *Between Naturalism and Religion*. Translated by Ciaran Cronin. Cambridge: Polity, 2009.

Haldane, John. *Faithful Reason: Essays Catholic and Philosophical*. London: Routledge, 2004.

Haughey, John C., SJ. *Where Is Knowing Going? The Horizons of the Knowing Subject*. Washington, DC: Georgetown University Press, 2009.

Hayard, Fernand. *The Vatican Council: A Short History*. Translated by the Earl of Wicklow. Dublin: Clonmore and Reynolds Ltd, 1951.

Hess, Peter M.J., and Paul L. Allen. *Catholicism and Science*. Westport, CT: Greenwood Press, 2008.

Hughes, Philip. *The Church in Crisis: A History of Twenty Great Councils*. London: Burns and Oates, 1961.

Jedin, Huber. *Crisis and the Closure of the Council of Trent: A Retrospective View from the Second Vatican Council*. Translated by N.D. Smith. London and Melbourne, VIC: Sheed and Ward, 1967.

John Paul II. *Fides et Ratio / Faith and Reason*. Encyclical. Rome: 14 September 1998. http://www.vatican.va/holy_father/john_paul_ii/encyclicals/ documents/hf_jp-ii_enc_15101998_fides-et-ratio_en.html (accessed 7 December 2014).

– *Address to UNESCO*. Paris: 2 June 1980. http://inters.org/John-Paul-II-UNESCO-Culture (accessed 4 May 2015).

– *Apostolic Exhortation Catechesi Tradendae / On Catechesis in Our Time*. Rome: 16 October 1979. http://w2.vatican.va/content/john-paul-ii/en/apost_exhortations/documents/hf_jp-ii_exh_16101979_catechesi-tradendae.html (accessed 7 April 2015).

Jordan, Mark K. "The Terms of the Debate over Christian Philosophy." *Communio: International Catholic Review* (Fall 1985): 293–311.

Kelty, Brian. "Catholic Education: The Historical Context." In *The Catholic School: Paradoxes and Challenges*, edited by Dennis McLaughlin, 9–29. Strathfield, NSW: St Pauls, 2000.

– "Toward a Theology of Catholic Education." *Religious Education* 94, no. 1 (1999): 6–23.

Kerr, Fergus. *After Aquinas: Versions of Thomism*. Malden, MA: Blackwell, 2002.

Knasas, John F.X. *Being and Some Twentieth-Century Thomists*. New York: Fordham University Press, 2003.

– "Whither the Neo-Thomist Revival." *Logos: A Journal of Catholic Thought and Culture* 3, no. 4 (Fall 2000): 121–49. http://muse.jhu.edu.myaccess.library. utoronto.ca/journals/logos/v003/3.4knasas.pdf (accessed 5 November 2014).

Knightley, Georgia Masters. "Vatican II: The Church's Self Understanding." In *Vatican II: The Continuing Agenda*, edited by Anthony J. Cernera, 1–24. Fairfield, CT: Sacred Heart University Press, 1997.

Laghi, Pio. "Letter from the Congregation of Catholic Education on the Document *Educational Guidance in Human Love*." Rome: 2 May 1997. http://www.wf-f.org/Laghi97sex-ed.html (accessed 7 March 2015).

Leckey, Dolores R. *The Laity and Christian Education: Apostolicam Actuositatem, Gravissimum Educationis*. New York and Mahwah, NJ: Paulist Press, 2006.

Leen, Edward. *What Is Education?* New York: Sheed and Ward, 1943.

Leo XIII. *Rerum Novarum / Of New Things. Encyclical Letter on Capital and Labor*. Rome: 15 May 1891. http://www.vatican.va/holy_father/leo_xiii/encyclicals/ documents/hf_l-xiii_enc_15051891_rerum-novarum_en.html (accessed 17 November 2014).

– *Spectata Fides / On Christian Education, Encyclical*. Rome: 27 November 1885. http://w2.vatican.va/content/leo-xiii/en/encyclicals/documents/hf_l-xiii_enc_27111885_spectata-fides.html (accessed 4 February 2016).

– *Aeterni Patris / On the Restoration of Christian Philosophy*. Rome: 4 August 1879. http://www.vatican.va/holy_father/leo_xiii/encyclicals/documents/hf_ l-xiii_enc_04081879_aeterni-patris_en.html (accessed 5 November 2014).

Lonergan, Bernard. *Early Works on Theological Method 2. Collected Works of Bernard Lonergan, vol. 23*. Translated by Michael G. Shields and edited by Robert M. Doran and H. Daniel Monsour. Toronto: University of Toronto Press, 2013.

– *Early Works on Theological Method 1. Collected Works of Bernard Lonergan, vol. 22*. Edited by Robert M. Doran and Robert C. Croken. Toronto: University of Toronto Press, 2010.

– *Shorter Papers. Collected Works of Bernard Lonergan, vol. 20*. Edited by Robert C. Croken, Robert M. Doran, and H. Daniel Monsour. Toronto: University of Toronto Press, 2007.

– *Phenomenology and Logic. Collected Works of Bernard Lonergan, vol. 18*. Edited by Philip J. McShane. Toronto: University of Toronto Press, 2005.

– *Philosophical and Theological Papers 1965–1980. Collected Works of Bernard Lonergan, vol. 17*. Edited by Robert C. Croken and Robert M. Doran. Toronto: University of Toronto Press, 2004.

– *Topics in Education. Collected Works of Bernard Lonergan, vol. 10*. Edited by Robert M. Doran and Frederick E. Crowe. Toronto: University of Toronto Press, 2000.

– *Verbum: Word and Idea in Aquinas. Collected Works of Bernard Lonergan, vol. 2*. Edited by Frederick E. Crowe and Robert M. Doran. Toronto: University of Toronto Press, 1997.

– *Philosophical and Theological Papers 1958–1964. Collected Works of Bernard Lonergan, vol. 6*. Edited by Robert C. Croken, Frederick E. Crowe, and Robert M. Doran. Toronto: University of Toronto Press, 1996.

– *Collection. Collected Works of Bernard Lonergan, vol. 4*. Edited by Frederick E. Crowe and Robert M. Doran. Toronto: University of Toronto Press, 1993.

– *Insight: A Study of Human Understanding. Collected Works of Bernard Lonergan, vol. 3*. Edited by Frederick E. Crowe and Robert M. Doran. Toronto: University of Toronto Press, 1992.

– *Understanding and Being. Collected Works of Bernard Lonergan, vol. 5*. Edited by Elizabeth A. Morelli and Mark D. Morelli. Toronto: University of Toronto Press, 1990.

– *A Third Collection: Papers by Bernard J.F. Lonergan SJ*. Edited by Frederick E. Crowe, SJ. London: Geoffrey Chapman, 1985.

– *The Way to Nicea: The Dialectical Development of Trinitarian Theology*. Translated by Conn O'Donovan from the first part of *De Deo Trino*. London: Darton, Longman, and Todd, 1976.

– *Second Collection: Papers by Bernard J.F. Lonergan SJ*. Edited by William F.J. Ryan, SJ, and Bernard J. Tyrrell, SJ. London: Darton, Longman and Todd, 1974.

– *Method in Theology*. New York: The Seabury Press, 1972.
– *Doctrinal Pluralism*. Milwaukee, WI: Marquette University Press, 1971.
Marique, Pierre J. *The Philosophy of Christian Education*. New York: Prentice-Hall, 1939.
Maritain, Jacques. *Untrammeled Approaches: The Collected Works of Jacques Maritain, vol. 20*. Translated by Bernard Doering. Notre Dame, IN: University of Notre Dame Press, 1997.
– *The Education of Man: The Educational Philosophy of Jacques Maritain*. Edited with an introduction by Donald and Idella Gallagher. Westport, CT: Greenwood Press Publishers, 1976.
– *Art and Scholasticism and the Frontiers of Poetry*. Translated by Joseph W. Evans. Notre Dame, IN: University of Notre Dame Press, 1974.
– *Integral Humanism: Temporal and Spiritual Problems of a New Christendom*. Translated by Joseph W. Evans. Notre Dame, IN: University of Notre Dame Press, 1973.
– *The Person and the Common Good*. Translated by John J. Fitzgerald. Notre Dame, IN: University of Notre Dame Press, 1972.
– *Ransoming the Time*. Translated by Harry Lorin Binsse. New York: Gordian Press, 1972.
– *Freedom in the Modern World*. Translated by Richard O'Sullivan, KC. New York: Gordian Press, 1971.
– *On the Church of Christ: The Person of the Church and Her Personnel*. Translated by Joseph W. Evans. Notre Dame, IN: University of Notre Dame Press, 1973.
– *The Peasant of the Garonne: An Old Layman Questions Himself about the Present Time*. Translated by Michael Cuddihy and Elizabeth Hughes. New York: Holt, Rinehart and Winston, 1968.
– *Moral Philosophy*. London: Geoffrey Bles, 1964.
– *On the Use of Philosophy: Three Essays*. Princeton, NJ: Princeton University Press, 1961.
– *Distinguish to Unite; or, The Degrees of Knowledge*. Translated by Gerald B. Phelan. New York: Charles Scribner's Sons, 1959.
– *St. Thomas Aquinas*. New York: Meridian Books, Inc., 1958.
– *An Essay on Christian Philosophy*. Translated by Edward H. Flannery. New York: Philosophical Library, 1955.
– *Scholasticism and Politics*. Translated by Mortimer J. Adler. London: Geoffrey Bles, 1954.
– *Creative Intuition in Art and Poetry*. New York: Pantheon Books, 1953.
– *The Range of Reason*. New York: Charles Scribner's Sons, 1953.
– "Angelic Doctor." *Proceedings of the American Catholic Philosophical Association* 25 (1951): 4–11.
– *Man and the State*. Chicago, IL: The University of Chicago Press, 1951.

— *Christianity and Democracy*. Translated by Doris Anson. New York: Charles Scribner's Sons, 1950.

— *Existence and the Existent*. Translated by Lewis Galantiere and Gerald B. Phelan. New York: Pantheon, 1948.

— *The Rights of Man and Natural Law*. Translated by Doris C. Anson. New York: Charles Scribner's Sons, 1947.

— *Education at the Crossroads*. New Haven, CT, and London: Yale University Press, 1943.

— *A Preface to Metaphysics: Seven Lectures on Being*. London: Sheed and Ward, 1943.

— *The Twilight of Civilization*. Translated by Lionel Landry. New York: Sheed and Ward, 1943.

— "Religion and Culture." In *Essays in Order*, edited by Christopher Dawson and T.F. Burns, 3–61. New York: Sheed & Ward, 1940.

— *Theonas: Conversations of a Sage*. Translated by F.J. Sheed. London and New York: Sheed & Ward, 1933.

Maritain, Jacques, and Raïssa Maritain. *Prayer and Intelligence*. Translated by Algar Thorold. New York: Sheed and Ward, 1943.

Maritain, Raïssa. *We Have Been Friends Together: Memoirs*. Translated by Julie Kernan. New York: Longmans, Green and Co., 1942.

Mathews, William A. *Lonergan's Quest: A Study of Desire in the Authoring of Insight*. Toronto: University of Toronto Press, 2005.

Maurer, Armand A. "Gilson and *Aeterni Patris*." In *Thomistic Papers VI*, edited by John F.X. Knasas, 91–105. Houston, TX: Center for Thomistic Studies, University of St Thomas, 1994.

Mayer, Mary Helen. *The Philosophy of Teaching of St. Thomas Aquinas*. New York: The Bruce Publishing Company, 1929.

McCarthy, Timothy G. *The Catholic Tradition: Before and After Vatican II 1878–1993*. Chicago, IL: Loyola University Press, 1994.

McCool, Gerald. *The Neo-Thomists*. Milwaukee, WI: Marquette University Press, 1994.

— *From Unity to Pluralism: The Internal Evolution of Thomism*. New York: Fordham University Press, 1989.

— *Nineteenth Century Scholasticism: The Search for a Unitary Method*. New York: Fordham University Press, 1989.

McEvoy, James Gerard. *Leaving Christendom for Good: Church-World Dialogue in a Secular Age*. Latham, MD: Lexington Books, 2014.

McInerny, Ralph. *The Very Rich Hours of Jacques Maritain: A Spiritual Life*. Notre Dame, IN: University of Notre Dame Press, 2003.

McLaughlin, Terrence, Joseph O'Keefe, SJ, and Bernadette O'Keefe, eds. *The Contemporary Catholic School: Context, Identity and Diversity*. London: The Falmer Press, 1996.

McLean, George F., ed. *Philosophy and the Integration of Contemporary Catholic Education*. Washington, DC: The Catholic University of America Press, 1962.

Miller, J. Michael, CSB. *The Holy See's Teachings on Catholic Schools*. Manchester, NH: Sophia Institute Press, 2006.

Moran, Gabriel. "Religious Education after Vatican II." In *Open Catholicism: The Tradition at Its Best: Essays in Honor of Gerard S. Sloyan*, edited by David Efroymson and John Raines, 151–66. Collegeville, MN: The Liturgical Press, 1997.

Morris, Andrew B., ed. *Catholic Education: Universal Principles, Locally Applied*. Newcastle-upon-Tyne, UK: Cambridge Scholars Publishers, 2012.

Nédoncelle, Maurice. *Is There a Christian Philosophy?* Translated by Illtyd Trethowan, OSB. New York: Hawthorn Books, 1961.

O'Connell, Marvin R. *Critics on Trial: An Introduction to the Catholic Modernist Crisis*. Washington, DC: The Catholic University of America Press, 1994.

O'Donnell, Charles. "Jacques Maritain – Political Philosopher." In *Jacques Maritain: The Man and His Achievement*, edited with an introduction by Joseph W. Evans, 161–79. New York: Sheed and Ward, 1963.

O'Malley, Frank. "The Education of Man." *The Review of Politics* VI (1944): 3–17.

O'Malley, John, SJ. "Introduction." In *After Vatican II: Trajectories and Hermeneutics*, edited by James L. Heft with John O'Malley, SJ, x–xxii. Grand Rapids, MI: William B. Eerdmans Publishing Company, 2012.

– *What Happened at Vatican II*. Cambridge, MA: The Belknap Press of Harvard University Press, 2008.

O'Shea, Paul. "The 'Critical Realism' of Jacques Maritain and Bernard Lonergan." PhD thesis. Dublin: Milltown Institute of Theology and Philosophy, 1989.

Papal Teachings: Education. Selected and arranged by the Benedictine Monks of Solesmes and translated by Reverend Aldo Rebeschini. Boston, MA: St Paul Editions, 1979.

Paul VI. *Evangelii Nuntiandi / On Evangelization in the Modern World, Apostolic Exhortation*. Rome: 8 December 1975. http://w2.vatican.va/content/paul-vi/en/apost_exhortations/documents/hf_p-vi_exh_19751208_evangelii-nuntiandi.html (accessed 4 March 2015).

– *Pastoral Constitution on the Church in the Modern World / Gaudium et Spes*. Rome: 7 December 1965. http://www.vatican.va/archive/hist_councils/ii_vatican_council/documents/vat-ii_cons_19651207_gaudium-et-spes_en.html (accessed 28 November 2014).

– *Decree on the Apostolate of the Laity / Apostolicam Actuositatem*. Rome: 18 November 1965. http://www.vatican.va/archive/hist_councils/ii_vatican_council/documents/vat-ii_decree_19651118_apostolicam-actuositatem_en.html (accessed 29 April 2015).

– *Dogmatic Constitution on Divine Revelation / Dei Verbum.* Rome: 18 November 1965. http://www.vatican.va/archive/hist_councils/ii_vatican_council/ documents/vat-ii_const_19651118_dei-verbum_en.html (accessed 28 November 2014).

– *Declaration on Christian Education / Gravissimum Educationis.* Rome: 28 October 1965. http://www.vatican.va/archive/hist_councils/ii_vatican_council/ documents/vat-ii_decl_19651028_gravissimum-educationis_en.html (accessed 30 November 2014).

– *Declaration on the Relation of the Church to Non-Christian Religions / Nostra Aetate.* Rome: 28 October 1965. http://www.vatican.va/archive/hist_councils/ ii_vatican_council/documents/vat-ii_decl_19651028_nostra-aetate_en.html (accessed 10 November 2014).

– *Dogmatic Constitution on the Church Lumen Gentium.* Rome: 21 November 1964. http://www.vatican.va/archive/hist_councils/ii_vatican_council/ documents/vat-ii_const_19641121_lumen-gentium_en.html (accessed 29 November 2014).

Pegis, Anton C. *Christian Philosophy and Intellectual Freedom.* Milwaukee, WI: The Bruce Publishing Company, 1955.

– ed. *A Gilson Reader: Selected Readings of Etienne Gilson.* Garden City, NY: Image Books, 1957.

Phelan, Gerald B. "First Award of the Cardinal Spellman Aquinas Medal." *Proceedings of the American Catholic Philosophical Association* 25 (1951): 1–4.

Pieper, Josef. *The Silence of St. Thomas.* Translated by John Murray, SJ, and Daniel O'Connor. South Bend, IN: St Augustine's Press, 1999.

– *Happiness and Contemplation.* Translated by Richard and Clara Winston. South Bend, IN: St Augustine's Press, 1998.

Pius X. *Pascendi Dominici Gregis / On the Doctrines of the Modernists, Encyclical.* Rome: 8 September 1907. http://w2.vatican.va/content/pius-x/en/ encyclicals/documents/hf_p-x_enc_19070908_pascendi-dominici- gregis.html (accessed 4 February 2016).

– *Acerbo Nimis / On Teaching Christian Doctrine, Encyclical.* Rome: 15 April 1905. http://www.vatican.va/holy_father/pius_x/encyclicals/documents/hf_p-x_ enc_15041905_acerbo-nimis_en.html (accessed 30 November 2014).

Pius XI. *Divini Illius Magistri / On Christian Education, Encyclical.* Rome: 31 December 1929. http://www.vatican.va/holy_father/pius_xi/encyclicals/ documents/hf_p-xi_enc_31121929_divini-illius-magistri_en.html (accessed 30 November 2014).

– *Quadragesimo Anno / On the Fortieth Year, Encyclical Letter on the Restoration of the Social Order.* Rome: 15 May 1931. http://www.vatican.va/holy_father/ pius_xi/encyclicals/documents/hf_p-xi_enc_19310515_quadragesimo-anno_ en.html (accessed 17 November 2014).

Pontifical Council for Culture. *Where Is Your God? Responding to the Challenge of Unbelief and Religious Indifference Today.* Rome: 13 March 2004. http://www.vatican.va/roman_curia/pontifical_councils/cultr/documents/ rc_pc_cultr_doc_20040313_where-is-your-god_en.html (accessed 10 April 2015).

– *Towards a Pastoral Approach to Culture.* Rome: 23 May 1999. http://www.vatican.va/roman_curia/pontifical_councils/cultr/documents/ rc_pc_pc-cultr_doc_03061999_pastoral_en.html (accessed 14 January 2015).

Pontifical Council for Culture and Pontifical Council for Interreligious Dialogue. *Jesus Christ the Bearer of the Water of Life: A Christian Reflection on the New Age.* Rome: 3 February 2003. http://www.vatican.va/roman_curia/ pontifical_councils/interelg/documents/rc_pc_interelg_doc_20030203_ new-age_en.html (accessed 8 April 2015).

Pontifical Council for the Family. *The Truth and Meaning of Human Sexuality: Guidelines for Education within the Family.* Vatican City: 8 December 1995. http://www.vatican.va/roman_curia/pontifical_councils/family/documents/ rc_pc_family_doc_08121995_human-sexuality_en.html (accessed 21 December 2015).

Pontifical Council for Social Communications. *The Church and Internet.* Vatican City: 22 February 2002. http://www.vatican.va/roman_curia/pontifical_ councils/pccs/documents/rc_pc_pccs_doc20020228_church-internet_ en.html (accessed 26 March 2015).

– *Ethics in the Internet.* Vatican City: 22 February 2002. http://www.vatican.va/ roman_curia/pontifical_councils/pccs/documents/rc_pc_pccs_doc_ 20020228_ethics-internet_en.html (accessed 1 May 2015).

Ratzinger, Joseph. *A Turning Point for Europe? The Church in the Modern World – Assessment and Forecast.* Translated by Brian McNeil, CRV. San Francisco, CA: Ignatius Press, 1994.

Reardon, Bernard M.G. "Introduction." In *Roman Catholic Modernism,* edited by Bernard M.G. Reardon, 9–67. London: Adam & Charles Black, 1970.

Redden, John D., and Francis A. Ryan. *A Catholic Philosophy of Education.* Milwaukee, WI: The Bruce Publishing Company, 1949.

Reilly, James P. *The Leonine Enterprise: An Exercise in Historical Discovery.* Villanova, PA: Augustinian Historical Institute, Villanova University, 1982.

Rice, Valentine. "Jacques Maritain and the Problem of Christian Philosophy." *Hermathena,* no. 135 (1983): 7–34.

Riordan, Patrick. *A Grammar of the Common Good: Speaking of Globalization.* London: Continuum, 2008.

Roberts, Alexander, and James Donaldson, eds. *The Ante-Nicene Fathers: Volume 1 The Apostolic Fathers: Justin Martyr, Irenaeus.* Peabody, MA: Hendrickson Publishers, Inc., 1995.

Rusembuka, Muhigirwa F. *The Two Ways of Human Development According to B. Lonergan: Anticipation in Insight.* Rome: Editrice Pontificia Università Gregoriana, 2001.

Sacred Congregation for Catholic Education. *Educational Guidance for Human Love: Outlines for Sex Education.* Rome: 1 November 1983.
http://www.vatican.va/roman_curia/congregations/ccatheduc/documents/
rc_con_ccatheduc_doc_19831101_sexual-education_en.html (accessed
11 January 2015).

– *Lay Catholics in Schools: Witnesses to Faith.* Rome: 15 October 1982.
http://www.vatican.va/roman_curia/congregations/ccatheduc/documents/
rc_con_ccatheduc_doc_19821015_lay-catholics_en.html (accessed
7 December 2014).

– *The Catholic School.* Rome: 19 March 1977. http://www.vatican.va/
roman_curia/congregations/ccatheduc/documents/rc_con_ccatheduc_doc_
19770319_catholic-school_en.html (accessed 11 January 2015).

Saracino, Michele. *On Being Human: A Conversation With Lonergan and Levinas.* Milwaukee, WI: Marquette University Press, 2003.

Schultenover, David G., SJ. *A View from Rome: On the Eve of the Modernist Crisis.* New York: Fordham University Press, 1993.

Sen, Amartya. *Identity and Violence: The Illusion of Destiny.* London: Allen Lane, 2006.

Shea, William M. "From Classicism to Method: John Dewey and Bernard Lonergan." *American Journal of Education* 99, no. 3 (1991): 298–319.

Slavin, Robert J., OP. "The Thomistic Concept of Education." In *Essays in Thomism*, edited by Robert E. Brennan, OP, 312–31. New York: Sheed and Ward, 1942.

Smith, Vincent Edward. *The School Examined: Its Aim and Content.* Milwaukee, WI: The Bruce Publishing Company, 1960.

Sullivan, John. "Catholic Education as Ongoing Translation." *International Studies in Catholic Education* 4, no. 2 (2012): 200–7.

Sullivan, Maureen, OP. *The Road to Vatican II: Key Changes in Theology.* New York and Mahwah, NJ: Paulist Press, 2007.

Taylor, Charles. "Why We Need a Radical Redefinition of the Secular." In *Power of Religion in the Public Square*, edited and introduced by Eduardo Mendieta and Jonathan Vanantwerpen, 34–59. New York: Columbia University Press, 2011.

– *Multiculturalism and the Politics of Recognition.* With commentary by Amy Gutmann (ed.), Stephen C. Rockefeller, Michael Walzer, and Susan Wolf. Princeton, NJ: Princeton University Press, 1992.

Tierny, Michael. "M. Maritain on Education." *Studies: An Irish Quarterly Review* 33, no. 129 (March 1944): 21–9.

Thompson, Philip M. *Between Science and Religion: The Engagement of Catholic Intellectuals with Science and Technology in the Twentieth Century*. Lanham, MD: Lexington Books, 2009.

Topley, Raymond. "Meeting Lonergan's Challenge to Educators." In *Lonergan Workshop*, edited by Fred Lawrence, vol. 21 (2009): 369–81.

Ventresca, Robert A. "A Plague of Perverse Opinions: Leo XIII's *Aeterni Patris* and the Catholic Encounter with Modernity." *Logos: A Journal of Catholic Thought and Culture* 12, no. 1 (2009): 143–68.

Walker, Timothy. "Lonergan, Science, and Religious Education." *The Lonergan Review: The Journal of the Bernard J. Lonergan Institute* V, no. 1 (2014): 139–50.

Wallace, William A., OP. *The Elements of Philosophy: A Compendium for Philosophers and Theologians*. New York: Alba House, 1977.

Ward, Leo R. *New Life in Catholic Schools*. St Louis, MO: B. Herder Book Co., 1958.

Warner, Carolyn M. *Confessions of an Interest Group: The Catholic Church and Political Parties in Europe*. Princeton, NJ: Princeton University Press, 2000.

Watzlawik, Joseph. *Leo XIII and the New Scholasticism*. Cebu City, Philippines: San Carlos Publications, 1966.

INDEX

Adler, Mortimer, 71
American Catholic Philosophical
    Association, 54
Archimedes, 99
Aristotle, 30, 32, 38, 63, 109, 133,
    138, 166, 202; *Metaphysics*, 109,
    248n130; *Nicomachean Ethics*, 202
Augustine, Saint, 28, 29, 63, 101, 203,
    230

Benedict XVI, 44
Bergson, Henri, 56
Bloy, Leony, 56
Bonaventure, Saint, 29
Boys, Mary C.: *Educating in Faith:*
    Maps and Visions, 47–8

Cardinal Spellman–Aquinas Award,
    54
Catechism of the Catholic Church: and
    definition of the common good,
    181. *See also* Catholic education:
    role of catechesis in
Catholic Church, 10–11, 27, 36,
    38–45, 46, 87, 88, 110, 119, 146,
    150, 185, 186, 187, 211, 217, 220,
    221, 224; and crisis of modernism,

30–1; and culture, 21–2; and distinction between philosophy and
theology, 39, 49, 68–9; intellectual
life of, 26–31, 51–2; position and
role of in education, 13, 14–15,
16–17, 23, 25–52, 54, 61, 79, 84–5,
87–90, 107, 111–12, 115, 127, 153,
155, 182–3, 187, 210, 211, 216, 217,
224; and religious education, 16,
32, 43, 45, 46, 48–9, 51, 53, 80, 81,
88, 114–16, 128, 140, 145–6, 182,
215; and Tradition, 14, 40–1
Catholic education: and activity
versus activism, 212–13; Catholic
philosophy of education distinguished from philosophy of
Catholic education, 14–16, 26; and
the challenge of globalization, 120,
176, 180; and the common good,
4, 8, 9, 11, 47, 81, 111, 117, 150,
180, 181–4, 191–3, 205, 206, 207,
209, 218–19, 224, 227; criticisms
of, 12, 13, 39, 115, 216–17, 224;
curriculum of, 7, 8, 10, 11–12, 19,
34, 37–8, 65–7, 75, 79, 80, 83–4,
86–9, 90, 92, 94, 95–6, 97, 107–8,
112–13, 115, 116, 121, 125–6, 128,